THE TYSELEY STORY

Tyseley Collection's GWR 'Castle' Class 4-6-0 No. 5043 *Earl of Mount Edgcumbe* at speed – privately owned steam locomotives are now permitted to run up to 75mph on the British national railway network. No. 5043 has been painstakingly restored from scrapyard condition by Tyseley Locomotive Works and has now run several celebratory non-stop specials, including 'The Bristolian', 'The Cheltenham Flyer' and 'The InterCity'. She is seen here in her BR(WR) rebuilt condition, with four row superheater, double chimney and blastpipe, and Hawksworth tender. In this modified form, she ran at speeds of up to 100mph for British Railways on 'The Bristolian' during the introduction of the diesel hydraulics in the late 1950s. A true 'GTI Castle.' [Photo: Robin Coombes]

Cover: The pioneer express engine of our story, BR(WR) 'Castle' Class 4-6-0 No. 7029 *Clun Castle*, climbs Sapperton bank on 6th April 2019. *Clun Castle* was one of the first privately preserved express steam locomotives to operate over British Railways, having earned her preservation by securing the fastest point to point timing from Plymouth to Bristol in 1964, beating *City of Truro*'s 1904 record run. She hauled several 'last' trains in her BR days, including the very last time-tabled steam-hauled passenger train from Paddington. In preservation, she hauled the last through train on the GWR North Western main line from Birkenhead to Birmingham and she was the last steam engine to leave both Snow Hill and Moor Street stations in Birmingham before their closure. Following the 'Return to Steam' of privately preserved locomotives in 1972, after the infamous BR steam ban, she hauled the first public tour and went on to star in the 150th anniversary celebrations for the Great Western Railway in 1975. She was also the first privately owned steam locomotive to venture back into Cornwall over Brunel's Saltash Bridge. In 1988, HRH The Prince of Wales drove her to Tyseley depot, which is now her home. In this picture she seen is spearheading the first year's special train programme of Vintage Trains, currently the only publicly owned and charitably controlled train operating company in the world. [Photo: Robin Coombes]

THE TYSELEY STORY

SEVENTY YEARS OF
RAILWAY PIONEERING IN BIRMINGHAM

MICHAEL WHITEHOUSE

Lightmoor Press

GWR auto-fitted 0-6-0PT No. 6435 was purchased from BR to operate commercial tourist trains for the new Dart Valley Railway in Devon. She is seen here on 17th October 1965, taking water on the main line whilst on the first stage of her transfer to the DVR from Tyseley depot in Birmingham, where she had been repainted by the family firm of B. Whitehouse & Sons. Pat Whitehouse is on the footplate and, in the background, stands No. 7029 *Clun Castle*, which was double-heading the SLS Special but was then still in BR ownership. No one knew then that she would shortly also move to be shedded at Tyseley, begin the collection now promoted by Vintage Trains and enable Tyseley proudly to continue its unbroken service of having a steam locomotive available for service every day since June 1908, when the depot originally opened. [PHOTO: C.M. WHITEHOUSE COLLECTION]

Published by LIGHTMOOR PRESS

© Lightmoor Press & Michael Whitehouse 2021
Designed by Neil Parkhouse

British Library Cataloguing-in-Publication Data.
A catalogue record for this book is available from the British Library

ISBN: 9781911038 92 4

LIGHTMOOR PRESS

Unit 144B, Harbour Road Trading Estate, Lydney, Gloucestershire GL15 4EJ
website: www.lightmoor.co.uk
email: info@lightmoor.co.uk

Lightmoor Press is an imprint of
Black Dwarf Lightmoor Publications Ltd

Printed in Poland
www.lfbookservices.co.uk

CONTENTS

Learning to drive. On selected Sunday afternoons I was allowed private steam locomotive driving lessons during school exeats. I practised on unkempt No. 7029 *Clun Castle* in the depot yard at Tyseley in 1966, under the watchful eye of a depot driver. The original name and number plates were left in safekeeping in the shedmaster's office whilst the engine was shedded in the original 1908 roundhouse. Little did I know then that this track would become the starting point for Vintage Trains' main line excursions, that the depot would become one of Britain's premier steam locomotive workshops and that I would have the privilege and the duty of chairing its charity for over forty years. [Photo: P.B. Whitehouse]

INTRODUCTION

This is the story of railway preservation pioneering in the city of Birmingham. It is a story of how people give freely of their time to achieve impossible dreams. Even as the stakes continue to rise, these pioneers seek to ensure that one of Britain's most important inventions, the steam locomotive, still has a useful purpose in society in the 21st century.

Steam engine pioneering was very evident in Birmingham long before the preservationists arrived on the scene. The steam engine was a force for change during the Industrial Revolution. Boulton & Watt, based at Soho Works in Birmingham, improved the efficiency of the atmospheric pumping engine and enabled steam technology to power machinery reliably. The power of steam was a transformational and disruptive technology which changed the world for ever. Steam engines made possible a dramatic increase in industrial productivity. They provided relief from the drudgery of hard and repetitive physical labour and also enabled improvements in public health, especially in pumping fresh water and the safe disposal of sewage.

Thus Birmingham became the largest manufacturing centre the world had ever known. In 1838, the London & Birmingham Railway was connected to the Grand Junction and Liverpool & Manchester railways to create the first inter-city network in the world. The power of steam, once again, became transformational, by providing power to operate a railway system. Steam locomotion enabled faster and cheaper transport of people and goods than ever before, connecting hitherto inaccessible places all over the world. Curzon Street station, at the edge of the City of Birmingham, was designed as one of Birmingham's three great buildings, along with the Town and Market halls: buildings for governance, the people and a gateway for export to the world. The railway became '*that mighty iron missionary of civilization and progress*'. (Reverend Dr Bowles of Hereford*)*.

The quality of life for city people improved. Fresh food could be delivered rapidly, fresh water and sanitation reduced disease. Leisure opportunities increased – excursion trains ran from Birmingham to Buxton in Derbyshire and Church Stretton in Shropshire, and employers treated their workforces to a day out in the countryside. In September 1863, manufacturers John Reynolds & Son hired a special train to take two hundred of their workers, families and friends from New Street station for a day trip to Malvern.

Railway companies competed to reach Birmingham. The Liverpool & Manchester, the Grand Junction and the London & Birmingham railways amalgamated into the London & North Western Railway, self styled the 'Premier Line.' The Great Western Railway created a near parallel route from Paddington, through Birmingham's Snow Hill and on to Chester and Birkenhead. The Midland Railway ventured in from Derby and on to Bristol, connecting with the L&NWR at Birmingham New Street station. In BR days, the 'Premier Line' was electrified in the 1960s and ran trains at up to 110 mph. In the privatised era from 1994, it competed with Chiltern (on the GWR route) and Cross Country (on the Midland Route).

Now, Birmingham is designated to be the first provincial terminus of High Speed 2, providing journey times of forty-five minutes from London back to Curzon Street, where express steam trains began. This new HS2 station will be immediately adjacent to the original GWR Moor Street city terminus, built in 1909, to cater for the expanded suburban service within Warwickshire. As luck will have it, this will enable 'The Shakespeare Express', one of Britain's few time-tabled express steam trains, to connect directly with HS2. The founders of this train were amongst the world pioneers of voluntary run railways, a story which began in Birmingham in 1950.

Parallel to this story but interwoven with it, in 1951, the men of Birmingham created a Museum of Science & Industry in Newhall Street, at the edge of the city's commercial centre and Jewellery Quarter. Here, relics of past industrial success were lovingly kept and admired by the public. Many of the industrial steam engines were kept in working order and demonstrated to visitors, the smell of warm steam oil often pervading the museum. Even now, in its current incarnation as Thinktank, many engines can be seen in steam regularly, including the oldest working steam engine in the world – the Smethwick Engine. This was installed in 1779 to pump water on the Birmingham to Wolverhampton canal and became the first steam engine to use both the expansive force of steam and a vacuum at the same time.

These museum pieces had their own devotees and volunteers who gave their time to help ensure they kept working. One such was Tom Hunt, who owned Hunt Bros (Oldbury) Ltd, a family foundry business and he gladly used his workshop's equipment to repair and make new parts for the museum when needed. His main interest in steam engines was with fairground equipment and as early as 1948, he acquired the 15ins gauge Sutton Miniature Railway based at the Crystal Palace funfair, operated by Pat Collins with his Showman steam engines. This was one of the earliest public miniature railways, having opened in 1907, later operated by the famous Bassett Lowke enterprise under the Miniature Railways of Great Britain brand. On the demise of the fairground after the Second World War, Tom also acquired one of Collins' glamorous

The Smethwick Engine, the world's oldest working steam engine, on display at Thinktank in Birmingham.

Showman engines, *The Leader*, together with his Wonderland organ. Tom Hunt was an early volunteer pioneer of steam engine preservation. He and friends co-operated with Norman Bertenshaw, the curator of the Birmingham Science Museum, to stage an annual steam engine rally in Newhall Street, outside the museum, attended by many hundreds of cognoscenti and families. These activities, coupled with membership of the Birmingham Locomotive Club and the Stephenson Locomotive Society, attracted many like-minded enthusiasts from the region. Seeking a return to some normality after the terrors of the war, they sought solace in friendship and discussions about steam engines, whether they be models, traction engines or railway locomotives.

Seventy years ago, Government began to recast the relationship between the state and its citizens by nationalising industries which were on their knees following the depression and the Second World War. Many people began to feel that the state was closing openings for individual initiative, throttling enterprise and initiative with red tape. Tom Rolt, a well known historian of the Industrial Revolution and pioneer of canal preservation, felt this keenly and so strove to keep alive a spark of the fine traditions of loyalty and service of former times. Working with Bill Trinder from Banbury, they pioneered the concept of voluntary run railways in Britain. Rolt encouraged a team, initially largely led by Birmingham enthusiasts, to innovate successfully to save a Welsh narrow gauge slate quarry line, the Talyllyn Railway, and rebuild it to become the world's first successful volunteer run railway.

Some of this team then began to scale greater heights, moving into standard gauge railway preservation, first buying locomotives to run on British Railways, then re-opening a Devon branch line as a commercial tourist railway. Not satisfied with that, they went on to rescue famous express steam locomotives from the breaker's

ABOVE: Steam for pleasure. A traction engine rally in Newhall Street, Birmingham, outside the Museum of Science & Industry in 1968. In the foreground is Pat Collins' Showman's engine, *The Leader*, and his Wonderland organ, from the Sutton Coldfield Crystal Palace fairground, both rescued by Tom Hunt, the Midland's industrialist who began the journey into voluntary run railways with his acquisition in 1948 of the former Bassett Lowke 15ins gauge miniature railway which operated there. He ran both this railway and his traction engines with his son, Bill, who remains a founder trustee of Vintage Trains at Tyseley – connections from the very beginning of voluntary railway preservation. [PHOTO: P.B. WHITEHOUSE]

OPPOSITE PAGE TOP: Not all special trains were run for enthusiasts. Here at New Street Station, Birmingham is a 'City of Birmingham Holiday Express' ready to leave, probably for the seaside, behind ex-LM&SR 'Black Five' 4-6-0 No. 44914. [PHOTO: DAVE WALDREN COLLECTION]

OPPOSITE PAGE BOTTOM: Expanding the Birmingham collection into railways. Ex-LM&SR 'Coronation Pacific' No. 46235 *City of Birmingham* is manoeuvred into position in its retirement home at the Birmingham Museum of Science & Industry in 1964. [PHOTO: E.S. RUSSELL]

torch and to ensure that they continued to operate at speed on the main line on special trains.

To do so, they built enduring relationships with railwaymen and others so enabling the steam locomotive not only to survive after the end of steam on the British railway system, but to continue to run at speed, as it was designed to do.

All the while, the effort to ensure success was obliged to increase. From being given a railway to do with as they pleased and then buying standard gauge locomotives as a hobby, in the same way as some people buy old cars or motorbikes, they moved onwards and upwards. They learned political and commercial persuasion, necessary to allow their locomotives to continue to be used well after their working life sell by dates. They created a new workshop to repair their locomotives. They raised significant finance to rebuild them

Meeting a new friend. Record breaker and last of her class, No. 7029 *Clun Castle* and I meet each other for the first time at Worcester shed in 1966. Next to me in the picture is Richard Rolt, son of Tom Rolt who began the voluntary run railway movement, together with a shed cleaner. [PHOTO: P.B. WHITEHOUSE]

anew as they wore out, establishing engineering apprenticeships to perpetuate skills. More recently, their successors have even gained operating licences to run their own main line railway company, with a view to ensuring these icons of British history survive and continue to run at speed on the national railway.

This journey continues to ensure the steam locomotive serves a useful purpose and skills are passed on to future generations. Steam trains have been proven now to contribute to our tourist industry, our education and training, and to our economic development generally. Perhaps best of all, very many people have gained satisfaction from their 'business hobby' as well as ensuring that one of Britain's greatest inventions survives and thrives against all the odds.

So it is no co-incidence that this story is based on Birmingham people, following in the footsteps of the innovators of the steam age and the industrial revolution which made the City the 'Workshop of the World'. It would have been a travesty for the steam engine to sink into oblivion and remain only in museums. By the efforts of these pioneers, and those of many other like-minded people in the country and now worldwide, the steam locomotive has been kept in service and run at speed on special trains on the main line railway for over seventy years.

This story is told largely through my own eyes and also featuring the very last Great Western Railway express steam locomotive to survive on British Railways, *Clun Castle*, as one of the heroes but also recognising the huge contributions of others elsewhere who enriched the story.

Whilst in retrospect it seems that we have followed a fairly logical process, in reality most of the steps were taken without any preconceived strategy or business plan determined at the outset. We have just done the next thing which seemed the right choice at the time. Hindsight is a wonderful thing. We have jolted along from being enthralled by watching steam trains, photographing and riding as many steam trains as possible before their withdrawal, to owning, repairing and operating our own trains, all requiring ever increasing expertise, money and determination. We have succeeded beyond our wildest dreams. And we must keep on doing so, whatever the pitfalls ahead.

Michael Whitehouse
Worcestershire, June, 2021

ACKNOWLEDGEMENTS

J.H.L. Adams, P.M. Alexander, Reverend Canon Brian Arman, Hugh Ballantyne, Andrew Bell, *Birmingham Post & Mail*, Tony Bowles, Malcolm Briggs, Richard Cadge, Roger Carpenter, Ray Churchill, David Cobbe, Colour-Rail, Ken Cooper, Martin Creese, Robin Coombes, Taliesin Coombes, Carole Cuneo, Frank Dumbleton, Richard Elliott, Robert Falconer, Bob Green, Joan Green, L. Hanson, G.R. Hounsell, Lacey's Studios, Russell Leitch, Bob Meanley, Milepost 82^1/$_2$, Neil Parkhouse, David Postle/Kidderminster Railway Museum, Bill Potter, Dick Potts, Malcolm Ranieri, David Russell, Matt Spencer, Tim Stephens, Paul Strong, Eric Treacy, Dave Waldren, David Ward, John Whiteley, T.E. Williams.

Special trains have run through family life for the whole of their seventy year existence and there have been many highs and lows for the Whitehouse family but, to date, perhaps none higher than the visit to Tyseley by HRH The Prince of Wales on 14th September, 1988. The visit was to celebrate the then Birmingham Railway Museum's remarkable success in retraining some eight hundred previously redundant craftsmen pursuant to a Government funded Community Programme. My father, 'PBW', deserved recognition for leading that venture, securing funding and organising a scheme to give people their confidence back, so I asked the Lord Lieutenant if a Royal visit could be arranged – and it could. Moreover, Cyril Bleasdale, then General Manager of the London Midland Region, kindly arranged a Royal Train from Birmingham Snow Hill to Tyseley depot to collect Prince Charles from his previous engagement. So, father and son stand proudly in front of 'their' flagship locomotive No. 7029 *Clun Castle*, at the rebuilt Snow Hill station before the Royal arrival. It was not lost on us that No. 7029 hauled the last steam train from Snow Hill and here she was back again but we were not to know that a few years later we would be promoting regular time-tabled trains from the station under the title of 'The Shakespeare Express'. [PHOTO: C.M. WHITEHOUSE COLLECTION]

The World's Fastest Train – 'The Cheltenham Flyer'. On 11th May 2013, Vintage Trains promoted a non stop charter train (operated by West Coast Railways) from Cheltenham to London (Paddington), so recreating this famous train. [PHOTO: ROBIN COOMBES]

1. BEYOND OUR WILDEST DREAMS

'There was not a well thought out strategy to cut teeth on the Talyllyn, move to establish a Great Western branch line in Devon, buy the last Great Western designed express engine and run it, establish a well equipped railway workshop in Birmingham and then develop it for commercial heritage use, and to run regular steam express dining car trains, even though that might sound logical – but that is exactly what happened!'

PBW, newly betrothed to Thelma, with both leaning out of one of the original Talyllyn Railway 4-wheeled carriages chatting to Tom Rolt on Abergynolwyn station platform. The adventure begins!

On the wall in my study is a framed black and white photograph of Royal Air Force D Wing, 15 Squadron, A Flight, showing my father standing at the end of the third row of the team. He was a navigator in Bomber Command, not allowed to fly their Lancasters because his eyesight was not good enough. So the next best thing was to decide where they were going to fly by becoming a navigator, carefully tracking depots, marshalling yards and junctions as targets rather than stations or trains themselves; that way, the bombs would kill fewer people but do more strategic damage. After surviving three German bombing raid missions, somewhat against the odds, he was posted to the Middle East Air Transport Corps on freight haulage with Dakotas. That actually turned out to be more dangerous as his plane was shot from a ship in the Mediterranean and irreparably damaged. First the cargo was thrown out to help lighten the load on the failing plane – sheep! – then the machinery carried and then, when neither stemmed the inevitable, he found himself one of two survivors floating in a dinghy waiting to be rescued by a Greek merchant ship. His colleague died. All this put survival and determination to succeed in very clear perspective.

My father learned a great deal in the war, both in action and in the transport corps. He applied this knowledge, once safely back on the ground, with both his own family and the B. Whitehouse & Sons family construction firm, which was a key part of Birmingham's business community. Whilst building a model of the L&NWR Harborne Branch and attending Birmingham Locomotive Club and Stephenson Locomotive Society meetings, he soon brushed up against other like-minded Birmingham and Black Country men who were all determined to make a difference and get things done, especially now they were and would remain free men.

My father met Pat Garland this way. Garland was Chairman of the Midlands Area of the Stephenson Locomotive Society. Both men modelled in 4mm scale, 18.1mm gauge and were interested in all things Great Western too. Pat Garland performed the honours as best man at PBW's wedding in 1948. 'PJG' knew Jim Russell as well, also a 4mm scale GWR modeller and photographer. Russell introduced Garland to Rolt and Bill Trinder, who had a hardware shop in Banbury where Rolt was then living on his canal boat. Trinder was then in cahoots with Rolt to do something to save the Talyllyn Railway and so 4mm model railways proved key to voluntary railway preservation originating in Birmingham, rather than anywhere else, just on account of who knew whom.

So, it was easy when Tom Rolt, the same man who had largely been responsible for saving Britain's canal network, asked Pat Garland to call the now famous 1950 meeting at the Imperial Hotel in town to discuss saving the Talyllyn Railway in mid Wales. All Dad's friends knew the line and had visited it. Known by his initials as 'PBW', he now takes up the story:

"The meeting had been seized with a spirit of crusade and even the sceptics showed more interest than they had intended to – the idea of saving a railway in those days when all people said was "You can't do it" or "You can't have it" was beginning to appeal.

Afterwards, myself, Pat Garland who was an accountant and several others interested in the venture met in Garland's office to put the whole idea down on paper. We knew that to put the line in order would cost more than £15,000. We could not afford to pay for it ourselves.

We decided to form a committee. Our first move was successful. We approached Lady Haydn, who agreed to hand over all her shares to a holding company without payment. The oldest surviving steam narrow gauge passenger railway in the world was ours. Now that we had the railway, the problem was what were we going to do with it? Nobody had ever thought of trying to save a railway before, and we had nobody to guide us."

But with the 'Birmingham Committee's' background in survival and business, they instinctively knew what to do. They asked for money. Leaflets were printed and these reached out to 300 new members, each of whom was charged £1, given a vote at the AGM and free travel on the line. By the end of the first season this had grown to £652 in ordinary subscriptions, £840 from life memberships and £903 in donations. Traffic in the first two operating seasons was also successful, with passenger numbers up from 15,000 in the first season to 22,000 in 1952. A team had emerged: The Jones family who had driven the engines for years were employed, Tom Rolt agreed to become the first General Manager and volunteers started to arrive to run the trains, and undertake essential maintenance and repairs, all supported by the Board of Directors in Birmingham. Some may say this was remote management, which is true, but the directors all had busy lives at home rebuilding their businesses and looking after new and growing families. Moreover, they were able to use their businesses to help.

Tom Hunt had a foundry in Oldbury and a great interest in steam machinery. He and his son Bill owned several traction engines bought from Pat Collins, who ran the fairground and miniature railway at Sutton Coldfield we read about in the Introduction; they took over the 15ins gauge railway and together with John Wilkins, who brought 'Servis' washing machines to a new household market, they also re-invigorated the 15ins gauge Fairbourne Miniature Railway, not far from the Talyllyn; in fact, both these miniature lines could really be said to be the real pioneers in running railways voluntarily but the Talyllyn took on the public mantle. Financial, moral and physical support emanated from Hunt Bros, Wilkins & Mitchell, Garland Impey and B. Whitehouse & Sons. The firms' lorries

The Miniature Railway, Fairbourne, purchased in 1947 by John Wilkins, a Midlands' industrialist, as a railway he could enjoy, was actually the first preserved railway but the TR took the mantle. John was a good friend to the TR, providing advice and helping its cash flow, and he also purchased GWR pannier tank No. 6435 for the Dart Valley Railway. The locomotive in the picture, *Count Louis*, was the last 15ins gauge product made by Bassett Lowke, originally for Count Louis Zborowski who, together with Captain Jack Howey, planned the famous Romney, Hythe & Dymchurch Railway. Sadly, Count Louis was killed racing his Bentley at Monza in the Italian Grand Prix, so his engine passed to the Fairbourne Railway where it was the mainstay of services for many years. Now, it too is preserved by descendants of the Tyseley pioneers and friends, and kept in working order for celebrations. [FROM AN OLD POSTCARD]

This Andrew Barclay 0-4-0WT was rescued from Ableson's scrapyard in the Midlands and refurbished free of charge for the TR by Hunt Bros (Oldbury). It was named *Douglas* after the scrapyard owner.

groaned over the Cambrian mountains with never-ending supplies of castings, wood and paint. Even Talyllyn steam engines were transported to and from the Midlands: *Douglas*, an Andrew Barclay 0-4-0WT, was rescued from a scrapyard, regauged by Hunts and sent over the mountains. Both *Talyllyn* and *Dolgoch* were brought back for major rebuilding at Hunts and Gibbons Bros, all entirely free of charge, and locomotive livery was standardised as GWR green. Pat Garland kept the books and hosted the committee meetings, where issues were committed to paper for visibility and good decision-making. Cognoscenti and enablers visited PBW at home to plot.

Step by step, the Talyllyn Railway was rebuilt, so that, by its centenary in 1965, the line had been largely re-equipped and was now carrying some 100,000 passengers a year. This was largely thanks to the flourishing summer holiday trade in caravans and bed & breakfast establishments along the sea coast within a day's reach of the Midlands and the North West. On the Cambrian Coast line, Saturday trains ran 'block to block,' double headed on changeover day.

The success of the adventure had been watched with interest by others, who were inspired and given confidence to try even more difficult things themselves. The Ffestiniog Railway, further up the coast, was re-opened after significant apparent legal problems were solved. Amateur enthusiasts revived a narrow gauge line in Australia's Victoria, which became known as the Puffing Billy Railway; they even had to move their railway lock, stock and barrel! The BBC and

the film industry became fascinated by railway enthusiasts playing with their own trains. The Talyllyn benefitted from a surge in visitors from a 1957 outside broadcast and Ealing Studios got the idea of *The Titfield Thunderbolt* comedy film from a visit to the railway.

So far so good but success was not won as of right. As PBW put it: "*If the financial problems of an undertaking such as ours are not taken lightly, but with determination, all obstacles can be overcome.*"

But the next adventure was about to happen. There was not, as now looks to be the case, a well thought out strategy to cut teeth on the Talyllyn, move to establish a Great Western branch line in Devon, buy the last Great Western designed express engine and run it, establish a well equipped railway workshop in Birmingham and then develop it for commercial heritage use, and to run regular steam express dining car trains, even though that might sound logical – but that is exactly what happened! The growing team, adding new friends and family generations, just morphed through the steps … at least to start with.

Once the Talyllyn Railway was up, running and able, more or less, to run itself from Towyn, other opportunities arose, this time standard gauge. 'PBW' and 'PJG' (the initials Pat Whitehouse and Pat Garland were known by) moved onto the next square on the railway preservation chessboard. They were both good friends with Arthur Camwell, the Midlands Area Secretary of the Stephenson Locomotive Society, who had a penchant for running special trains to mark the closure of lines or the withdrawal of locomotive classes;

On 26th September 1964, the TRPS AGM special train rounds the curve into Morfa Mawdach, having just run over Barmouth viaduct for the return trip. It was hauled by two engines which, by chance, both found their way to the Dart Valley Railway – 'Small Prairie' No. 4555 and 'Manor' 4-6-0 No. 7827 *Lydham Manor*. [PHOTO: M. POPE]

indeed he organised over a hundred, all of which were great fun and provided a magnet to both Pats to ride on the train, on the footplate and to photograph. The Talyllyn Railway Preservation Society ran its own train to the AGMs, with an amazing variety of motive power; 'Kings' and 'Castles' from Paddington of course but also *City of Truro* and, over the Cambrian section, an incredible variety of engines and not just GWR ones – an L&SWR 'T9', an SE&CR 'D' Class 4-4-0 and an L&YR 2-4-2T all appeared at Towyn. It was easy enough to fix all this once contacts and friends had been made and so it was then really just a small step to buy an engine of their own.

B. Whitehouse & Sons had had a particularly trying time doing some bridge work at Walsall station and BR were not very helpful. In sorting the muddle out, PBW ended up meeting Sir Stanley Raymond, London Midland Region's General Manager, who, once the matter was settled, made the mistake of asking PBW if there was anything else he could do for him whilst he was in the meeting. Quick as a flash, PBW said: "*Well, as a matter of fact, yes, there is. I'd like to buy a steam engine.*" So it was that both Pats became the proud owner of ex-GWR 'Small Prairie' 2-6-2T No. 4555, selected by the many friends they had both made on SLS trips and during the filming of a classic BBC TV programme of the 1950s – *Railway Roundabout*. The deal was the purchase of the engine, a light casual overhaul at Swindon, a spare boiler, a van full of parts and a trial run to Kemble in return for £750! At the time they bought the engine, neither Pats were aware that No. 4555 was originally delivered new

to Tyseley – the locomotive was to begin both its GWR career and its new preserved one at the same depot. This step was to have far reaching implications for the future of both the Whitehouse family and steam preservation.

The ultimate plan now was to buy and operate a GWR Devon branch line as a commercial venture with steam trains but running for tourists – and that is just what these two men did, working with numerous others such as Bob Saunders from Devon and Ian Allan, who needs little introduction. From the outset, the Dart Valley Railway was to be a business. Shares were sold to the public, a Light Railway Order granted and, after Dr Beeching had been invited to re-open the line he had closed, the branch carried 22,358 passengers in the first three weeks of its operation in 1969 and, by 1971, annual passenger numbers had increased to 125,000. Because initially there was no run round loop or station at the Totnes end, the services were run by GWR auto-fitted engines with up to four trailer cars, a far cry from the one or two coaches in public service days. The aim was to be authentic but commercial.

The DVR board were dedicated to making their railway a success but as pioneers it was not an easy start. The A38 road improvements bi-sected the line just north of the main intermediate station at Buckfastleigh, which denied them access to the wonderful Brunel timber-covered terminus at Ashburton. This was a blow from which the pioneers never really recovered as, instead of making Buckfastleigh the intermediate passing station for a two train service, the sleepy halt at Staverton now had to be converted to fulfill this

The essence of a Great Western branch line? No, this picture was not taken in the 1930s but on 9th July 1969, during the DVR era, and shows the 6.03pm Totnes (Riverside) to Buckfastleigh auto train service hauled by GWR pannier No. 6412. The train is running through Stretchford woods, near Staverton, on the preserved Dart Valley Railway. [PHOTO: JOHN M. BOYES]

role. Also, it wasn't economically sustainable to take trains back into Totnes station and so further compromises had to be made. Of course the volunteer preservationists wanted to keep their branch line running, and why not, but PBW became a little disenchanted.

But no matter. The next surprise and opportunity was on its way – onwards and upwards! *Clun Castle* made a record run from Plymouth to Bristol as part of the 'Castle Swansong' tour in 1964 and enthusiasts clamoured for the engine to be kept. British Railways were not interested of course, as *Caerphilly Castle* had already been reserved for the nation. Railwaymen at Bristol Bath Road tried to raise the money, then two Cornishmen, Jack Trounson and John Southern, established a fund but the asking price of some £3,000 just could not be raised. In 1964 such a sum was a lot of money but luck stepped in.

PBW sold the family construction business to international giant Cubitts in 1964, pocketed a reasonable sum and gained the position of a Cubitts main board director on the princely annual salary of £8,000. The Whitehouse family was able to step up a gear and moved house to Edgbaston, upgraded from Austins to Jaguars and bought a mechanical Castle! PBW and fellow DVR director, John Evans stumped up the balance of the money and put No. 7029 in a trust from day one, with Jack Trounson representing the fund's subscribers. The idea was to run a few specials for the SLS and the Locomotive Club of Great Britain, then retire the engine to Buckfastleigh goods shed where she could be displayed and perhaps

rolled out into the sunshine on summer Sundays. No one thought of keeping her running on the main line or at least no one knew how to do that. Even Alan Pegler, who had bought *Flying Scotsman*, and Captain Bill Smith, who acquired his lovely GNR 'J52', could only run their engines if BR staff actually did all the work.

Clun Castle also came to Tyseley. PBW knew Tommy Field, the shedmaster, well by now, as a steady steam of GWR tank engines had passed through the depot for repainting by our family construction firm and had hauled several 'Cam' excursions. *Clun* might as well come along too, especially as the stay was only to be temporary.

Once *Clun Castle* arrived at Tyseley, fortunately railwaymen 'came out of the woodwork' to help. This team was ably led by Bernard Rainbow and Phil Gloster, who were to become stalwarts at ensuring No. 7029 survived the increasing number of special trains she was asked to run, including a sojourn on the East Coast at the invitation of Gerry Fiennes, running from King's Cross to Newcastle, York and Leeds, and over Shap. These runs did three things in my Dad's mind: First, the engine was not going to Devon to sit in a museum; second, he had been led towards buying another steam locomotive, ex-LMS 'Jubilee' Class 4-6-0 No.5593 *Kolhapur*; third, he now realised (if he didn't already know) that if these two express engines were to be kept running we needed a place to keep them, a workshop to fix them in and a team to run them. A whole new ball game was about to arrive, as the costs and implications were beyond just raising money by members' subscriptions and raffles,

Hauling a Paddington-Worcester-Nottingham special train, *Clun Castle* breasts the summit of the Lickey Incline at Blackwell on 29th March 1965, still in BR service but with the future guiding mind, PBW, waving from the footplate. There is really very little better than riding on 'one's own' express steam locomotive up hills …!

'Castles' at Tyseley. There is much historical precedent for people having their family portraits painted but the Whitehouses only commissioned portraits of its mechanical family. This is a drawing commissioned privately from Terence Cuneo after the March 1967 final express steam train runs to Chester and Birkenhead. It was done as a test for an oil painting and, intriguingly, if you look closely shows two *Clun Castles* inside the roundhouse.
[PHOTO:
C.M. WHITEHOUSE COLLECTION]

and relying on friendly engineers to fix things when they went wrong. Running an express steam engine on British Rail at 75 mph was an entirely different undertaking but by now the team was wiser after learning some of the ropes on the narrow gauge, branch lines and occasional special trains, whilst PBW also had an enthusiastic son to collaborate with, which was perhaps the best part of all for both of them. Now PBW and I could egg each other on, discuss prospects interminably and put ideas down on paper to see how they looked as frequently as we liked, without even leaving home.

The rules of the game now changed and the steps taken in the late 1960s were to lay deep and satisfactory foundations for main line preserved steam to survive well into the future, although success took some time to come and required some lessons to be learned along the way. A charity was established which reached out to industry and enthusiasts alike to raise enough money, and beg and be given cash, machines and peoples' time to create a new workshop on land rented at Tyseley. This was faith indeed, especially as BR had by then imposed a steam ban. However, this was only to last three years and was actually a blessing in disguise as the new and enlarged team could concentrate on building up the facility and collecting as much machinery and tooling as possible whilst it was being thrown out as scrap. Far greater challenges were to occur in the years ahead but for now the bi-annual Tyseley Open Day became famous for showing off 'caged lions' stalking around the depot – all for 7s 6d (35p). Enthusiasts queued all down the Warwick Road to get in – 24,000 people came to the first one in 1968 – and there was really nowhere else to see main line steam engines at work, even if they were only storming up the steep grade of the Tyseley goods loop for half a mile.

BR relented and allowed steam back on its metals in a controlled way in 1972, following the good work done by Peter Prior of Bulmers. Tyseley was on the approved list as a trusted depot with most of its locomotives as well. PBW had seen to that through good connections, by having people like Terry Miller of High Speed Train fame and Bill Thorley of the BR Board as associates. It was to prove a challenging time getting track time for the GWR engines though, as the BR and Steam Locomotive Operators' Association

politics were tough to play out and GWR engines were slightly wider than their competitors, so route availability was restricted. But we played the game and survived and, some of the time, even excelled. *Clun Castle* made numerous main line trips on ex-Great Western main lines and the advent of 'The Shakespeare Express' in GW150 year were to lay foundations for the future, although the team and basis were largely going to have to change before these sorts of operations could be repeated on a frequent basis. National politics would also need to change to allow steam trains to run regularly and much more money would be needed. The deep 1980s recession also played its part in showing the way. There is nothing like a good downturn to fire up change!

I busied myself in battling with the main line politics, sometimes succeeding: one year *Clun Castle*, *Defiant* and *Kolhapur* all ran on the main line! A somewhat understandably irritated David Ward, BR Special Trains Manager, demanded to know at one SLOA AGM how many more engines would be proposed for the main line by members as he, quite rightly, thought there were already too many to cover the costs of their future repairs. He insisted on going around the room to ask members how many more engines they might want to add to the list. Most people said one or maybe two but when it came to me, I said eight in total! The room went very quiet. I had been counting up the Tyseley collection of three 'Castles', a 'Jubilee', a 'Hall' and three panniers. So who turned out to be right? Well, we have run all eight engines on the main line at one time or another, *plus* a Class '47' diesel and hosted several other engines after effecting repairs. Dreams are possible to put into practice, provided the right people and money are there to effect them, relationships are sound to put them in place and, most importantly, there is a sustainable way to keep them going. Neither PBW or I knew what might transpire of course but, by then, we did know what we wanted to do. It would take another thirty years or so for all the stars to become aligned.

Meanwhile, PBW busied himself unravelling the public sector grant matrix. He learned what he termed 'grant speak' and gained literally millions of pounds from the public exchequer to employ hundreds of redundant craftsmen to give them another

On 3rd October 1971, 18,000 people paid 7s 6d to come and gawp at *King George V* and *Princess Elizabeth* shuttling up and down the Tyseley goods loop without so much as a rope between them and the trains. Tyseley Open Days became nationally famous after the end of BR steam as being pretty much the only place where main line steam could be seen working at all, due to much persuasion and a profit sharing incentive for BR by PBW. This kept the pressure up and main line steam returned the following year, with the first train hauled by *Clun Castle* as some recompense for the sheer guts, determination and hard work put in behind the scenes [PHOTO: C.M. WHITEHOUSE]

chance in life. This new team helped rebuild both our section of Tyseley depot, from the cavernous drains upwards (even aspiring to rebuilding a roundhouse!), and as many engines as we could muster. Hallucinations played their part of course. We thought we could run GWR tank engines No's 4160 and 5637 on the main line from Birmingham to Stratford-upon-Avon – they seemed an ideal size – but BR was having no truck with small engines or 'The Shakespeare Express' and so the tank engines were sold to help defray the increasing capital spend on the remainder of the fleet. However, the Community Programme was successful beyond its dreams. Not only was much good construction and engineering work done but over eight hundred people were given work and regained the confidence to re-enter society in full time jobs. HRH The Prince of Wales came to approve. A red letter day for us all.

However, all good things come to an end and so did the job scheme, when we were least expecting it. Government turned off the tap when policies changed of course. The redundancies which resulted put our Tyseley operation on its knees and were enough to make PBW retire and enjoy a directorship on the Great Central Railway. I had sent our flagship engines there to be repaired and used, as we did not then have the funds to fix them.

During this time there were very many extremely long telephone conversations between Bob Meanley and me, somewhat about 'Bloomers' (which we will read about later), but also about making dreams work again. I had met Bob during a Settle & Carlisle trip when LMS 'Jubilee' Class 4-6-0 *Leander* made a superb return trip over the scenic line. The engine was always well presented and worked properly, and Bob Meanley had largely delivered that result, which fact I had noticed. Then two more pieces of luck presented themselves. Bob had spent a great deal of time working on a team designing Corby power station and had managed to accumulate sufficient funds to allow him a bit of a much-needed break, so he 'volunteered' to come to Tyseley to spend six months to see if something could be made of the workshop. Secondly, railway privatisation came along and enabled 'anyone' to run their own trains if they complied with the process. I was by then a commercial lawyer working deeply in this field in my day job advising the likes of ABB and so knew the ropes.

With this collective knowledge and lots of sessions putting the ideas down on paper to test them, we both popped along to an SLOA meeting and gently announced that 'The Shakespeare Express' would start running as England's only regular summer express steam train. The people in the room went very quiet and understandably so, as it had by then been some years since Tyseley locomotives had ventured out on the main line and many had given us up – but 'The Shakespeare Express' is still running over twenty years later …

Interestingly, we know PBW would have approved of all this, as right at the beginning of privatisation we discussed the concept of establishing our own Train Operating Company and also the possibilities of running some of what are now the Chiltern services. We even went to discuss all this with the Department of Transport but, whilst they were interested in the concept, they were not then prepared to invent the micro-franchise of a small Birmingham suburban network.

So we buckled down to make the new operation prosper as best we could with little or no capital but still with good connections and much elbow grease. I had 'bumped into' Ed Burkhardt, an American with Wisconsin Central Railroad who now led English Welsh & Scottish Railways, the new owner of British Rail's long haul freight business which, co-incidentally included its steam operating licence. After a good dinner at the Grand Junction Club (established by PBW and associates for the good company of friends and the persuasion of whomsoever required), Ed came to Tyseley to try his hand at driving *Rood Ashton Hall* up and down our depot sidings, after which he kindly agreed to run our trains for us. He gave us a great leg up and we never even received a bill for the first year's operations. As he told me later, everyone needs a leg up to get started. He was most kind.

Bob put his shoulder to the wheel and, with the equipment we had rescued from the demise of steam, built up an engineering business which has become the envy of many – Tyseley Locomotive Works (TLW). We entered the steam locomotive contracting business and step by step, the business grew, with apprentices trained to become skilled engineers and team leaders. All manner of contracts were won and delivered, our 'shop window' being our express steam trains, which ran shining and sparkling in the sun at speed on the main line. The Institute of Mechanical Engineers likened TLW to the steam engine equivalent of the E-Type Jaguar and Concorde. We had become a national asset, which must not now be lost on any count; the Heritage Lottery agrees with that too. As luck (and great family relationships) would have it, Bob's son Alastair showed an interest in engineering at a very early age and took to Tyseley. He has been there ever since and is now leading the development of TLW, having cut his teeth with friends on rebuilding 'Halls' and 'Castles' to exacting standards.

Fairly quickly Bob developed a method of operation which the small team could manage: two charters a month in the season, with 'The Shakespeare Express' in the summer school holidays. This paid the bills and allowed slow but steady fleet development. HSBC sold us a train of Mark 2 vacuum braked carriages for a total of £1 (Bob and I contributed 50p each!) and TLW rebuilt *Rood Ashton Hall* and pannier tanks No's 9600 and 7752. They then took on the gargantuan task of rebuilding *Earl of Mount Edgcumbe*, a thoroughbred GWR 'Castle' modernised with a four row superheater and a double chimney to become the 1950s 'GTI version'. Of course, this was just the practice run for overhauling *Clun Castle*, one of the few 'original' privately preserved steam engines that had started off the main line special train movement run by the voluntary sector.

By now, West Coast Railway Company were operating our trains and a good twenty-year partnership evolved which delivered our programme very well and with minimal fuss. Indeed, an operating licence was all we did not have from the essentials needed to sustain main line steam – locomotives, a train, a workshop and running depot, skilled people, a tour promoter and an operating licence. Apart from operations, our policy of 'insourcing' stood us in great stead, as we could make our own decisions, keep our own surpluses and avoid factions. We just did not control the railway we ran on but we made up for that somewhat by ensuring we had good friends in many places. David Smith and WCRC were very good to us.

One of our friends was (and remains) former Tyseley volunteer and EWS Charter Train Manager Matthew Golton, who was by now high up in First Group, which operated much of the remaining Great Western Railway. Matthew enabled us to operate *Earl of Mount Edgcumbe* on several high profile non stop expresses: 'The Bristolian', 'The Cheltenham Flyer', 'The Inter City' and IZ48, a re-run of *Clun Castle*'s Plymouth to Bristol record run from 1964. On that trip, we were running well and steadily at the regulation 75mph for mile after mile, when one of the Network Rail team on board exclaimed that, if we continued at this rate, we would shave a few minutes off No. 7029's record and did we wish to do that or slow down a bit? What a silly question! So now we have two record breakers on the same route.

If you take a snapshot of what you are doing every ten years or so, it is instructive to consider your progress both generally and also when compared with what is happening in the 'outside world'. In fact, it is dangerous not to do so. We were now in the 21st century and rapidly approaching the next 'tipping point' in our journey. Fortunately, we recognised it with just a few moments to spare.

We had moved up the steep hill from enjoying other people's special trains, understanding how to rebuild and operate narrow gauge and also branch lines, to acquiring an express steam engine and having it run for us, then translating all that into creating a workshop and team to be able to do everything except operate ourselves, whilst just about keeping our head above water with the available time and money. All good – or was it?

We were getting older, most steam locomotives were really life expired and the good work which TLW was able to do showed us that we really needed to enter the complete renewals business, find more and younger people, and much more money. It was rather like Lewis Carroll's Red Queen in *Alice Through The Looking Glass*; we had to run very fast indeed just to stay in the same place and if we wanted to get into the next square, we had to run even faster – but how?

Even worse, people with real knowledge and experience in maintaining and operating steam locomotives were becoming as scarce as hens' teeth. The network was beginning to experience some high profile steam locomotive failures, with bits dropping off engines and even our friendly operator, WCRC, suffered a suspension of its operating licence due to safety breaches. Was the main line heritage movement past its sell by date? Would our stakeholders pull the rug or support us? What should be done to climb the further and much steeper hill?

I was invited to an Italian lunch in Birmingham by two of our railway industry non executive trustees and asked if I wanted to form our own operating company. This would naturally require us to seek significant capital funds to take this step to be masters of our own destiny and gain a seat at the 'table' of the main line railway. We consulted and were encouraged to do so by our friends in industry and in our city – the relevant movers and shakers wanted steam to survive and thrive on the main line. 'The Shakespeare Express' was seen as an ideal and realistic operation to form a core component of the long term future. The route retained much of its Great Western heritage and the destinations at either end were to die for: Shakespeare's Stratford-upon-Avon is on everyones' bucket list and Birmingham is within reach of ten million people and would, we thought, eventually be connected to the world via London by HS2. The West Midland Rail Executive agreed to partner with us on the journey. My meeting with its Mayor, Andy Street, to explain our proposition was accelerated as he did not need to listen to the justification – he simply wanted delivery!

Business plans are all very well and, indeed, must be written, but you need fire in your belly and a steady nerve to deliver. And sometimes, one just has to try something and see if it works, We sat round our boardroom in my law firm, Wragge & Co., and debated. We had all the attributes we needed, except an operating licence and bags of money. We had the political support. We knew how to proceed but we had no real fundraising experience. We probably needed a million pounds.

We decided on a Community Benefit Society. A co-operative corporation owned and run by its shareholders but charitably controlled to avoid sqabbles and to try to provide longevity. We felt that ferroequinologists* would like to own an operating company which ran express steam trains. And they did. We raised £1,150,000, wrote a safety management system, recruited and were in business in 2017. This was a major change indeed. For the first time a community, which was not either owned by a state corporation or a man of significant net worth, had been granted an operating licence to run express steam trains on the main line. We did treat ourselves to a very good dinner.

We were just in time. To undertake such a step now would be even more difficult and just possibly too difficult; key people have retired, whilst the pandemic of 2020-21 removed the immediate prospects of significant fundraising and even stopped our trains running. Yes, there have been growing pains and learning points but we are still alive, solvent and have no commercial borrowings.

*A student of ferroequinology; a person who studies trains.

Perhaps the crowning glory of the first innings for all PBW's hard work was fixing for HRH The Prince of Wales to come and say 'thank you' in September 1988, for all the effort in enabling over eight hundred people to find confidence in work again during the 1980s recession and regain full time employment. Of course, Tyseley's infrastructure benefitted as well but that was the deal. Here PBW and I take a bit of a flier with Royalty, introducing Prince Charles to construction workers, even one wearing a T shirt emblazoned with 'Loadsa Money', but it was a good chat and, just sometimes, one has to run with the wind. [Photo: Alan Wood]

We have done the same as we did in the last great recession of the 1980s. We have taken the time during the pandemic lockdown to learn from the growing pains and reinvent how we deliver, step by step. Furthermore, we have resolved to deliver a sustainable succession, perhaps the hardest task yet as new generations approach life differently and steam age skills are becoming rare.

The trick now is to make ourselves relevant. Nostalgia for outmoded trains is all well and good but the future does not owe us a living. We are now buckling down to create a purpose for our express steam trains. After all, as a disruptive technology in the 19th century, railways helped change the world, create the Commonwealth, enable the City of Birmingham to become the greatest manufacturing centre the world had ever seen and encourage migrants to settle. If we can show our diverse community where they fit in this evolving story by using our beloved steam engines, then just maybe we can inspire them to innovate for themselves, as we have done. And by working within a community enterprise which runs a vibrant engineering business and a growing travel and entertainment company, everyone can learn and work together as a team to deliver results and gain satisfaction from what they contribute. Steam engines cannot run just by computer and the internet. They rely on people working together as a team, bringing their disparate skills to play to advantage in a competitive world.

So we will create Britain's first main line heritage railway along the Shakespeare Line, running turn and turn about with commuter trains, delivering excellent and unusual services to distinguish ourselves and appeal to everyone.

This then is the 'Tyseley Story' from its inception to date, delivered by dedicated people from the Midlands and Birmingham. This book will delve into aspects of this story in both words and pictures and seek to place it within the national context of main line steam. Whilst writing and collating all this, I pinched myself in the realisation that I have actually been some part in this story all the way through – from an enquiring child humoured by PBW, to delivering family delegated tasks and then assuming the mantle. Of course, delivery is by a team of friends who have many different skills. Over the very long time we have now been on this express steam train journey, we have largely learned what works and what does not but we are still learning. I do not have a crystal ball to determine the future but that does not matter. What does matter, is finding the right dedicated and determined team to hand the baton on to.

Echoing the words of Tom Rolt in his classic *Railway Adventure* about the first two years of the Talyllyn Railway Preservation Society, it has been an adventure which I shall remember all my days.

2. IN THE BEGINNING: THE TALYLLYN RAILWAY

'By this time the meeting had become infused with a spirit of crusade and even the sceptics, of which I was one, showed more interest than they intended.'

Pat Whitehouse

Early in October 1950, I received a circular signed by that redoubtable preserver of lost causes, author L.T.C. Rolt. It told of a forthcoming meeting at the Imperial Hotel, Birmingham to consider the future and possible preservation of the Talyllyn, the oldest surviving steam hauled narrow gauge railway in the world.

This was the first time that any serious proposal for this form of railway preservation had ever been put forward[1] and on the day of the meeting, 11th October, *The Birmingham Post* carried mention of it on the front page of its newspaper.

About seventy people attended, many of them hardened and somewhat sceptical enthusiasts from the Midlands. The lead was taken by Rolt and he was supported by Edward Thomas, then general manager of the TR. It appeared that this line could no longer carry on because heavy renewals were necessary. Unless help was forthcoming it would have to close.

Rolt led with his chin. He said he hoped that the meeting would result in the formation of a strong working committee to investigate the possible acquisition of the railway and the formation of a supporting society which would keep the line running.

Mr Thomas then spoke – he confirmed the bad state of the track and equipment but added that 1950 had been a record season with passenger receipts at £400, representing 5,235 passengers. He estimated that this figure might have been increased to 8,000 had accommodation been adequate.

By this time the meeting had become infused with a spirit of crusade and even the sceptics, of which I was one, showed more interest than they intended. The idea of saving a railway in those days of 'You can't do it' or 'You can't have it' was beginning to appeal. A committee was formed to investigate the possibilities. I found myself agreeing to be its Secretary, thus beginning a lifetime of involvement in steam preservation.

A lot of hard work and fun led to the Talyllyn being turned round and becoming a real success story, followed quickly by the resuscitation of the Ffestiniog, which in turn was followed by the Welshpool & Llanfair. The echo even rebounded to Australia, where the Puffing Billy Society joined forces with the Victorian Government Railways in rescuing and making viable the 2ft 6ins gauge line near Melbourne.

The original conspirators. One of the most important pictures of the preservation era, taken on the first day of Talyllyn Railway Preservation Society operations, 14th May 1951. Left to right: David Curwen (Engineer), Bill Trinder (Chairman), Pat Whitehouse (Secretary), Tom Rolt (General Manager) and Pat Garland (Treasurer) line up at Towyn Wharf station in front of *Dolgoch*.
[PHOTO: *THE TIMES*, TR COLLECTION]

'The Old Lady' – the sole working steam locomotive on the Talyllyn Railway on takeover by the preservationists in 1951. Manufactured in 1866 by Fletcher, Jennings of Whitehaven, 0-4-0T No. 2 *Dolgoch* stands at Rhydyronen station. At that time the Talyllyn was a total anachronism, untouched by eighty-five years of trundling trains up and down the Afon Fathew Valley from Bryn Eglwys Quarry in the foothills of the Cambrian mountains to the sea at Towyn. On entering preservation, the railway still had its two original locomotives and Midlands-built Brown Marshall carriages, with no continuous brake and wrought iron rails kept roughly in gauge by the turf which lay between them. [PHOTO: JOHN ADAMS]

Right: The Talyllyn Railway Preservation Society's First Progress Report, showing the initial committee elected to take the world's first volunteer run railway forward. This team included Pat Garland (accountant), Pat Whitehouse (building contractor), Ken Cope (Midland Red buses publicity manager) and Jim Russell (businessman, ex-GWR railwayman and 4mm GWR modeller, who introduced Tom Rolt to Bill Trinder, the two pioneers).

Below: Riding the Talyllyn in a former Penrhyn Railway quarrymens' open carriage. PBW is seen on the extreme right.

TALYLLYN RAILWAY PRESERVATION
SOCIETY.

First Progress Report.

At the preliminary meeting held at the Imperial Hotel, Birmingham on October 11th 1950, a Committee was set up as follows:
W.G.Trinder (Chairman) P.B.Whitehouse (Hon.Sec.)
P.J.Garland (Hon. Treas.) L.T.C. Rolt (Hon.Pub.Officer)
J.H.Russell, G.Walker, A.L.F.Fuller, E.E.Smith, W.Oliver, R.K.Cope, H.Gray, W.Tippetts, O.H.Prosser, E.S. Tonks.

In addition, the following members have since been co-opted onto the Committee: J.C.Wilkins, J.I.C. Boyd, E.Lees, W.Faulkner, D.C.Curwen.

In order to deal more effectively with the volume of business it was subsequently decided to divide the Committee into three sub-committees as follows:
Finance & General Purposes: Messrs. Trinder, Garland, Whitehouse,Fuller, Walker, Lees.
Advertising & Publicity: Messrs. Cope, Gray, Tippetts, Prosser, Tonks, Boyd.
Engineering: Messrs. Wilkins, Russell, Rolt, Smith, Curwen, Oliver.

John Snell

What is now a tidy, well maintained and very respectable operation was, some seventy years ago, anything but. I first rode on the Talyllyn Railway when it was still owned by Sir Henry Haydn Jones, on Easter Monday 1948. By then, things were at a pretty low ebb; two or three men were still employed in the quarries at Bryn Eglwys but since the last underground workings had been condemned as unsafe, all they could do was split and size rock which had already been brought to the surface. Two men, father and son Hugh and Dai Jones, were still employed by the railway, repairing track or stock or the locomotive, as required and within their capabilities. That day a handwritten notice in the window at Wharf and another in the ironmonger's window in Towyn High Street advertised three trips. The morning run had brought down a few wagons of slate. There were about fifteen people on the afternoon train, including me. It was an astonishing, lurching and bouncing ride, mainly along the interior of a thick hedge, which was also sometimes accompanied by sheep or cows. You glimpsed the scenery from time to time. Like the majority of trains, we stayed on the rails. But, by the 1950 season, that majority was down to about five out of six trips.

Before returning to my hotel and after *Dolgoch* had left with the evening train up the valley, I was allowed to look round the

railway's base at Pendre. The other engine, *Talyllyn*, was intact but out of action, with an alarming swelling on one side of the firebox and a hen's nest on the cab floor. The famous mobile booking office guard's van was parked in the workshop awaiting new wheel tyres. The whole operation was obviously in a fragile state and, in fact, a serious breakdown meant that few trains ran at all in 1949. I hardly thought I would ever see the railway again.

I was due to leave school in early 1951 and go up to Oxford that autumn. How to occupy that summer? I was delighted to see a news paragraph in the *Railway Magazine* announcing the project to preserve the Talyllyn following Sir Haydn's recent death. So I wrote to L.T.C. Rolt as instructed in the news item and, to cut a long story short, I found myself at the beginning of April meeting David Curwen in lodgings at Bryncrug, outside Towyn, and the following day starting to help him to prepare *Dolgoch* for its annual boiler inspection.

Pendre Works, at that time, had few amenities. One end of the combined locoshed and workshop was occupied by the then retired enginemen's four roomed house. There was no gas or electricity in any part of the building and only one water feedpipe in the non residential end, which ran to a rotten looking wooden tank in the roof. Washing had to be done in a bucket and, unless an engine was in steam, hot water came only from a small kettle on the works forge, which was encouraged by an enormous hand powered bellows and which was mainly used to make tea.

David and I got *Dolgoch* past the boiler inspector, although quite a lot of water poured out of the firebox as I worked away at the stirrup pump keeping the test pressure at 150psi. "*It will take up under steam,*" they said to each other. The inspector, rather suspicious of what was obviously an elderly boiler with an uncertain past, asked David to drill a small hole in the lower part of the barrel, and was pleasantly surprised to measure the thickness of the metal at that point and find it was a little less than the original $^3/_8$in.[2]

With the boiler passed for service at its rated 100lbs pressure, David started on the next job, which was to overhaul the suspension at the rear axle. The weight was carried by four volute springs, mounted on either side of the footplate in front of the firedoor. The four columns retaining these

springs were each attached to the frames by two 1in. diameter bolts which, after years of being banged about, had all stripped their threads, so that the engine subsided onto its axle boxes and the springs did nothing. In 1949, this had caused the frames to break, with the rear watertank remaining attached mainly through the cab roof. The frame was repaired by welding, after a delay which lost most of that year's business, but the cause of the problem was still there for us to deal with. We had to jack up the engine and drill out and re tap the eight holes in the frame to $1^1/_4$ins diameter, all using muscle power and an ancient ratchet drill – a very heavy job. Then there was reassembly, fitting the rotten old timber battens under the boiler lagging sheets, closing up the eccentric straps and brasses to reduce visible clearances, modifying the handbrake (which was the only brake) to bring the brake shoes into contact with the rear wheels and finally, after about three weeks, we were able to raise steam for the first time under the new management.

Meanwhile a gang had been assembled to work on the track, including the two previous employees, Hugh and Dai Jones, Bill Oliver (till then the local Kleen-E-Ze brush salesman) and three men lent by the nearby Fairbourne Railway to help us off to a start. They had relaid about half a mile of track some way up the line with rail purchased from the Harlech scrap merchant who had recently demolished the Corris Railway. This had been delivered to Rhydyronen station, with some ex-Corris sleepers as well, which were in a much better state than our own. These materials were then pushed down the line by manpower. In this way, we got a small float of re-usable original rails which we could use to replace broken ones. They broke quite often, generally with the web collapsing and the railhead going down an inch or so, often snapping but normally being held in line by the unbroken foot.

Meanwhile, Tom Rolt had arrived and was opening up the office down at Wharf, with which we could communicate by walking

half a mile down the line. One of Tom's first tasks was to organise the railway's first ever telephone; it took another year to install the second, a private line linking Wharf and Pendre. Since the track was in line with the BBC's local transmitter down on the coast, this telephone picked up the Welsh Home Service quite clearly. Things were still primitive.

A few days before I arrived, British Railways had delivered the two Corris locomotives, the brake van and all its surviving wagons to Wharf station from Machynlleth, where they had spent the last three years under tarpaulins on the remaining few sidings in the old Corris yard. Our first priority, once we had got steam on *Dolgoch*, was to bring this new equipment up to Pendre. As well as acting as David's fireman, I was commissioned by Pat Whitehouse to film this historic event for publicity purposes. Then David and I went for a joyride, taking the Corris van up the line for the first time. I had earlier walked the track as far as Dolgoch, noticing that all the rails were still there, though the long cutting above Brynglas was flooded and alive with about a million tadpoles. We got to Dolgoch without trouble, rather surprisingly, but then had a problem as the station water tank was, for the first time, empty, and so very nearly was the tank on the engine. There was nothing to do but return at once to Pendre, letting the fire die down. We were lucky; we got there without dropping the plug, and nothing worse than stalling with no fire and no steam in the middle of the level crossing. We barred the engine clear of the road and there it stayed until morning.

The next task was to start work on Corris locomotive No. 3, which we then called '*The Falcon*', after the name of its builder. It had been the only serviceable machine on the Corris for the last year or so, and David judged it could be got going fairly quickly, and so it proved, although the boiler inspector reduced the allowable pressure from 160lbs to 100lbs in view of the age of the tubes. Unlike the TR engines, whose boilers were lagged with wood, the

Family on the Talyllyn. My mother and sister, Thelma and Maggy, in conversation with the loco crew of former Corris Railway 0-4-2ST No. 3 *Sir Haydn* at Abergynolwyn. No. 3 had kept its original number throughout Corris, GWR, BR and Talyllyn ownership, and had been named after Sir Haydn Jones, the MP for Merionethshire and owner of the TR since 1910. He paid the expenses of the 2ft 3ins gauge line from his own pocket so that it could, at least, continue running for the rest of his lifetime; maybe he should really be considered the preservation pioneer? [PHOTO: P.B. WHITEHOUSE]

Local hero. Gareth Jones from Towyn was interested in the goings on of the preservationists as they struggled to maintain the train service. John Snell, a student down from Oxford, was helping drive and fire the 'Old Lady' *Dolgoch* and encouraged Gareth to join in at only thirteen years of age. Here Gareth is seen fixing the Coronation headboard on 2nd June 1953, Coronation Day, to former Corris Railway Kerr, Stuart 'Tattoo' Class 0-4-2T No. 4 *Edward Thomas*, named after the last General Manager before the preservation era. Edward Thomas joined Tom Rolt at the pioneering Birmingham hotel meeting in 1950 and eloquently put the case for continuing operations on the Talyllyn. Gareth went on to become Chief Traction Inspector for steam locomotives for English, Welsh & Scottish Railways/DB Cargo and encouraged many footplatemen in their work, including on 'The Shakespeare Express'. It is a small world. [Photo: John Adams]

Corris more up to date boilers were lagged with blue asbestos plaster. Nobody thought evil of that material back then. David and I broke it all off the boiler of No. 3, avoiding dust by wetting it all first and then putting the fragments in a wooden barrel for re-use. David ordered up some more blue asbestos to build up the body of this insulation and I brought the paper sack of crocidolite up from Sir Haydn's ironmongers in the High Street in a wheelbarrow. Nowadays, Health & Safety inspectors would be standing three deep to prevent anything like that happening but, although David and I were both liberally plastered up in the stuff to our elbows, we survived. But I admit we kept it wet as we did not fancy the dust it made. The other thing we noticed was that No. 3's wheels had narrow treads, quite unlike the other TR engines and indeed also Corris No. 4. This obviously made No. 3 an uncertain runner on the deteriorated TR track but we had no choice as No. 4 needed a great deal of work.

This got us to the Whitsun holiday weekend, when we were due to re-open for the Monday, running only as far as Rhydyronen. But on the Saturday, we ran a train all the way to Abergynolwyn for the first time, because many Preservation Society members had arrived and it was intended to put up posters and publicity in all the stations. And all went well on both days; passengers flooded in, and photographers, and we had a page of pictures in the next day's *Times* newspaper. The age of railway preservation had arrived.

But we now had to contemplate running ten trains a week for the main season, starting early in June, instead of only six the year before. Hugh Jones would be needed to supervise the track gang, whose daily labours were going to be essential, while David Curwen would still be needed in the workshops. So Dai would drive and I would fire and I found I had a job for the summer at £5 a week.

Unfortunately, the Joneses found the changes brought about by the more adequate management were not to their liking and first Hugh then Dai left, with the result that by the end of July, I was the regular driver of a public passenger train service, aged just nineteen. Very soon, we recruited a new fireman to replace me: Gareth Jones, a big strong local lad who bicycled round the town delivering meat for the butcher but who always seemed to be looking over the wall when the train was at Wharf. After he accepted the job, I found that he was barely thirteen! But that did not matter then and he was as keen as mustard and never needed to be told anything twice. Although retired now, his last job was as traction inspector for DB Cargo on main line steam special trains.

During that first season, several more people joined the railway's paid staff, since it was going to be essential to press ahead with track renewal as quickly as possible. John Bate became a volunteer in the first year, rising to Chief Engineer for many years and still volunteering today – something of a record. David Curwen had to go back to run his own business after the first season and Tom Rolt had to do the same at the end of the second. I worked on the paid staff for the first three years, and as a volunteer during my university vacations but then other commitments pulled me away too. But it was all an adventure never to be forgotten.

And things were touch and go for a while. In spite of a maintenance and renewal effort many times greater than for thirty years at least, the physical collapse of the railway was still proceeding faster than its recovery and, during the 1953-54 winter, it became impossible for a time to operate over the worst three quarters of a mile through the woods at Dolgoch. It was not until the Royal Engineers arranged a two week summer camp for one of their railway operating units in 1953, during which they completely resleepered and overhauled that length, that as it proved, the corner was just about turned. It was a close run thing but the Talyllyn nowadays is a very respectable railway.

References

1. Not strictly true. In the 1930s there had been a local attempt in the USA to preserve the Maine 2ft gauge Bridgton & Harrison line but, sadly, this came to nothing and it closed in 1941, largely due to the outbreak of war restricting tourist traffic. But much equipment was saved and ran on a recreated Edaville Railroad in Cape Cod.
2. Later, when the boiler was eventually replaced, it was found that had the hole drilled in the boiler been a little either side of the actual place, the boiler thickness would have been found to be some 1/8in. – then the story that unfolded might have been quite different!

Harborne station in 4mm scale. This model was scratch-built by PBW as early as 1948 and still survives in working order. It was exhibited at various local model railway shows in Birmingham at the time when PBW and PJG first met and developed the friendships which led them to help rescue the Talyllyn Railway, and then engage in standard gauge railway preservation. The train in the platform is an Exley-manufactured two coach LM&SR set ready to return to Birmingham New Street, hauled by an L&NWR 'Chopper' 2-4-2T made by Guy Williams, locomotive builder from the exquisite Pendon Museum of railway models. [PHOTO: C.M. WHITEHOUSE]

3. HARBORNE

'Cam's first excursion was to Harborne in 1950.'

Our special train story really begins in the Birmingham 'village' of Harborne – a prosperous suburb of the city – as that is both where my family lived and to where W.A. 'Cam' Camwell ran his first special train in 1950, two years before I was born. The Harborne Branch intrigued many people. Branch lines conjure up fairly set images in the minds of most enthusiasts but Harborne was different.

The Harborne Railway Company was incorporated on 28th June 1866, to build a railway only just over two miles long and worked, from the outset, by the London & North Western Railway who undertook, in 1874, to work the line in perpetuity for fifty per cent of the gross receipts. Originally, the proposal was to link Harborne with Halesowen on the outskirts of Birmingham, connecting with the Great Western Railway at Old Hill, but plans were changed. Intriguingly, the line from Old Hill to Halesowen was still built by the GWR and the very last steam locomotives to operate it were based at Tyseley depot but we will come to that later.

The first train left Harborne at 8 o'clock on Monday 10th August 1874, the locomotive being decorated with red, green and white flags but, otherwise, without ceremony. Initially, there were six daily trains and three on Sundays, until the residents of the arterial Hagley Road objected strongly to the disturbance of their Sabbath.

This service was increased to the rather amazing total of twenty daily trains, except on Sundays of course, which only took fifteen minutes for their journey. Additionally, each day there were a couple of goods trains delivering household requirements to suburbia, mainly coal for domestic fires. The reason for the very frequent service was to take commuters from Harborne into the centre of Birmingham at New Street station. So useful was the branch that my grandfather was able to nip home on the train for lunch before returning to his office in the afternoon. The postal service was also so

good, that he used to send a postcard from his office in the morning to tell my grandmother what time he would be arriving for lunch that day. A sort of postal email service. The time table was really excellent, with the first train leaving Harborne at 6.45am and the last train leaving New Street at 11.30pm, allowing theatre-goers to return home after shows but also enabling the 'Peaky Blinder' lads to ride with them, often causing some distress to passengers.

Services were mainly hauled by L&NWR tank locomotives but, in the early days, an occasional 'Jumbo' 2-4-0 put in an appearance on through trains from Burton and Walsall, enabling *Sirius*, *Sister Dora* and *Snowdon* to grace the turntable at Harborne station, another unusual feature for a branch line. Loads were often heavy, with crowded trains of eight coaches.

The problem with operation of the line was the junction with the L&NWR main line at Monument Road. Branch trains would habitually be held up by more important, late running express trains, as the access into New Street station was only by the double tracked main line. Soon, Birmingham City Corporation buses had won the traffic and passenger services ceased in 1924.

Cam's first excursion was to Harborne in 1950. Although the line was by now goods only, he chartered the Dudley two-coach push-pull 'motor' set hauled by L&NWR 'Radial' 2-4-2T No. 46747, normally shedded at 3C, Monument Lane. This left New Street station at 3.10pm on Saturday 3rd June and was almost certainly the first and the last push-pull formation on the branch. As advanced notice of the special appeared in the press, considerable interest was aroused and the train was even seen off at New Street by its stationmaster, who specially donned a top hat and tails for the occasion. Once the branch was reached, there were small crowds of well-wishers to wave at the first passenger train for nearly thirty years. The short train was packed to capacity with

The train at the bottom of the garden. My great grandmother took this picture in around 1909 of the 'Harborne Express' passing the bottom of the family garden on Westfield Road, showing an L&NWR 2-4-2T climbing the 1 in 66 incline towards the city with a train of 4-wheeled carriages.
[Photo: C.M. Whitehouse Collection]

OPPOSITE PAGE TOP: Watch the birdie! Former L&NWR 2-4-2T No. 46747 arrives at Harborne on Saturday 3rd June 1950, to be photographed by man and boy on the left; note the bowler hatted inspector on the right-hand side of the engine guarding the foot crossing. This was 'Cam's' first steam SLS Special and was almost certainly the first non-stop passenger train on the branch. [PHOTO: C.M. WHITEHOUSE COLLECTION]

RIGHT: The second SLS Special along the Harborne Branch (and also to Halesowen) ran on 30th May 1959, top and tailed by two former Midland Railway '2F' 0-6-0s. Here No. 58271 brings the train back down the branch towards the city, passing the 'Harborne tip' along Gillhurst Road. The tip now has houses built on it and, until very recently, my mother was able to look out of her lounge window onto this view, although trees have now obscured it and the whole branch line is a public cycle and walkway. [COLOUR-RAIL]

enthusiasts, including some rather wistful former regulars of the branch passenger service and the guard of the last passenger train. Also on board was that veteran local traveller, Mr TR Perkins, the Leamington chemist who set out to travel over every possible railway line in the United Kingdom and finally succeeded in his mission when he arrived at a remote country station in the middle of Southern Ireland.

The train was the first true 'Harborne Express', as it ran non-stop up the branch from Monument Lane. Mitchell & Butler's had a private network leading off the branch and they turned out their Aveling & Porter locomotive *John Barleycorn* to whistle its greeting as the 'Chopper' appeared from under Rotton Park Road bridge.

So well remembered was this trip, that Cam ran two more. One was topped and tailed by two Midland '2F' 0-6-0s on 30th May 1959 and, of course, Cam just had to run a last special train on Saturday 2nd November, 1963, when the goods service ceased. This was also top and tailed, this time by a couple of ex-LM&SR 'Mickey Mouse' 2-6-0s, No's 46429 and 46522, the latter in fully lined green livery. I was fortunate to travel on both these special trains and Cam kindly made sure I had a window seat right next to the engine. Amazingly now I think of it, Dad convinced the driver of No. 46522 to let me ride the footplate on the very last journey of all from Harborne back to New Street and I was only just eleven years old! What I did not know then and didn't even find out until 2020 was that Ray Churchill, our first steam driver for Vintage Trains, was the fireman on that locomotive! Small world indeed. Such was the introduction to riding steam specials which has continued all my life.

OPPOSITE PAGE BOTTOM: Excited children at Harborne station on 3rd June 1950. Passenger services ceased in 1924 and the station platform was used as a wood store for the Chad Valley toy factory which made, amongst many other things, wooden jigsaw puzzles for railway companies to sell as souvenirs. [PHOTO: BIRMINGHAM POST & MAIL]

RIGHT: The very last passenger train on the Harborne Branch was another 'Cam' special run on Saturday 2nd November 1963, when the goods service ceased. This was again top and tailed but by LM&SR 'Mickey Mouse' 2-6-0s No's 46429 and 46522. The latter, in fully lined green livery, is seen here again from the tip, leading the train away from Harborne station. Even at the tender age of eleven I was allowed a footplate ride on this journey. [PHOTO: LACEY'S STUDIOS]

The first public enthusiast trip was run by the Railway Correspondence & Travel Society, who chose an icon in steam locomotive engineering: the preserved Great Northern Railway single-wheeler No. 1, exhumed from the York Railway Museum and chartered together with period East Coast Joint Stock coaches, to run on 11th September 1938 from London King's Cross to Peterborough and back. A phenomenal experience even then. *The Times* reported: *'The departure from King's Cross was suitably cheered by a crowd on the platform. The trip was a matter of genuine enjoyment to the railway enthusiasts. They got their notebooks out and jotted down 'King's Cross, 0.00.' At intervals some other place and some other figure was jotted down. Crossword puzzles and the other normal pastimes associated with railway travel were entirely absent from this strange journey. Cameras were used with the utmost vigour and for the strangest purposes. There were people who deliberately took photographs of the mouth of each tunnel that the train entered. The train was spoken of in terms of affection. "Now she's pulling,"* someone would say with an emotional disregard for the sex of the 'Flying Scotsman' and his locomotive which is technically known as Patrick Stirling No. 1.'
[Photo: A.W.V. Mace/Milepost 82½ collection]

4. THE SOCIETY SPECIAL
Pat Whitehouse

This essay is taken from the 1960s Ian Allan Railway Roundabout Annual

'There can scarcely be an historic class of engine that has not been used to haul them, nor have many branch lines closed in recent years without a last train chartered by one society or another.'

One of the most important developments of the 1950s has been the Society Special Train and so I would like to tell you about some of these exciting trips and why they are run. The two big railway societies, the Stephenson Locomotive Society and the Railway Correspondence & Travel Society, have been with us for a long time; the SLS being the older, having celebrated its Golden Jubilee in 1959. Both cater for the average enthusiast as well as the real specialist and, in both cases, their membership runs into the thousands and they have centres in most of the large towns. Naturally, there is a tremendous variety of interests as far as members are concerned but I think it is safe to say that locomotives and railway histories are the two subjects which attract the greatest support.

In these days of transition and modernisation on our railways, these particular interests have become obsolete but the whole of the transport system is becoming more integrated and many railway routes are becoming uneconomic, due either to road competition or the fact that two or more lines of railway (because of the fierce competition of the old companies) were built to serve towns A and B. This means that, in addition to many classes of steam engine disappearing for ever, a very large route mileage of our railways is also going; sometimes there is only the removal of passenger services but often all services. So before long there will be a generation grown up who will not know what it is like to travel on an express behind a 'King' or an 'A3' 'Pacific', or a 'Duchess' or a 'Lord Nelson,' and

No. 3454 *Skylark*, the very last GWR 'Bulldog' 4-4-0 in service, waits in the centre road at Birmingham Snow Hill on 17th June 1951, with the first of what became an annual series of SLS Specials to the GWR 'mecca' at Swindon. Note the 'G W R' lettering was still on the tender despite Nationalisation having taken place three years previously. [Photo: P.B. Whitehouse]

GNR 'Atlantic' 4-4-2 No. 251 on Doncaster shed, having been exhumed from York Railway Museum and put back into service for Alan Pegler's 'Plant Centenarian' train celebrating the works' centenary. This engine double-headed the special with *Henry Oakley*, another Ivatt 'Atlantic' from the museum. Alan Pegler and Trevor Bailey simply persuaded BR to agree to temporarily removing them and putting them back into traffic for the specials. Both people subsequently went on to be seriously involved in resurrecting the Ffestiniog Railway and Pegler subsequently purchased *Flying Scotsman*. [Photo: P.B. Whitehouse]

even now there are a vast number of enthusiasts who have rarely, if ever, travelled behind a pre-Grouping locomotive on an express train and a similar number who have never travelled over a country branch line on a regular passenger train.

The Society Specials have come into existence to bring a little piece of the past into the present, and in general these trains are hauled by older classes of locomotive over closed sections of railway, though this is not always quite the case, as a number of specials combine modern motive power over the main lines with high-speed running, before proceeding over the closed branch behind the veteran. One of the first society sponsored specials must have been on 11th September 1938, when the RCTS promoted a train

behind the restored Great Northern Railway Stirling 'Single' wheeler No. 1, which the London & North Eastern Railway fetched out of York Museum specially. What a sight this old lady was with her train of period piece 6-wheeled coaches and it was a real enthusiasts' event; the train having been chartered for a trip from King's Cross to Peterborough and back. Even in these days when nearly everyone owns a camera, I doubt if many trains have been photographed so much in such a short space of time for it really was an occasion.

So, over twenty years ago, the seeds of the Society Special were sown and most of the passengers were those sufficiently old enough to be sampling afresh a type of railway journey they must have thought to be gone for ever. But there was also a younger

A former L&SWR 'T9' 4-4-0 on foreign ground. No. 30304 double heads a GWR double-framed 'Dukedog' 4-4-0 on a Talyllyn Railway Preservation Society Special, round the curve past the golf links at Aberdovey, on the last lap of the journey from London and Shrewsbury to Towyn. [PHOTO: P.B. WHITEHOUSE]

generation who did not know the golden age of railways and who had come to find out for themselves. It must have been about 1948 that the post war specials began to run and, in those days, it was very much of a novelty both to the railwaymen and the amateur; one or two are freshly fixed in my mind and of them the first is the SLS 'Swansong for a Skylark' from Birmingham to Swindon one June Sunday in 1951.

There was something about the 'Bulldogs' that appealed to me: their outside frames, huge brass nameplates, sometimes on the outside of the cab and oval shaped, and sometimes over the leading pair of driving wheels, a great arc of polished brass letters. Like many other Great Western engines, they used to snort and make rather rude noises when they were standing in a station and I think this appealed to me very much as a boy. They also used to have lovely names: how well I remember *Pershore Plum*, *Brasenose*, *Kingfisher* and *Sir Massey Lopes*. Our engine for the special was one of the two remaining in the class, and it was an engine I had never seen before: *Skylark*. We had a train packed to the doors and really to make a job of it my good friend O.S. Nock rode on the footplate, recording the running. What a red letter day it was!

The next special I want to mention was even more stirring and to many railwaymen and enthusiasts a very sad occasion; it was the last run of one of the most famous of locomotive classes: the Ivatt 'Atlantic'. The trip was a public excursion organised for enthusiasts by the Eastern Region of British Railways. The date was 26th November 1950, the engine No. 62822 and the journey from King's Cross to Doncaster. To show how popular the train was, all seats were booked in a little more than a week after it was first advertised. The special left King's Cross at 11.00am, the engine carrying a specially designed headboard showing the first larger boilered Ivatt 'Atlantic', No. 251 built in 1902, already withdrawn and now preserved at York. In spite of fog, No. 62822 arrived on time at Doncaster at 2.15pm and a chapter in the locomotive history

of the East Coast route to Scotland came to an end. To mark the occasion Mr K.C. Bird, the Chief Regional Officer, Eastern Region, presented one of the engine's works plates to Mr H.G. Ivatt, the designer's son (and incidentally at that time the Chief Mechanical Engineer of the London Midland Region). In a special goodwill message handed to the driver of No. 62822 by the stationmaster at King's Cross and addressed to the stationmaster at Doncaster, it was said of the Ivatt Atlantics '*they helped to make the East Coast route justly famous and no doubt that proud tradition will go on in yet further brilliant pages of our railway history.*' It will be a long time before the old Great Northern enthusiasts forget the sight of the last Great Northern 'Atlantic' slipping off her train at the north end of the Down platform at Doncaster, moving off down the line, giving a crow on her whistle for the signalman, and then back down on the other side of the platform past her train and run quietly into the works, her job done. For the rest of the afternoon she was placed alongside No. 251 and several other famous engines for us to inspect.

Since 1951, these special trains have been more and more frequent and they have run over every Region. There can scarcely be an historic class of engine that has not been used to haul them, nor have many branch lines closed in recent years without a last train chartered by one society or another. In the running of these trains there has been real cooperation between the railway authorities and the societies, for the detailed work involved can be terrific, especially if the train has to work over semi-abandoned sections of track. There are, somewhat naturally, several schools of thought as to the make up of these trains and no one section of specialists thinks exactly the same as another. To some, it is the engine that counts, to others, the quality of the locomotive's running and, to the historians, the very fact that they are riding on a piece of track on which they have never travelled before, and never mind whether the power be a Stirling 'Single' or a multiple unit diesel set. Even

'PBW' being helped into his overalls by his co-conspirator Pat Garland on Ruabon station on 28th September 1963, before taking a cab ride on GWR 'Manor' Class 4-6-0 No. 7827 *Lydham Manor* over the Cambrian lines on a Talyllyn Railway Preservation Society Special. [Photo: J.J. Davis/TR Collection]

the locomotive enthusiasts are sometimes purists and there was once a most tiresome gentlemen who complained bitterly that a pre-Grouping engine should never run on a section of line that it did not use in the days of its old company!

This reminds me of another kind of special train which has grown up during the past seven years or so. This is the Preservation Society Special. The Talyllyn Railway, of course, was the first in the field and it was the Talyllyn Railway Preservation Society who ran the first of the preservation specials, the idea being to take society members along on annual general meeting day to see their railway. To start with the numbers were small and the train was only a former Great Western Railway diesel railcar but it wasn't long before the numbers increased far beyond this, making a steam train essential. All kinds of engines have been used for the run between London and Towyn; usually a large express engine as far as Shrewsbury and then, after that, over the winding and hilly road over the mountains, two smaller engines.

I have seen all these trains and when the day is over at Towyn and everyone has had his fill of the narrow gauge, the special waits at the main line station for the journey home. The first of these steam specials had an ex-L&SWR 'T9' 4-4-0 rostered. I remember that evening as we walked down the main street of Towyn in the darkness. The rain had stopped but there was a wind blowing up

from the sea and we could hear a safety valve hissing as we stepped out of the hotel into the road. The train had been in for some time when we arrived and the lighted coaches stood alongside the Up platform. At the head, two locomotives glittered under the combined lights of the platform lamps and the glow from their fires, while plumes of steam rose from safety valves and were caught by the wind to be pushed downwards towards the black shadowy figures standing in admiring groups beneath the footplates of the veterans. We joined them, men (and women too) from Portsmouth, London, Birmingham, Manchester and even Ireland, together with a few of the locals who had come to see the train depart. In the flickering light we saw the beautiful curves of the leading engine, the 'T9', and, behind her, the solid respectability of the 'Dukedog,' her outside cranks symbolic of an age now past. The driver of the 'T9' sat waiting on the left of his footplate (contrary to good Great Western practice, where they drive on the right-hand side), clad in an old mackintosh with his trousers tied round his ankles with string. Soon the key man, our old friend Headquarters Inspector George Holland, was aboard, the signal light changed from red to green, the guard's whistle blew, his lamp too showed green and they were away, two whistles sounding in unison, arms waving from the engine cabs and from the train, detonators exploding as the wheels passed over them, to disappear into the distance, London-bound.

5. THE 'CAM' SLS SPECIALS

*"Do you want to go up to Mallard's speed record or to 130mph, or what?
You have two minutes to make up your mind."*

William Arthur Camwell was simply 'Cam' to all his very many friends. Born in Handsworth, Birmingham on 18th November 1906, Cam was soon introduced to transport. His journey to grammar school involved travelling either by L&NWR into Birmingham New Street or by Birmingham Corporation Tram and on these journeys was born his lifelong passion for both railways and trams. His entire career was spent in banking and he became manager for the Birmingham Municipal Bank, retiring from the Kingstanding branch in 1971 after forty-seven years service. He was popular and well liked, always working hard to ensure his customers received fast, efficient and courteous service. He carried this through into his service as Secretary for the Midland Area of the Stephenson Locomotive Society.

The SLS was a long standing railway society of some repute and, by now, well over a hundred years old, having been founded in 1909 to gather information about locomotives and to arrange visits to depots.

Like many societies, the SLS had its characters. One such was the President from 1925 until as late as 1960 – J.N. Maskelyne. He had an affection for the London, Brighton & South Coast Railway and was a man of great charm, which he put to good use in persuading the Southern Railway to preserve *Gladstone*, a Stroudley 0-4-2 tender engine. Maskelyne simply asked Sir Herbert Walker if the railway would present the locomotive to the SLS who would look after it. For £150, *Gladstone* was returned to Brighton Works where she was built in 1882 and retro-fitted with a Stroudley boiler and repainted in full and glorious LB&SCR 'improved engine green'! Maskelyne then charmed the L&NER into finding *Gladstone* a place in their York Museum free of charge. This rescue of an historic locomotive by a society of volunteers must rank as pioneering private preservation. Not satisfied with that, the Society ran its first recorded railtour on 19th March 1932, when it arranged with the LM&SR to take a trip for members only on the petrol-driven, rubber-tyred Micheline railcar, which was then being tested between Bletchley and Oxford. The railtour phenomenon had begun.

The first public enthusiast trip, however, as we have already seen, was run by the Railway Correspondence & Travel Society. It chose another icon in steam locomotive engineering: the preserved Great Northern Railway single wheeler No. 1, exhumed from the York Railway Museum and chartered by the Society, together with

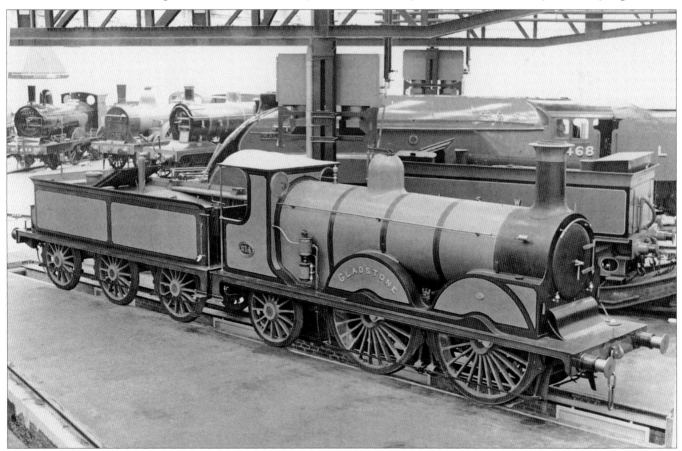

LB&SCR 0-4-2 No. 214 *Gladstone*, originally preserved by the SLS in 1927 and presented to the British Transport Commission when the National Collection was formed. *Gladstone* is believed to have been the first locomotive preserved privately rather than by the state and is seen here in the National Railway Museum at York shortly after arrival. [Photo: J.H.L. Adams/Colourviews Ltd]

LEFT: Cam's first steam SLS Railtour was to Harborne.
Here, ex-L&NWR 'Radial' 2-4-2T No. 46757 stands at
Monument Lane, the junction for the Harborne Branch
and where she was shedded, on 3rd June 1950.
[PHOTO: DAVID WALDREN COLLECTION]

BELOW LEFT: Ex-Midland '2F' 0-6-0s No's 58271 and 58177
at Halesowen on 30th May 1959, during the second 'Cam'
special to Harborne and Halesowen.
[PHOTO: DAVID WALDREN COLLECTION]

of Squadron Leader, he was deputised to take Pandit Nehru out of British captivity in Burma back to Calcutta.

All this excitement over, Cam resumed his banking career and his railway hobby, becoming the first Secretary of the SLS Area in the Midlands in 1946, a position which he maintained for nearly forty years. He travelled on a joint Birmingham Locomotive Club/SLS railtour over the Welshpool & Llanfair Railway on 2nd July 1949 (repeated a week later on 9th due to its popularity), hauled by one of their 0-6-0Ts, No. 823 *Countess*. Cam subsequently organised a GWR railcar special from Birmingham to Welshpool, running via Kidderminster, Ludlow, Shrewsbury and returning via Wellington.

We have already read about the 'Harborne Express' of 3rd June 1950. This was in fact a tour of the 'Birmingham Circle' and various branches (including Harborne) made possible by the use of the Dudley push-pull set hauled and propelled by ex-L&NWR 'Radial' 2-4-2T No. 46757.

There were seven tours that year, including a nine day tour of Ireland in May, organised by a joint committee of the SLS, RCTS and the Irish Railway Record Society, which covered all the Irish railways, even the Fintona horse tram, at an estimated cost of about £20.

Cam quickly expanded his special train repertoire, working with a small team of friends who assisted him in making these tours so successful: N.A. Tandy, D. Woodhouse and J.C. Wilkins helped by surveying the routes, writing the itineraries in such fine detail and producing them at minimal cost. Specialists such as the renowned Dr Hollick, a Staffordshire GP and historian par excellence of the Potteries, North Staffordshire and Peak District railways, brought his experience to bear on itineraries for tours in 'his' region. Undoubtedly, these SLS Special tours set the pattern and high standard for the railtours of other societies that were to follow.

Many memorable tours were run, covering the West Midlands of course, but expanding to all the railway branches in South Wales, the East Midlands and Staffordshire and, by others, further and further afield such as into L&NER territory throughout the 1950s and '60s. However, the 'maestro' organiser was definitely Cam. The tours were highly successful and enabled many enthusiasts to savour long and often complex itineraries, travelling for the last

period East Coast Joint Stock coaches, to run on 11th September 1938 from London King's Cross to Peterborough and back. A phenomenal experience even then.

In the early 1920s the journal *Locomotive News & Railway Contractor* had published a list of all British railway locomotive sheds, including all the sub-sheds, some of which were quite remote. This list fired Cam's enthusiasm to visit them all and record them for posterity, an ambition which began in 1934. At this time too, an increasing number of branches were being shut and so Cam also tried to travel and photograph the closing lines before they disappeared completely.

The Second World War curtailed these activities and Cam was called up into the RAF, seeing service in both India and Burma, being stationed in Calcutta and Rangoon where he was Secretary of the Air Priorities Board, which was responsible for controlling the limited air space available. In 1946, having reached the rank

Ex-GWR Railcar No. W7W, still in chocolate and cream livery, at Coleford Severn & Wye station on 23rd September 1950. [PHOTO: P.B. WHITEHOUSE]

The last GWR 'Bulldog' in service, No. 3454 *Skylark*, on arrival at Oxford with the first Swindon SLS Special on 17th June 1951. [PHOTO: P.M. ALEXANDER]

LEFT: Renowned and prolific author O.S. 'Ossie' Nock, who recorded much 'Locomotive Practice & Performance' in the *Railway Magazine*, on the footplate of *Skylark*.
[PHOTO: P.M. ALEXANDER]

BELOW: The last GWR 'Saint' still at work, No. 2920 *Saint David*, climbs Sapperton Bank towards the summit tunnel with six carriages on 15th June 1952. Wearing BR lined black livery, the 4-6-0 is hauling the second annual SLS Special from Birmingham Snow Hill to Swindon. [PHOTO: P.M. ALEXANDER]

time over many lines and often also behind the last survivor of a class of locomotive.

These times were very different to now; common sense prevailed and there was no bureaucratic policy of not permitting this or that for health & safety or other political reasons. The BR Modernisation Plan had made it clear that steam was not long for this world and, of course, railwaymen carried their job with pride. So enthusiasts were permitted (and indeed encouraged) to enjoy the railways. Generally, the SLS members in command were well connected and knew many senior railwaymen. Cam was certainly in this category and, combined his connections with an encyclopaedic knowledge of the railway network. The years ahead were to blossom with the unusual and the fast disappearing. And the tours were easy to organise. In those days, a simple telephone call to BR was all that was really needed. Once they understood what was ordered, they would work out the times, find the rolling stock, allocate the locomotive and send a simple contract sheet out for the booking. All Cam then had to do was sell the tickets. A far cry from the complex charter procedures today in the privatised world.

Perhaps the best remembered set of trips included the annual GWR trip to Swindon Works. The first of these, the 'Swansong of a Skylark' ran on 17th June 1951 when 'Bulldog' No. 3454 *Skylark*, an outside framed 4-4-0 and the last of her class took five coaches from Birmingham Snow Hill to Swindon and back. The legendary

O.S. Nock rode the footplate complete with his stopwatch. These trips became an institution, run each year, usually with the last member of a GWR class of famous locomotive: *Saint David*, *Princess Margaret*, *City of Truro*, *Pendennis Castle*, *King Henry VI* and *County of Chester* being amongst the notable names. All these engines came to the GWR depot at Tyseley in Birmingham to be prepared for the trip, being cleaned often by enthusiastic amateurs and having their GWR bufferbeam numbers restored by painters from B. Whitehouse & Sons, the family firm who also made the wooden headboards always carried by the locomotives. So began the long and continuing association of Tyseley depot with the special train.

Probably everyone who rode these specials has their favourite and certainly there were many deserving runs to choose from. The last Midland 'Compound' running in the pouring rain from New Street to Redditch; an L&NWR 'G2', from the last remaining few stabled at Bescot taking a seven hour tour round Birmingham in 1963; the last trains on the Ross & Monmouth in the winter snow; a spark arrested pannier on the Cleobury Mortimer & Ditton Priors Branch and the first BR blue-liveried train on the narrow gauge Vale of Rheidol line behind 2-6-2T No. 9 *Prince of Wales*, all come very readily to mind.

Cam was very accommodating and helpful, and made sure many a young enthusiast travelled if they were interested, even if the train was supposedly full and he recruited many hundreds of people into

No. 1335, a 2-4-0 built by Dübs originally for the Midland & South Western Junction Railway and then absorbed and modified by the Great Western, veers away from the island platform at Moreton in Marsh and onto the Shipston-on-Stour Branch on 31st August 1952. Note the rows of steam heated banana vans in the sidings behind. [Photo: P.M. Alexander]

the SLS. Everything on his trips just seemed to fall into place and even Cam was able to rush around with his cameras recording the passing scene along with everyone else. At stations, passengers would pour off the train, clamber up signals for better photographs and gather around the locomotive all the while. Due to demand, he even ran three identical last trains on the Shropshire & Montgomery army run line, on 14th, 21st and 28th September 1958 – two brakevans and two carriages full to bursting with enthusiasts. On the last train on the 2ft 6ins gauge Welshpool & Llanfair Railway on 3rd November 1956, hauled by No. 822 *The Earl*, enthusiasts rode in empty open coal wagons, some sitting on station benches thoughtfully put inside them by station staff from Welshpool. On the last train from Stafford to Bromshall Junction on 23rd March 1957, with Ivatt 2-6-2T No. 41224 and a three coach non-corridor motor set, saplings had to be cleared ahead of the train as the line had not been used for six years!

But just maybe the *piece de résistance* was on the East Coast Main Line. For their Golden Jubilee in 1959, BR were persuaded to provide one of Sir Nigel Gresley's finest, 'A4 Pacific' No. 60007, named after the great engineer himself, put in charge of legendary 'demon' driver Bill Hoole. This produced an incredible 110mph on the southbound journey from Doncaster, running down Stoke Bank, which proved to be the post-war world record for steam. *Sir Nigel Gresley* was in good working order and Hoole was recorded as saying: "*The engine is running beautifully – if she carries on like this, we should get what we want.*" On the footplate he asked the Inspector: "*Do you want to go up to Mallard's speed record or to 130mph, or what? You have two minutes to make up your mind.*" The Inspector made it plain that 110mph was to be the limit. Hoole reacted accordingly: "*I told my mate to save blowing off through Peterborough.*"

Most fittingly, the last steam tours organised by Cam were not one but two specials from Birmingham to the North West on 4th

ABOVE: A portrait of No. 1335 standing at the terminus at Shipston-on-Stour, still in GWR livery and with her driver leaning out of the cab and the train guard on the cab steps. [PHOTO: P.M. ALEXANDER]

LEFT: Ex-L&NWR 0-6-2T 'Coal Tank' No. 58903 on a 'Centenary of New Street Station' evening excursion on 1st June, 1954. [PHOTO: DAVID WALDREN COLLECTION]

Speed unrestricted! Double-headed former North London Railway 0-6-0Ts No's 58860 leading, and 58856 climb Britain's steepest adhesion worked railway incline at 1 in 14 at Hopton on the Cromford & High Peak line. Enthusiasts crowd in the open wagons of this Manchester Area SLS special on 25th April 1953. [Photo: E.S. Russell]

August 1968, to mark the end of main line steam on British Railways, with double-headed ex-LM&SR 'Black Fives' working the trains in Lancashire. But Cam continued organising specials way after that, including a well remembered electric-hauled day trip to sail on PS *Waverley* round the Isle of Bute and to Rothsay on a beautifully sunny day. We think the very last tour Cam organised was on 14th June 1969, running from Birmingham to Burton on Trent, Marehay Crossing on the Ripley Branch, Wirksworth and Derby, just over nineteen years after his first one.

Photographic Souvenir
in connection with the

LAST TRAIN
on the

SHROPSHIRE and MONTGOMERYSHIRE RAILWAY

SUNDAY, 20th MARCH, 1960

Organised by
THE STEPHENSON LOCOMOTIVE SOCIETY
(Midland Area)

Chronology of the line

Potteries, Shrewsbury and North Wales Railway o. 13th August, 1866, cl. 21st December, 1866, re-opened December, 1868, closed and abandoned as from 22nd June, 1880.

Re-opened as Shropshire and Montgomeryshire Railway on 13th Apl. 1911, (Criggion branch on 21st February, 1912).

Passenger services ceased from 6th November, 1933.

Government control assumed as from September, 1939.

1941—ma'n line (Shrewsbury-L'anymynech) requisitioned by WD.

1947—WD Military status to WD Civilian status.

1948—become part of B.R.—the Railway Executive, Western Region. (Only the Criggion branch was affected by this).

1959—Military depots closed and tracks lifted. Criggion branch closed completely after cessation of quarry traffic in December.

1960—29th February, civilian rail traffic facilities ceased; the last train actually worked from Abbey station, Shrewsbury, on 26th February, when work commenced upon a connection from Abbey goods yard to the Severn Valley branch of the W.R. From this date the outlet for military traffic became Llanymynech.

As soon as all W.D. equipment has been removed the line will be formally handed back to B.R. (W.R.)—dismantling will follow.

Ex-GWR '2021' Class pannier tank No. 2144, based at Kidderminster shed, passes over an occupation crossing on the Cleobury Mortimer & Ditton Priors Branch in 1955. Note the inspector riding almost outside the cab. The spark arrestor chimney was fitted especially for working this branch, which had been requisitioned in 1939 to serve a newly established Royal Navy Armaments Depot at Ditton Priors. The SLS headboard was made in the carpenter's shop at B. Whitehouse & Sons. [Photo: P.B. Whitehouse]

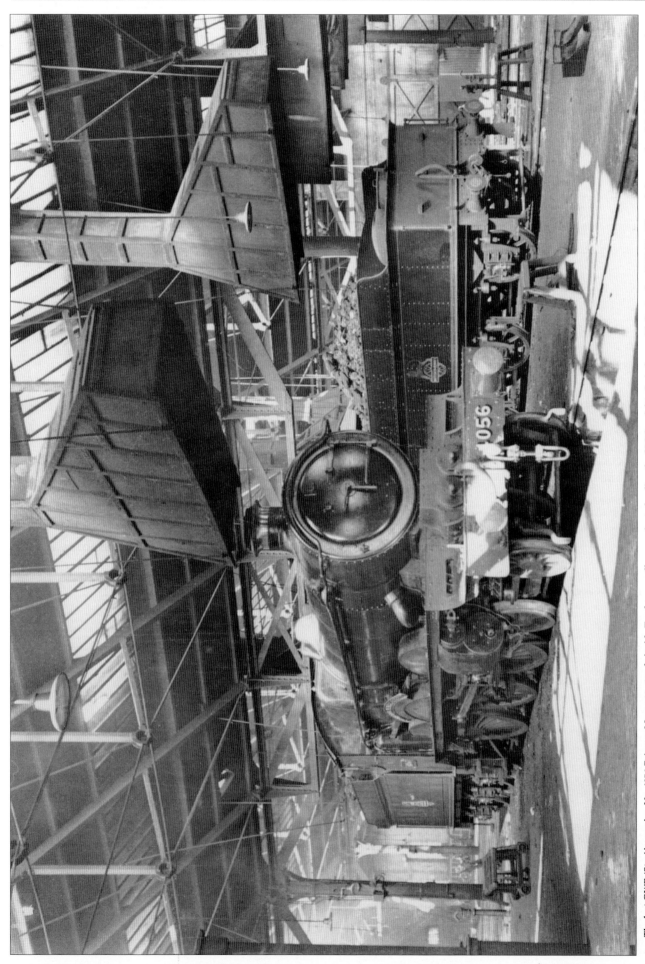

The last GWR 'Star' in service, No. 4056 *Princess Margaret*, stands inside Tyseley roundhouse prior to hauling the SLS Special to Swindon on 9th September 1956. Her BR smokebox numberplate had been removed and GWR number hand-painted on the buffer beam by a painter from B. Whitehouse & Sons. PBW took me to Tyseley for my first visit aged nearly four years old specially so I could see her and I still remember the occasion – the first of very very many visits! [PHOTO: P.B. WHITEHOUSE]

More lasts! The last active 'King', No. 6018 *King Henry VI*, stands on the Down Main line at Birmingham Snow Hill, preparatory to hauling its last passenger train, an SLS Special to Swindon works on 28th April 1963. The 4-6-0 had just run round the carriages, hence apparently being 'wrong line', which it would then shunt across into the Up platform for departure.
[PHOTO: DAVID WALDREN COLLECTION]

The last GWR Hawksworth 'County' Class, No. 1011 *County of Chester*, stands inside Tyseley passenger roundhouse, being bulled up by enthusiasts for its last trip to Swindon on 20th September 1964. Terry Jones was one of the gang (you can just see him climbing down from No. 1011 having cleaned her copper-capped chimney). He recalls: *"There were a group of lads at Saltley Grammar School who were keen trainspotters and I was asked if I was interested in going on the 'Last of the Counties' trip being run by the SLS to Swindon and because I wanted to see the works there I jumped at the chance. I was then 17 years old and lived in Shard End. I cycled to Tyseley on the 19th and was given a paraffin rag and told to get stuck in. I think we did a good job to see her off looking her best."* [PHOTO: P.B. WHITEHOUSE]

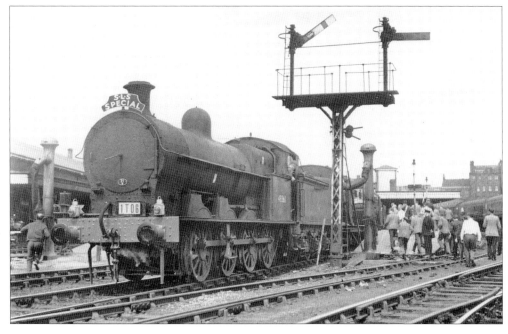

Ex-L&NWR 'G2' 0-8-0 No. 49361, from the last remaining few members of the class still stabled at Bescot, hauled a seven hour tour round Birmingham on 12th December 1964, during which the engine is seen here taking water at Walsall. I was lucky enough to have a footplate ride for part of the journey when only twelve years old!
[PHOTO: P.B. WHITEHOUSE]

Cam had two birthday special surprises run in his honour, both organised by David Russell of BR Derby. On Saturday 18th October 1986, for his 80th birthday, he travelled with a hundred and fifty of his friends behind ninety-eight year old L&NWR 'Coal Tank' 0-6-2T No. 1054 from Shrewsbury to Stockport. Of course, Cam had previously hired this lovely locomotive to double head L&NWR 'G2' 0-8-0 No. 49121 over the Abergavenny to Merthyr line on 5th January 1958. Co-incidentally, this was the first train filmed for the BBC TV series *Railway Roundabout* by John Adams and Pat Whitehouse, both SLS members and part of the team who established the Talyllyn Railway Preservation Society. To celebrate Cam's 85th birthday, David organised a trip on 19th October 1991 with BR 'Standard' Class '4' No. 75069 from Crewe via Chester, Shrewsbury and Hereford, and onto Kidderminster, where Class '47'

diesel No. 47222 (temporarily renamed *W.A. Camwell* for the day) took the train back to Crewe.

Of course, not all the SLS trips were organised by Cam and other areas had their glory too. Although this book is primarily a 'Birmingham record', mention must be made of one trip organised by Harold Bowtell and Fergus Johnson in the North West. They ran a 'Potteries Railtour' behind ex-Lancashire & Yorkshire 2-4-2T No. 50703 and LM&SR 2-6-2T No. 40201. The tour attracted a reporter from the Manchester Guardian who described the participants as '*locomotologists*', who dangerously rivalled the ancient hobby of ornithology. He reported excitedly as the special was skirting the shores of Rudyard Lake on the Churnet Valley line: '*One member of the group held up a finger for silence and all hands stood obediently, the only sound being the steady drumming of the wheels in our ears. Hear that! – exclaimed the man who had called for silence, the clickety-click has changed to clicks in groups of three. We must be running on old 30 ft. rail! And it was true enough, the standard 90ft and 60ft pieces of steel had been succeeded temporarily by shorter lengths on this historic line. It was an exciting moment for everyone!*' Locomotive No. 50703 was borrowed from Warrington and the journalist wrote about her too: '*Old 50703 proved to have at least two of the infirmities of old age, a finicky appetite and some sort of kidney trouble.*'.

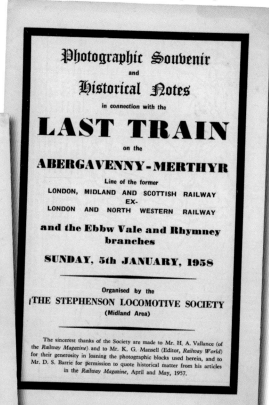

ABOVE: A couple more examples of the photographic souvenir brochures that were produced by the SLS for last trains organised by 'Cam': Abergavenny to Merthyr of 5th January 1958 and the 'Farewell to Steam' special of 4th August, 1968. WHITEHOUSE COLLECTION

RIGHT: On Saturday 18th October 1986, for his 80th birthday, Cam travelled with 150 of his friends from Shrewsbury to Stockport behind 98-year old 'Coal Tank' 0-6-2T No. 1054. [PHOTO: C.M. WHITEHOUSE]

6. THE TALYLLYN RAILWAY PRESERVATION SOCIETY AGM SPECIALS

*'A quite remarkable series of locomotives were rostered on these trains,
both on the GWR main line from Paddington and over the Cambrian.'*

Perhaps learning from Cam's determination to run so many last trains, the Talyllyn Railway also began organising a special train each year for its annual general meeting at Towyn, combining the useful service of transporting members to the meeting with an enjoyable experience. The trains were run from London but also served the Midlands. AGMs were initially held on a Saturday evening, with the special arriving at Towyn after lunch and special trains being provided on the TR too, so that members could also ride 'their' railway. The return main line trip left around midnight, with arrival back in London on the Sunday morning. As the Cambrian section normally closed at midnight, this arrangement involved all manner of after hours special signal box openings.

Not to be outdone by Cam's exploits, a quite remarkable series of locomotives were rostered on these trains too, both on the GWR main line from Paddington and over the Cambrian. On occasion, the train set from 'The Bristolian' was used and, from 1963, sleeping cars were added for the return journey, which seldom left Wales before midnight. The first two specials in 1953 and 1954 were with ex-GWR railcars but then, up until 1966, all trips were steam. *Clun Castle* hauled that train from Banbury to Shrewsbury and then double-headed 'Standard' Class '4' 4-6-0s No's 75002 and 75029 took over for the run to Towyn on the Cambrian section.

Over the years the following steam locomotives hauled these trains, as well as several 'Dukedog' outside framed 4-4-0s over the Cambrian section (ex-GWR unless stated):

• Ex-L&SWR 'T9' Class 4-4-0 No. 30304
• Ex-SE&CR 'D' Class 0-6-0 No. 31075
• Ex-L&YR 'Radial tank' 2-4-2T No. 50781
• 'Star' Class 4-6-0 No. 4061 *Glastonbury Abbey*
• 'City' Class 4-4-0 No. 3440 *City of Truro*
• Ex-MR 'Compound' 4-4-0 No. 41123
• 'Castle' Class 4-6-0 No. 7007 *Great Western*

The second TRPS special, on 25th September 1954, used GWR railcars No's W33W, and W38W, sandwiching carriage No. W1096W, all in carmine and cream livery. The train is seen here in the bay platform at Ruabon, where it reversed to continue to Towyn along the Dee Valley line to Barmouth Junction, where it would reverse again and continue down the coast. This longer journey necessitated a 6.20am start from London (Paddington) and departure from Towyn at 11.50pm!

'T9' at Towyn. For the 1955 trip, which was the first steam special, the TRPS secured an L&SWR 'T9' 4-4-0, which ran solo from Shrewsbury to Welshpool, where GWR 'Dukedog No. 9008 was coupled inside for the rest of the journey. The train is seen here on arrival at Towyn, where the passengers changed for the Talyllyn Railway, but the special carried on to Barmouth for servicing and the locomotives to be turned on the turntable at Barmouth Junction. [Photo: P.B.Whitehouse]

- '47XX' Class 2-8-0 No. 4701
- 'King' Class No. 6000 *King George V*
- Ex-SR 'Battle of Britain' Class 4-6-2 No. 34064 *Fighter Command*
- 'County' Class 4-6-0 No. 1011 *County of Chester*
- 'Castle' Class 4-6-0 No. 4079 *Pendennis Castle*
- BR-built 'Castle' Class 4-6-0 No. 7029 *Clun Castle*

The first such special was on 26th September 1953, using GWR diesel railcar No. W13W. It was a very long day, especially as the railcars had no toilets, the passengers taking advantage of station and refuelling stops. The railcar left Paddington at 6.45am, with refreshments loaded at Birmingham and arrival at Towyn at 2.20pm, in time for members to take a ride on the TR to Abergynolwyn and back behind the ex-Corris Railway 0-4-2T No. 3 and then have their AGM. John Slater, TR magazine editor, reported on the return run: '*We then returned to the station, boarded our railcar and left for London. Tea was taken on board at Moat Lane (there was a refreshment room there which must have been specially manned), but just before Lapworth disaster struck. We stopped just at the platform edge in a cloud of steam. It was found that all our cooling water had run away through a loose connection. This was repaired and the radiator filled from the station fire buckets but, on trying to start, it was found that the engine had seized up solid. After an abortive attempt on our part to push it into a loop (it wouldn't budge), a GWR 2-8-0 No. 2830 was detached from its train on the Down line and hauled the car into the loop, ran round it and hauled it back to where we were waiting. We had stopped at 3.30am and at 4.15am we continued on our way, hauled by a freight loco, running tender first with 'express' headlamps at a speed between 15-20 mph! Eight miles further on, we stopped at Leamington Spa, only just in time as something else was very hot and the rear bogie was smoking heavily. Another railcar, W22W, was laid* on for us here and we boarded it, thanking the crew of the freight engine on our way past them. The second car was only a 48 seater, so 20 or so people had to stand. But we got to Paddington without further incident, an hour and a half late. I reckon that British Railways can write off any profit they may have hoped to make out of the trip.'

The year 1955 was to see the first steam hauled special, which then set the pattern for the next twelve years. This used GWR 'Star' No. 4061 *Glastonbury Abbey* as far as Shrewsbury, where ex-L&SWR 'T9' 4-4-0 No. 30304 took over, having been brought up from the Southern specially for the trip. The 'T9' ran solo to Welshpool where GWR 'Dukedog' 4-4-0 No. 9008 was coupled inside for the rest of the journey, so beginning a long association with the class on these specials. This continued until 1960, when the last of them, No. 9017, hauled the train before later moving to be preserved on the Bluebell Railway.

The motive power for 1956 was even more extraordinary: SE&CR 'D' Class 4-4-0 No. 31075 double-heading with GWR 'Dean Goods' 0-6-0 No. 2538 on the Cambrian line, with the Paddington-Shrewsbury leg and return handled by 'Star' Class No. 4056 *Princess Margaret*. But this was topped by the 'visiting' locomotive in 1957 – former Lancashire & Yorkshire Railway 'Radial' 2-4-2T No. 50781 double-heading with 'Dukedog' No. 9021. Sadly, the L&YR tank failed at Machynlleth shed, where it ran from Towyn for turning and servicing, and this proved to be the last time a 'foreigner' was used on the Cambrian section of these tours.

The TR didn't give up on their quest for unusual motive power on these trains though and, in 1961, the train was double-headed from Shrewsbury by GWR 'Small Prairie' No. 5555 and 'Collett Goods' and No. 2222 – the latter in fact being No. 2217 but renumbered for the occasion so to be in harmony with the 55XX! In the 1960s,

ABOVE: The motive power for 1956 was extraordinary, comprising SE&CR 'D' Class No. 31075 double-heading with 'Dean Goods' No. 2538, with the pair seen here near Talerddig. [PHOTO: P.B. WHITEHOUSE]

RIGHT: The 'visiting' locomotive in 1957 was former L&YR 'Radial' tank No. 50781 double-heading with 'Dukedog' No. 9021. Sadly, the 2-4-2T failed at Machynlleth shed, to where it had run from Towyn for turning and servicing, and this proved to be the last time a 'foreigner' was used on the Cambrian section of these tours. Here the train is seen at Welshpool on the outward journey with No. 50781 surrounded by passengers whilst taking water at the column. [PHOTO: P.B. WHITEHOUSE]

once the 'Dukedogs' had been retired, it became the practice to use double headed GWR 'Manor' 4-6-0s, which were to an extent synoymous with the Cambrian in any case. In 1963, after the TR's own No. 4 *Edward Thomas* had been fitted with an oblong Giesl ejector, the TR chartered Southern 'Battle of Britain' No. 34064 *Fighter Command*, which also had a Giesl fitted, complete with a whole train of Southern green carriages. The Bulleid disgraced itself at Shrewsbury, failing to restart the train from a signal check on the station approach, having to be banked in by an Ivatt 2-6-2T. Double headed 'Manors' then took over for a spirited run along the Cambrian main line to Towyn, recovering a sixty minutes late departure from Shrewsbury to be only ten minutes behind time on arrival! Pat Garland, then still TR Treasurer (but later President), was a staunch GWR man and, wearing a GWR tie for the occasion

of the trip, retorted that if there was ever a Southern engine on the special again, he would wear a black tie!

Perhaps he saw to it, as the following year's special arrived at Shrewsbury behind No. 1011 *County of Chester* and then ran with double-headed locomotives over the Cambrian section both of which ended up preserved on the Dart Valley Railway in Devon: his and PBW's own 'Small Prairie' No. 4555, together with No. 7827 *Lydham Manor*. The very last steam hauled TRPS special was, of course, hauled from Banbury by none other than *Clun Castle*, by then the last of her class and quickly racking up an impressive range of 'last' trips and interesting itineraries. No. 7029 became the last Western Region steam engine out of both Paddington and Snow Hill and, later in preservation, also Birmingham Moor Street, having joined the Tyseley Collection once No. 4555 had left for Devon.

The AGMs were initially held on a Saturday evening, with the special arriving at Towyn after lunch and special trains also being provided on the Talyllyn so that members could also ride 'their' railway. At Towyn (Wharf) station on 24th September 1955, two trains are ready to take members up the line, utilising all available rolling stock and running with both former Corris Railway locomotives: on the left is No. 4 *Edward Thomas*, a Kerr, Stuart 0-4-2T named after the last General Manager before take over, and on the right is No. 3, a Falcon 0-4-2T named *Sir Haydn* after the previous owner, who had kept the line alive since 1910 paying expenses out of his own pocket if necessary. In the left foreground is the Welsh Highland Railway 2-6-2T *Russell*, forming part of the nascent narrow gauge museum collection. [PHOTO: P.B. WHITEHOUSE]

ABOVE. The special of 27th September 1960 was the last to use one of the outside-framed 'Dukedog' 4-4-0s. No. 9017 was withdrawn shortly after the trip and a collection was taken on the train towards its purchase for preservation on the Bluebell Railway, organised by Birmingham enamel badge manufacturer Tom Gomm. On the special, which is seen here calling at Moat Lane Junction, No. 9017 was pilot engine to Churchward 'Mogul' No. 7330.

RIGHT: On 29th September 1962, the special ran via Ruabon, over what is now the Llangollen Railway, the first steam special to do so. The train was hauled from London to Ruabon by 'King' Class No. 6000 *King George V* from where it was then double-headed by 'Manor' 4-6-0 No. 7801 *Anthony Manor* and 'Mogul' 2-6-0 No. 7314 to Morfa Mawddach and Towyn. The pair are seen here at Ruabon waiting to depart having just taken over the train.

A little later on from the previous picture, No. 7801 Anthony Manor and 'Mogul' No. 7314 pass Corwen with the train, which was mostly formed of appropriately liveried chocolate & cream stock. [PHOTO: DAVE COBBE]

7. BR DID IT TOO!
Pat Whitehouse

"'Reggie' Hanks lit a spark which brightened into flame on other regions.'

It all really began in 1957. This was the time of sparkling 'Castles' and chocolate and cream coaches on 'The Bristolian', running hard towards 100mph and Reggie Hanks as Chairman and General Manager of the Western Region. It was he who first thought of getting *City of Truro* out of York Museum and putting her to work on enthusiasts' specials whilst earning her day to day keep on the Didcot, Newbury & Southampton run. He lit a spark which brightened into flame on other regions.

The greatest light came from Scotland, where General Manager James Ness put four veterans back into working order and even repainted them into their old pre-Grouping colours: the beautiful blue Caley single-wheeler No. 123, the brown North British 4-4-0 *Glen Douglas*, the yellow Highland 'Jones Goods' 4-6-0 No. 103 and the Great North of Scotland *Gordon Highlander*, a delightful green 4-4-0. These old locomotives gave pleasure to thousands and one, the Caley 'Spinner', even made its way down to Birmingham Moor Street for an exhibition with *City of Truro*, then paused at Tyseley depot before running all the way south to the Bluebell Railway.

Two other old ladies also showed their paces: the restored Midland 'Compound' No. 1000, perhaps the finest of British Transport Commission Curator John Scholes' relics, whilst not to be outdone, the Southern Region provided a 'T9' 4-4-0 in L&SWR light green.

I covered the Midland 'Compound' story for the BBC childrens' television show *Railway Roundabout*. Even more so than the *City of Truro*, she shows those who did not know the pre-Grouping companies the glory of those days – a truly resplendent engine, painted in Midland lake colour, shining fit for a Queen and a tribute to those who took so much trouble to see that she was restored so beautifully. I had the privilege and pleasure of going with her on her steam trials from Derby to Leicester. What pictures were brought back to my memory when I saw her standing in the roundhouse at Derby with that typically Midland chimney, the lovely red colouring and the huge numerals on the side of the tender.

Those were the days of the 'Indian Summer' and, like so many of the October days ahead, it heralded cold and bleak winters. But at least we saw them at work again and we are forever indebted to those in authority for that.

GWR 'City' Class 4-4-0 No. 3440 *City of Truro* waits for the 'right a way' at Andover Junction on a BR Western Region service train. 'Reggie' Hanks, the Chairman of the Western Region, had exhumed the engine from York Museum for specials and shedded her at Didcot so she could limber up on the Didcot, Newbury & Southampton trains. Her No. 3717 was also changed to an earlier number, 3440, to avoid confusion with a pannier tank. [PHOTO: P.M. ALEXANDER]

LEFT: *City of Truro* waits at Wolverhampton Low Level station on 16th June 1957 with an excursion train. The locomotive is immaculate and has its front coupling correctly hooked up to the buffer beam. The driver is oiling round the motion inside the frames and a couple of lads are looking curiously into the cab. [DAVE WALDREN COLLECTION]

BELOW: Exhibition at Moor Street station, Birmingham. *City of Truro* and Caledonian 'Single' No. 123 stand in the terminus platforms on 13th April, 1960 Both engines were kept at Tyseley depot to be prepared for the exhibition. I was seven years old when PBW took me there to see them both in steam inside the roundhouse. Curiously, he allowed me on to the footplate of only one of them and I chose *City of Truro*. A reasonable choice at the time but, subsequently, I have had other opportunities to 'cab' No. 3440 but never to go on the footplate of No. 123, especially in steam. [DAVE WALDREN COLLECTION]

BELOW: Midland Railway 'Compound' 4-4-0 No. 1000 was completely rebuilt at Derby Works, with many new parts and to the order of John Scholes, Curator British Transport Commission. When the engine was in use on specials, he ordered the tender to be hand coaled lest it got scratched. [PHOTO: JOHN ADAMS]

North British Railway 'Glen' or 'K' Class 4-4-0 No. 9256 *Glen Douglas* at Garve on 20th May 1960. She was repaired and repainted in NBR colours in 1959 and set to work on special trains in Scotland. The class were particularly associated with the West Highland line between Fort William and Mallaig, on which 'The Jacobite' steam tourist train now runs. *Glen Douglas* was put into Glasgow Transport Museum in 1965 and lent to the Scottish Railway Preservation Society in 1992. [PHOTO: E. S. RUSSELL]

Great North of Scotland 'F' Class 4-4-0 No. 49 *Gordon Highlander* was built in 1920 for general traffic use to the north and west of Aberdeen. No. 49 was based for much of her working life at Keith Depot and was named after the local regiment; in the local dialect the engine was nicknamed *'the Sojer'* ('the Soldier'). She was retired from regular service by BR in 1957 but repainted for special trains and continued to run until 1966, when she was placed in the Glasgow Transport Museum. [PHOTO: E.S. RUSSELL]

ABOVE: Caledonian Railway 'Single' wheeler 4-2-2 No. 123 was built in sixty six days by Neilson & Co. and exhibited at the Edinburgh International Exhibition in 1886, where she won a gold medal as an example of cutting edge technology. No. 123 ran frequently from Carlisle to Edinburgh and so participated in the 'Great Race to the North', in competition for the fastest journey from London to Scotland between the West Coast and East Coast railways. [PHOTO: E.S. RUSSELL]

BELOW: Caledonian 'Single' No. 123 and Highland Railway 'Jones Goods' No. 103 double head an excursion at Kelvin Hall in Glasgow, where both locomotives are now kept at the Glasgow Museum of Transport. [PHOTO: KEN COOPER]

Highland Railway 'Jones Goods' No. 103 was notable as the first type of steam locomotive with a 4-6-0 wheel arrangement in the British Isles. No. 103 was the first of fifteen such locomotives and built in 1894 by Sharp, Stewart & Co. At that time, they were the most powerful main line locomotives in the country and originally intended for freight but they also hauled passenger trains, particularly in the summer season. No. 103 was returned to working order by BR in 1959, having been presciently set aside by the LM&SR for preservation as early as 1934. She spent several years operating special trains, including a charter photographic special for the BBC TV programme *Railway Roundabout*, running from Kyle of Lochalsh to Inverness in place of the usual 'Black Five' 4-6-0. The engine is seen here at Forres station on 23rd August 1965, coupled to two Caledonian Railway carriages which BR had repainted in their original livery in 1958 and which are also now preserved by the Scottish Railway Preservation Society. [Photo: Ken Cooper]

8. A TALE OF TANK ENGINES
Pat Whitehouse

"Well, I don't know who you are Mr. Whitehouse, but I do know that you have got some good friends",
which, as they say, was a good start to the day.'

It was sometime during the summer of 1963 that Pat Garland and I thought of the idea of owning a standard gauge engine. We had both day dreamed a bit about this over the years but where would one keep the beast and who would look after it anyway? The spark which lit the final fire came from David Garnock's *The Great Marquess*, for I was, at the time, a trustee for this engine and she had a home up in Leeds – maybe the Middleton Railway could do with another engine? Pat and I talked this over not once but a dozen times – we even considered purchasing a 'Castle' but the thought of the maintenance and housing costs frightened us off that one – then. Eventually, the idea crystallised and it was decided that if we ever made the jump into the loco-owning field it should be a GWR small wheeled 2-6-2 tank. Fortunately, we had the privilege of knowing Reggie Hanks who, apart from being the previous Chairman, was then also a member of the Western Region Board. He was a great steam enthusiast and a GWR man to boot. Reggie fixed up a meeting for me with Mr Stanley Raymond, who was in the Chair at Paddington and the deal was on.

At that time, of course, there was no queue of enthusiasts all wanting to buy engines and run them on BR and, as far as Mr Raymond was concerned, this was a straightforward commercial transaction, so the matter was handed over to the mechanical side in the persons of George Robinson and Tommy Matthewson-Dick. Between us and with the able assistance of Locomotive Running Inspector Jack Hancock of Paddington, we spent some weeks looking for a suitable engine, a spare boiler and relative spare parts. Jack examined and reported on the condition of all the remaining '45XX' Class engines still in traffic. In January 1963, six of the '45XX' with the flat top side tanks were still in service. No. 4555 at Laira shed was selected as being in the best mechanical condition and arrangements were made for the engine to be brought to Swindon for inspection and any necessary repairs. Eventually, the deal was done with George Robson, who was extremely considerate. The spare boiler was the last to go through the late GWR works at Wolverhampton and, if we had only known what we know now, the present day situation could have been eased considerably, for the works were on their eleventh hour, fifty-ninth minute of their existence. The waste and despoliation seemed fantastic on closure, and some tens of thousands of pounds of machinery, tools and spares were literally thrown out – that this happened at a small works like Wolverhampton made one wonder what really happened at Swindon and Crewe – in a way it was Army surplus equipment all over again. Time and time again we have come

'Small Prairie' No. 4555 stands in the top of the yard at Tyseley depot, to which she had been delivered by the GWR when new in 1924. The original 1908 coaling stage (still standing today) is behind her. Here, some forty years later in 1965, she had returned 'home' once again but this time in the hands of two private individuals, Pat Garland and Pat Whitehouse, who simply wanted a steam locomotive of their own to enjoy. And enjoy they did! [PHOTO: P.B. WHITEHOUSE]

LEFT: Auto-fitted 0-6-0PT No. 6435 had been bought for the new Dart Valley Railway by John Wilkins, inventor of the Servis washing machine, who then owned and ran the 15ins gauge Fairbourne Railway in Wales and was a significant help to the nascent 2ft 3ins gauge Talyllyn Railway when it was getting onto its feet in the early 1950s. Following acquisition, No. 6435 was initially sent to Tyseley depot for repainting by B. Whitehouse & Sons, the family construction firm, and then undertook a few SLS special trains around the Midlands. Here she is seen standing at the top of the shed yard in light winter snow in 1965, with the new diesel depot being constructed in the background. [PHOTO: P. B. WHITEHOUSE]

RIGHT: GWR 0-4-2T No. 1420 stands resplendent at Worcester on 19th September 1965, after repainting into GWR colours that featured the 1930s roundel on her side tanks.
[PHOTO: K.C. COOPER]

LEFT: Preserved tank engines still thrive at Tyseley and even now run on the main line. Vintage Trains is home to three '57XX' Class 0-6-0PTs: No's 7752, 7760 and 9600. Built in November and December 1930 respectively, No's 7752 and 7760 had survived after being sold to the London Transport Executive after withdrawal, No. 7752 in 1959 and No. 7760 in 1961. With London Transport lettering and painted in Metropolitan Railway red, their new identities had been as No.'s L94 (7752) and L90 (7760), in which guise both continued in traffic until 1971.
[PHOTO: C.M. WHITEHOUSE]

The handover. No. 4555 stands with full boiler pressure inside the shed at Swindon after a light casual overhaul in the works to the order of the 'two Pats' who had bought her, with help and advice from many Western Region men, including the former Chairman of its Board, Reggie Hanks, seen on the right-hand side in front of No. 4555's bunker. The 'Small Prairie' is still in BR unlined black but would soon move to Tyseley for repainting in authentic Great Western green. For now though, she was being prepared for her acceptance test run to Kemble in September 1963. [PHOTO: P.B. WHITEHOUSE]

RIGHT: No. 4555 at Kemble in September 1963, on her test run in private ownership with the assembled top brass who had 'made it happen.' Standing in front of the cab (L to R) are Reggie Hanks, former Chairman of the Western Region Board, Jack Hancock, Locomotive Running Inspector, and Mr Ridgway, WR CME. [PHOTO: P.B. WHITEHOUSE]

BELOW: No. 4555 shrouded by steam at Snow Hill station, after arriving with the empty stock for the 5.27pm commuter train from Knowle & Dorridge one day in the summer of 1964. Pat Garland, one of its new proud owners, looks on happily at his engine running a time-tabled passenger service for British Railways. [PHOTO: BIRMINGHAM POST]

across this waste when seeking out spares and tools for our engines, and now I believe that even some of the 'Great Powers That Be' in the Railway admit that this panic transition from steam to diesel for the sake of an image was wasteful to say the least. There is no question that the transition was necessary but surely as a planned and rational campaign.

But as far as No. 4555 was concerned, she was well cared for – part of the purchase price was an arrangement for her to go through Swindon Works. It was a memorable day when we all (including Reggie Hanks) turned up to call on Mr Ridgway, the CME to the Western Region, on the day of her test run after overhaul. I think this was probably the first time he had come up alongside serious railway preservation and the enthusiasm it engenders at all levels, for I can well remember him saying on introduction, "*Well, I don't know who you are Mr Whitehouse, but I do know that you have got some good friends*", which, as they say, was a good start to the day.

The original idea for the test run was to be to Wootton Bassett but as this was only three miles from Swindon, it was not considered anything like long enough to enable a sound judgment to be made. An application was successfully made for a trip to Kemble (28

miles there and back) with a train of three coaches, as running light engine would not be a test of the locomotive's ability.

Kenneth Leech, the well known GWR locomotive enthusiast and former Chief Engineer of the Westinghouse Brake & Signal Company, acted as an adviser to us two Pats. He had practical engineering knowledge and, along with both of us, had unofficially enjoyed regular footplate travel on GWR locomotives; he had achieved quite a high mileage riding, firing and even driving locomotives between his home at Chippenham and many stations on the GW main line. Kenneth Leech rode on No. 4555's footplate on the test run to Kemble, when Pat Garland took the regulator while the train was shunted, Indeed Pat showed his hand somewhat when buffering up very gently to the coaches at Kemble, for Reggie Hanks was heard to remark that Pat "*hadn't learned that trick without a lot of practice*". The team retired to the inn opposite the station for a small celebration, well pleased with their purchase!

Our engine never went north to Yorkshire after all, for by the time she had gone through the works, we had joined forces with our friends down in Devon and her future would obviously be down there in due time. The question was where should she go during the interim period. As we both lived in Birmingham, our good friends on the London Midland Region agreed that she should come to Tyseley and this was the beginning of the story. We had been very fortunate in the price we were able to negotiate for our purchases and part of the bargain was that we would allow the engine to be used on specials or other occasions from time to time, to give BR a share of the benefits too. How things have changed in a few short years.

So, No. 4555 came to Tyseley towards the close of the year. Tom Field, then shed foreman, found space for her in the 'factory' – adjacent to the shed, whilst she was repainted from un-lined BR black to authentic original GWR green with 'Great Western' in full on her tanks. Later, when the factory and one of the two roundhouses were demolished, so that the diesel locomotive repair shops could be built, she went into the remaining steam shed. 1964 was a happy year and the late Tom Field and his staff were pleased to have this shining green acquisition on their books. In return for her accommodation, she was made available for use on selected light duties on ordinary passenger and freight duties. What an amazing sight that made! We used her on specials from time to time, including a last run up to Bromyard, a trip on the remaining part of the Severn Valley line, another over the Wombourn Branch, on the last train to and from Brecon and, of course, on the inevitable Talyllyn Railway Special – this time from Ruabon to Towyn. The South Wales trip was quite an achievement, for clearances between Cardiff and Merthyr were extremely tight and it was really only goodwill that got her there at all. In addition, Tom used her about once a week to keep her fit, usually on local pick-up freights but sometimes on the 5.27pm semi-fast passenger train from Snow Hill to Knowle & Dorridge. No. 4555 would run light engine

from Tyseley sheds to Queen's Head sidings (between Soho & Winson Green and Handsworth & Smethwick stations) to collect her coaches, which she then worked empty stock to Snow Hill station. On these occasions, apart from the natural joy of riding on the footplate of one's own engine, the sight of commuters coming down the steps at Snow Hill to spot a highly polished engine in Great Western green and lettered as such was worth seeing!

Pat Garland was a keen amateur engine driver and his part ownership of No. 4555 enabled him to keep his hand in. Regularly, he would dress in his boiler suit at his office, a short walk from Snow Hill station, and he would linger in the gloom of the station's blue brick arches until it was time for No. 4555 to depart, then he would step smartly onto the footplate and take the regulator. A long blast on the whistle as the train passed his lineside home would confirm to the family that their father was at the controls! He found it such an enjoyable experience that he always wanted to take the locomotive back to the shed after working the train. In

RIGHT: No. 4555 stands in Queen's Head carriage sidings (between Soho & Winson Green and Handsworth & Smethwick stations), in the company of GWR 'Mogul' No. 6364, as she picks up the empty carriage stock for a working of the 5.27pm all stations from Birmingham Snow Hill to Knowle & Dorridge in the summer of 1964.
[PHOTO: P.B. WHITEHOUSE]

BELOW: The then unique spectacle of a privately owned steam locomotive working a regular BR passenger train. No. 4555 stands at Knowle & Dorridge station taking water from the column on the platform after arriving with the 5.27pm train from Snow Hill.
[PHOTO: P.B. WHITEHOUSE]

LEFT: In 1964, No. 4555 was 'common user' engine at Tyseley shed, probably being in the best mechanical condition of any of the steam fleet that the shed foreman, Tommy Field, then had available. So, she was increasingly used on freight workings and could often be seen working trains of forty wagons and more towards Hatton and Leamington Spa. Here, she is seen entering Birmingham Snow Hill station from the west on one of these workings on 8th August 1964. [PHOTO: L. HANSON]

OPPOSITE PAGE TOP: No. 6435 running between Stratford-upon-Avon and Stratford Old Town, with the SLS 'Farewell to the Stratford-upon-Avon & Midland Junction Railway' tour of 24th April 1965. The special ran from Snow Hill to Woodford Halse and note that even the carriages were all of GWR origin! [PHOTO: T. E. WILLIAMS]

ABOVE: From time to time, No. 4555 was also used on special trains, often those organised by Arthur 'Cam' Camwell, Midland Area Secretary of the Stephenson Locomotive Society. Here she is seen in the company of '57XX' 0-6-0PT No. 3690, leaving Brecon with the last train to Merthyr on 2nd May 1964. Pat Whitehouse particularly enjoyed this steeply graded route, which had echoes of the earlier SLS special on the spectacular line from Abergavenny to Brynmawr, which had used two ex-L&NWR engines, a 'Coal Tank' and a 'Super D'. [PHOTO: C.M. WHITEHOUSE COLLECTION]

OPPOSITE PAGE BOTTOM: GWR auto-fitted 0-4-2T No. 1420 was delivered to Worcester shed to be fettled up by the Works Manager, Don Green, and repainted into true colours by B. Whitehouse & Sons, the family firm. Here she stands in the works alongside No. 4555, which was also receiving light maintenance, preparatory to both of them hauling the SLS 'Restored Locomotives Cavalcade' rail tour on 19th September 1965 and then moving on to their new home on the Dart Valley Railway. Don Green was to reappear later in the Tyseley story as he supervised the return to steam from Barry condition of 'Castle' No. 5080 *Defiant* in only eighteen months! [PHOTO: C. M. WHITEHOUSE]

LEFT: No's 4555 and 1420 stand at Worcester Shrub Hill station with the SLS tour on 19th September 1965. The train had arrived here behind L&NER No. 3442 *The Great Marquess* and the two tank engines then hauled it up the Severn Valley line from Hartlebury to Alverley Colliery sidings and then from Kidderminster to Wolverhampton Low Level, before heading back to Worcester, when this picture was taken. No. 3442 then returned the tour to Snow Hill. [PHOTO: C.M. WHITEHOUSE]

BELOW: No's 1420 and 6435 stand at Ashchurch on the Midland Main Line between Birmingham and Gloucester with the SLS 'GWR Cavalcade' tour of 17th October 1965, which was bound for Bristol and was being used to work the two tank engines south towards their new home on the Dart Valley. Organiser Arthur Camwell is making a forceful point in dialogue with PBW standing in cowgown with beret and hands in pockets before returning to the footplate. [PHOTO: C.M. WHITEHOUSE COLLECTION]

the end, he would drive to Tyseley shed in the morning, park and take the bus into town, so that the car would be waiting at Tyseley for him in the evening.

No. 4555 was also employed on some carriage shunting but by this time, in the run down of steam traction, she was quite the best engine, mechanically, that Tyseley had available and so she was increasingly used on freight working. She could often be seen on trains of forty wagons or more towards Hatton and Leamington Spa. So heavy did the usage become, that, in due course, we had to request that she did not go out quite so often!

On the whole, the engine's stay at Tyseley was reasonably uneventful and unrecorded but, on Monday 24th August 1964, No. 4555 had an adventure of the kind only usually found in railway fiction. It happened like this.

Cyril Tolley and his fireman had taken 'our engine' as he called it, on the local Bordesley Junction to Leamington pick-up goods. It had been quite a job to make it, for No. 4555 is one of the engines with smaller water tanks and they had quite a load, stopping to shunt at Hatton and Warwick cold store on the way. But they made it – just – and with no water in the tank – only a boiler full. They arrived at about 12.30pm, filled the tank and went to the shunters'

cabin for dinner. About 1.40pm an inspector came over: "*I've got a job for you*", he said.

Apparently instructions had been received from Control that the engine and crew were required to assist 'The Pines Express' from Leamington to Snow Hill up Hatton Bank. The train was being worked by steam engine *Acton Burnell Hall*, which had come on at Banbury after the diesel had failed and the driver had requested assistance from Leamington. Cyril's first thought was water but he told Control he would do his best. Away they went and coupled on between the 'Hall' and the train (this being good Western practice, as the train engine had a 4-wheeled bogie compared with No. 4555's pony truck). They set off at 2.40pm and arrived at Snow Hill (24 miles) at 3.08pm, and this included the climb at 1 in 100 up Hatton Bank. In a letter to me afterwards, amplified in good 'Black Country' tongue, Cyril said that the only time he had any grey hairs was through the platforms as she was rolling a good bit at speed. They looked in the tank at Snow Hill and found about a foot of water left, so they did well under the circumstances.

I was glad, yet sorry, not to have been on that rocking footplate and the thought of those little wheels going round at that speed is a trifle frightening, especially when it's your own engine! Maurice Long,

who was signalman at Lapworth, saw them swaying through and he swears they were doing 70mph and making up time. It was an experience to remember and savour. Cyril moved to work on the steam engines at Austin's, Longbridge and, at the Tyseley Open Day in May, 1970 he was in charge of their magnificent new Bagnall 0-6-0ST *Vulcan*. We talked of the run and he looked back on it with pride.

During the same year we began collecting engines for the Dart Valley Railway venture in Devon and another, this time a passenger pannier tank engine, No. 6435, arrived via Swindon. She, too, was repainted at Tyseley and put to work from time to time on the trip goods and specials. In particular, she worked what became the last steam train over the Stratford-upon-Avon & Midland Junction line, double heading an LM&SR

ABOVE: Later the same day, No. 6435 is seen now double-heading the tour with No. 7029 *Clun Castle* (still then in British Railways ownership) past Wick Bridge, between Berkeley Road and Charfield. There is some mystery as to why No. 1420 was taken off at Gloucester and replaced by *Clun*, which in the original itinerary was only booked to work the tour back from Bristol so the two tank engines could carry on south. [PHOTO: HUGH BALLANTYNE]

'4F' 0-6-0 as far as Stratford. We also acquired No. 1420, an auto-fitted 0-4-2T, which went directly to Worcester.

In 1965, it seemed as if the engines might be wanted down at Buckfastleigh before too long, so arrangements were made to work them down to Worcester, have a light overhaul in the works under the care of the Works Manager, Don Green, obtain a repaint and move on down to the South West. The first to go was No. 4555, which went right down to Exeter in October of that year to take a *Pendennis Castle* hauled special on to Totnes, coupled to No. 3205. The others followed later, having worked a Midlands SLS Special down to Bristol. It was almost the end of a unique period in our lives but not quite, for there was one more engine yet to come in late 1966. This was Swindon-built Hawksworth pannier tank No. 1638 from Croes Newydd shed, purchased for the Dart Valley like the others. She came down to Tyseley in the late autumn, was repainted in the spring and moved on to Devon via BR Western Region's open Day at Bristol Bath Road shed in October 1967.

All these engines were put to work on the Dart Valley Railway running between Buckfastleigh and Totnes. Smart and well kept, they are helping to give pleasure to many thousands of tourists every summer – something which gives us the feeling that it was all very much worthwhile. What an adventure in our lives!

RIGHT: No. 6435 and No. 7029 *Clun Castle* after arrival at Bristol Temple Meads with the SLS Special on 17th October, so ending the pannier tank's very last passenger run on the main line. Steam on the Western Region had only two and a half months left and *Clun Castle*'s fate still hung in the balance, as purchase for preservation was not until January 1966. PBW's thoughts – *"We even considered purchasing a 'Castle' but the thought of the maintenance and housing costs frightened us off that one – then"* – were not yet ringing in his head.

A wonderfully atmospheric shot of post-war, Hawksworth-designed '16XX' Class 0-6-0PT No. 1638, standing inside the passenger roundhouse at Tyseley in late 1966, having arrived for preservation on the Dart Valley Railway. She is seen here to prior repainting by the Whitehouse family firm but, sadly, had arrived too late to be used on any main line specials. Note the 6C Croes Newydd shedplate on No. 1638's smokebox door, the pannier tank's final home prior to withdrawal. [PHOTO: P.B. WHITEHOUSE]

9. THE DART VALLEY RAILWAY

'Unusually, the board set a policy that all its equipment must be owned by the company.
So it was that the early steam engines to arrive, such as No's 4555, 1420, 6412, 6430 and 6435,
were exchanged for shares and became company property.'

Terence Cuneo's delightful painting of No. 4555 crossing the River Dart, untypically with the Dynamometer carriage immediately behind the engine – but that was PBW's choice when he commissioned the painting. Through his *Railway Roundabout* connection, Pat became friends with Cuneo and featured his painting of the Talyllyn in one of the BBC TV programmes. The artist was also to paint many of the Tyseley Collection over the years. [Courtesy Carole Cuneo]

In the 1960s, if you were interested in model railways and favoured the Great Western Railway, it was likely that your layout would feature a typical branch line. In the 1950s, many people took holidays in Devon and enjoyed these quintessential former GWR branch lines during the summer holiday fortnight: Dartmouth, Moretonhampstead, Kingsbridge, Ashburton, St. Ives and Helston are just some destinations to conjure with. Fussy, small, green tank engines ran push-pull trains and branch shuttles, strengthened by main line coaches on holiday Saturdays to cater for the comings and goings of the changeover day. Happy memories are cherished by many people of summer days relaxing with families when the world seemed to run at a slower pace and the sun always shone.

Small wonder then that once the initial pioneering amateurs had cut their teeth on Welsh narrow gauge, they would hanker after re-creating holiday trains on Great Western branch lines. This

was especially so as they had also seen an array of Great Western engines pass their hotel window with the 'Cambrian Coast Express' during the last fling of Western Region finery – chocolate and cream carriages hauled by a fully lined out 'Manor' or 'Small Prairie'.

In the 1950s and '60s, British Railways was lopping branch lines off the arterial routes everywhere they could and holidaymakers were deserting trains for their cars, despite the long queues on the Honiton bypass and on the A38 to Devon. It was time to act; now or never. The hunt for the best branch line to buy began. Focus started with the line from Brent Junction to Kingsbridge but BR beat them to it by dismantling it. The Moretonhampstead Branch was still partly in use and the Paignton to Dartmouth line still very much so. Consequently, the focus shifted to the delightful branch line leaving the main line at Totnes. This ran alongside the River Dart, past the sleepy village of Staverton, through Buckfastleigh with its station halfway between the town and Buckfast, with its

ABOVE: On 7th September 1962, GWR 'Small Prairie' 2-6-2T No. 4555 shunts the last goods wagons in Ashburton station. A particularly poignant image as, of course, this engine also hauled the reopening train over the revived Dart Valley branch but neither No. 4555 nor the station were to survive there. The track was lifted and No. 4555 has moved to the Paignton & Dartmouth Railway. Shattered dreams.

LEFT: Ashes to ashes. Ashburton's Brunel wooden overall roofed train shed, to many the archetypal GWR branch terminus, waiting for the preservationists to arrive on 13th August 1966. They did arrive and also restored the station but, sadly, they had to leave again due to the widening of the A38. Ashburton has a station no longer, although most of the buildings still remain in commerical use. Under threat, efforts are being made to ensure their future survival but a plan to re-open the line back to the town has so far made little progress. [PHOTO: KEN COOPER]

famous Abbey, to terminate in the centre of Ashburton on the fringe of Dartmoor, under an original Brunel wooden overall station roof. A perfect model railway in reality and almost a perfect branch line to preserve, although it did not meet the main line quite at a junction station, unlike the Kingswear line. Moreover, Royalty would have approved, as the Royal train was often stabled along the quiet banks of the Dart overnight near Totnes, on what became known as 'the Royal Mile', so that the Queen could sleep in peace. If an early start was not required for the Royal train, then the first time-tabled branch train would be replaced by a bus; the branch always liked to accommodate itself to the requirements of its users.

The South Devon Railway built this ten mile branch to Brunel's broad gauge. Opened in 1872, it was regauged with the rest of the GWR network over an astonishing weekend in May 1892 but this proved to be a sad year for Ashburton; the tin mines in the area showed their first signs of flagging to produce profitable output and even the town's stannary court, established as long ago as 1285 by Edward I, was no longer necessary to 'assay' and set its mark on the ingots of tin; cheaper products were being imported in large quantities.

The GWR took over the South Devon Railway in 1878 and thus the branch also came under their remit. Both passengers and freight kept it going until the outbreak of the Second World War but it is doubtful if the line ever made a profit. Most of its traffic was coal, wool, cider and agricultural items. After Nationalisation in 1948,

A view from the signal box at Buckfastleigh on 8th April 1967, with No. 1420 seen through the open window. This was one of a series of publicity photographs taken before commercial services started. A picture from here today would be dominated by the A38 dual carriageway running close by. [PHOTO: J.M. BOYES]

road lorries increased and took away the traffic, resulting in 'Small Prairie' tank No. 4555 hauling the last freight train from Tavistock Junction to Ashburton on 7th September, with the branch closing completely three days later.

In the same month as the line closed, the *Western Morning News* of 29th September announced that a group of businessmen had a plan to save it. The Dart Valley Light Railway Limited was established with a view to reopening the branch as a commercial venture but operated with steam engines hauling tourist trains only in the summer season. This was a highly novel proposition as, hitherto, the majority of preserved lines had been established by enthusiasts who, whilst they clearly sought to run at a profit rather than a loss, perhaps did not establish their operation as an outright business. This is what distinguished the Dart Valley Railway from the others. It was also nearly to be its downfall, when the board later threw in the towel on the Ashburton line and moved their endeavours to the nearby Paignton & Dartmouth line, opening that as a private concern in 1973. Fortunately, when the company moved its loyalty to its other line and subsequently threatened the DVR with closure for a second time, the enthusiasts stepped in, taking over in 1991 so keeping the branch going – pioneering again in the same place! Pat Garland was still then on the DVR board and gave the new volunteer team much support.

The original 1960s DVR promoters were a mixed group of Birmingham friends, who built a team with other like-minded people in the movement from the local region in Devon. Pat Whitehouse stepped up to be Chairman this time, Pat Garland retained the Treasurer role and Bill Faulkner became Managing Director. All three of these people came from their endeavours on

the Talyllyn Railway. Ian Allan diversified from his ABC spotters books and publications to join the board, whilst Bob Saunders provided local input and indefatigable effort in sourcing redundant equipment. John Evans also lived locally and together with PBW was later to stump up the balance of the required cash to buy *Clun Castle*, after she took the point to point record run time from Plymouth to Bristol on Ian Allan's 1964 excursion; but that is another story which we will come to later.

This grouping of people came about largely as a result of Pat Garland being on holiday in Devon in 1963 and coming across the still extant rails on the Ashburton Branch. Thinking that they must still be there for a reason, he made enquiries and discovered that a group of local business men sought to buy the line and operate it as a tourist attraction. However, they had run into difficulties in their negotiations with BR. Garland and Whitehouse contacted the local team and, on account of their previous experience with the Talyllyn and good Western Region contacts, they joined in the scheme. At a meeting in Paddington with Gerry Fiennes, the General Manager, and Reggie Hanks, the remaining difficulties were solved and the Dart Valley Light Railway was born. No longer was No. 4555 to look for a home on the Middleton Railway in Yorkshire!

'The two Pats', in particular, had a track record by now of knowing how to rescue a railway and source material, so they started to amass a collection of suitable engines whilst the legal formalities for the DVR were in process. These engines were initially shedded at Tyseley and Worcester in the Midlands, near to their homes, where it was convenient to look after them. As we have already seen, after a spell of special train running around the Midlands and, for No. 4555, even running some service trains (mainly so Pat Garland

could drive his own engine home to Solihull after a day's office work!), these preserved tank locomotives made their way down to Totnes to begin their new life. No. 4555 most auspiciously had been delivered new to Tyseley in 1924 and also worked the last freight train to Ashburton in 1962, so her pedigree could not be faulted, as well as being a very suitable design for the line's traffic; all these events were remarkable coincidences and unknown to the two Pats when they bought the engine. Other locomotives collected in the Midlands included two auto-fitted tanks, 0-4-2T No. 1420 and 0-6-0PT No. 6435, together with small wheeled pannier No. 1638. All these were repainted by the Whitehouse family firm and No. 4555 even had a light casual overhaul at Swindon, coming with a spare boiler and wagon full of parts as part of her £750 purchase price.

Thus, on 2nd October 1965, the first items of rolling stock arrived: No. 4555 and also Collett goods 0-6-0 No. 3205, along with four BR(WR) push-pull auto trailers, which were to prove invaluable until a run-round loop was installed at the Totnes end of the branch. Much other useful and interesting equipment was also sourced. Many vans of spare parts were collected together when local sheds closed but also some very historic coaches: the Great Western's own Dynamometer car (although sadly stripped of equipment) and two of the famous 'Ocean Mails' wide-bodied saloons, *King George* and *Duchess of York*, together with Collett and Hawksworth design coaches for ordinary use. Perhaps the most exclusive coach to be acquired was the observation car originally used on the 'Devon Belle', converted from an ambulance car to a Pullman car in 1921, which had finished its working life at Oban in Scotland. Other engines sensibly duplicating types for ease of maintenance were also sourced: No's

Top: No. 1420 poses in Buckfastleigh station with an auto coach on 8th April 1967.

Middle: On the same occiasion, the 0-4-2T and newly repainted auto coach are now seen by Buckfastleigh signal box.

Bottom: Forming a typical GWR autotrain, the combination is now seen crossing the River Dart bridge near Buckfastleigh.
[Photos: All J.M. Boyes]

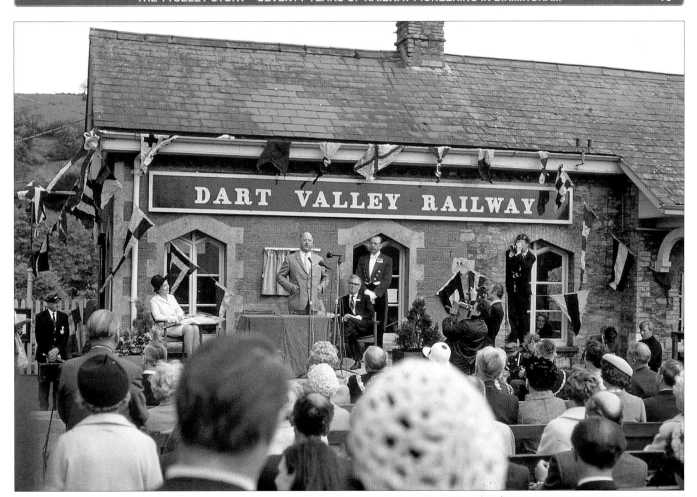

On 21st May 1969, Dr Beeching was invited to reopen the Dart Valley Railway at Buckfastleigh station. I recall my father saying that "as Beeching had closed the line, he could b... well re-open it then!" Indeed, Beeching himself alluded to the same thing in his speech, that he would not have been able to conduct the reopening ceremony if he had not closed the line in the first place. All of which, as railway historians will be aware, was not actually true! Whilst the good doctor was responsible for the closure of many lines and many more stations, he did not in fact close the Ashburton Branch. The so-called Beeching Report, actually named *The Reshaping of British Railways*, looked at all aspects of railway operation including the streamlining of goods services but closures were primarily concerned with the removal of unremunerative passenger services. However, it was published in March 1963, long after the passenger service to Ashburton had been withdrawn on 3rd November 1958, whilst the branch then closed completely with the cessation of goods traffic on and from 7th September 1962. But back in 1969, on such a fine day with a line actually reopening and the ceremony being performed by the villain who had shut so much of our railway system, why let the truth get in the way of such a good story!

ABOVE: No. 6435 leads a two coach auto train away from Buckfastleigh over the River Dart on 14th July 1969, the first year of commercial services.

BELOW: The same engine shunting auto trailers into Buckfastleigh goods yard at the end of the day's services on 7th July 1969. [BOTH PHOTOS: J.M. BOYES]

No. 6412 approaching the River Dart bridge just outside Buckfastleigh sandwiched by four auto trailers forming the 10.48am service from Totnes. This formation enabled the train to operate in true push-pull style, with the driver activating the regulator and the brake from the driving compartment of the auto trailer at the front, corresponding to the direction of travel. Meanwhile, the fireman remained on the footplate, in charge of providing steam and operating the reverser, the crew communicating by bell codes. Whilst this formation was highly convenient to the DVR, as there were then no run-round facilities at Totnes, it would not be so usual on a Devon branch line in GWR days, as four carriages were rarely necessary and, when they were, the train would usually be strengthened or made up entirely of main line stock running through. [PHOTO: J. M. BOYES]

A purely Great Western Railway view looking towards Buckfastleigh from the overbridge near Salmon Leap on 9th July 1969. This was a prescient picture, which sadly is no longer possible, as the A38 Devon Expressway dual carriageway was built through here in the early 1970s, crossing the River Dart at the same point as the railway. The line now terminates on the far bank. [PHOTO: J.M. BOYES]

GWR auto-fitted 0-4-2T No. 1420 crossing the River Dart at Salmon Leap, Buckfastleigh with a single trailer running down from Ashburton on 23rd May 1970. This is the bridge that was shortly to be lost to the road improvement scheme, plans for which had been put in place before the branch was saved for preservation. [PHOTO: J.M. BOYES]

No. 1420 poses in Ashburton station on 23rd May 1970. [Photo: J.M. Boyes]

1450, 6412 and 6430 (the latter intended for spares) together with the diminutive pannier 0-6-0PT, No. 1369, unusually with outside cylinders, which worked the Weymouth Quay Branch.

It took five years to negotiate the purchase of the line, raise the money and secure the necessary Light Railway Order for the transfer of running powers from BR to the new company. This was completed on 1st April 1969 and came into force the next day, which permitted the first passenger train to run on the branch under new ownership on 5th April, 1969 at 11.15am, carrying 300 passengers. It was an auspicious start, for over the Easter holiday, more than 8,000 single journeys were booked and, in the first three weeks, the total passenger journeys added up to 22,398. An official opening was performed a little later, on 21st May, by no less than Dr Beeching himself. There was lunch in a marquee after the opening speeches were made from a dais erected in the forecourt of Buckfastleigh station.

As outlined earlier, the approach of the board of directors of the new Dart Valley Railway was entirely different to most other heritage lines getting underway at this time. The railway was to be run by a company which raised its finance through issuing shares and employing a small but dedicated permanent staff of about a dozen people, assisted by volunteer support. During the summer season, the staff would concentrate on the efficient running of the train service but during the closed season in the winter, they would be engaged mainly on the track and in maintenance of the locomotives and carriages. Quite a proportion of the new permanent staff were former railwaymen who wanted to continue with steam engines, coming from both the Western and Southern regions. Others were enthusiastic amateurs who volunteered their services through

the Dart Valley Railway Association, helping with all aspects of operating and maintaining the railway. The Association became a significant shareholder in the company and had a representative on the board of directors. Also, unusually, the board set a policy that all its equipment must be owned by the company. So it was that the early steam engines to arrive, such as No's 4555, 1420, 6412, 6430 and 6435, were exchanged for shares and became company property. Some engines and equipment left the railway in the early days, mainly because of this policy: No. 3205 went to become the first engine to operate on the Severn Valley Railway in the Midlands and some of the early equipment collected by the Great Western Society and based in sidings at Totnes moved to a new home at Didcot.

There is little doubt that the railway was efficiently run. It quickly grew its passenger numbers to over 125,000 by 1971 and operated as economically as possible by virtue of only running a single train set. Turn round times were minimised by using the GWR push-pull auto train format, sometimes up to four coaches with the engine in the middle and driven from each end by means of mechanical linkages connecting the regulator on the engine to one in the front of the leading auto coach in each direction. Such an approach was initially necessary, as there was no station on the branch line at Totnes. It was not until the year following reopening that a run-round loop was installed at the end of the branch at what has now become known as Totnes (Riverside) and, even then, it was some time before the station was constructed. This true Great Western branch line could be said to be much like a full size model railway, with only one main intermediate station and a halt at Staverton; trains were prevented from running from either

The DVR team were able to be tempted by a fabulous range of GWR carriages to preserve (as were the Great Western Society at Didcot), even though they were unsuitable for commercial services. Here we see four lucky survivors in Buckfastleigh yard:

ABOVE LEFT: GWR Dean clerestory Engineers' Saloon No. 80978 on 9th July 1969; ABOVE RIGHT: GWR Churchward Engineers' Saloon No. 80977, ex-Gloucester, built in 1910, on 9th July 1969;

BELOW LEFT: Unique GWR Dynamometer car (sadly without its internal calibration equipment) on 25th May 1970; BELOW RIGHT: GWR 1931 built Ocean Saloon Duchess of York. [ALL PHOTOS: J.M. BOYES]

GWR outside cylindered 0-6-0PT No. 1369, saved as an indulgence from Weymouth Quay, as it was then thought too small for everyday commercial service, seen here on 12th July 1969 with two GWR open excursion carriages at Buckfastleigh, whilst preparing for the Buckfastleigh carnival. [PHOTO: J.M. BOYES]

the junction station or to the original terminus. A few years later, the DVR did experiment by having a train set certified to run on the main line into Totnes station but additional costs without any increased revenue soon saw this interesting operation withdrawn.

GWR 'roundel' device as applied to 0-6-0PT No. 6435.

Despite all good intentions, the whole branch could never be opened throughout to public trains. The last two miles from Buckfastleigh to Ashburton was severed from the rest in 1971 to enable the A38 trunk road to be made into a dual carriageway and the beautiful Brunel wooden overall roof station at Ashburton was lost to the heritage railway movement. Sadly, the design and route for the A38 widening had already been determined before the DVR obtained its running powers.

By now, Pat Whitehouse had caught the main line bug following his involvement with *Clun Castle*. At the time it was bought from BR, there was no realistic proposition of continuing to run it on the main line beyond, perhaps, a few final excursions prior to the end of steam in 1968. So the plan was to 'retire' her to the proposed museum at Buckfastleigh, where she could be steamed on occasion for exhibition. However, such was – and still is! – the lure of express steam trains on the main line and the determination of a new team of men at Tyseley depot in Birmingham, where No. 7029 had become based, that she never left. Instead, Pat stepped down from the DVR board to concentrate on his next step on the journey: the creation of a main line steam depot of the future at Tyseley.

10. HANCOCK'S CHOICE
THE GRAND FINALE OF THE 'CASTLE' CLASS LOCOMOTIVES

'It was the dream of the mechanical staff to see these fine 'Castles' go out in a blaze of glory and this small band of men became dedicated to achieving it in fine style.'

Avid train spotters will know that, by 1964, the only regular 'Castle' hauled express trains remaining were the Paddington to Worcesters; indeed, the Beyer, Peacock 'Hymek' diesels were already on their way. Our story begins there, for if one went to look over the fence at 85A by Shrub Hill station, an amazing array of clean 'Castles' could often be seen. In addition to home-based *Earl of Ducie*, *Penrice Castle* and *Sudeley Castle*, three more of the class had been moved there: *Cleeve Abbey*, *Bridgwater Castle* and *Hereford Castle*. They were all checked over by Shedmaster Harry Clinton and Works Manager Don Green, for this is a story about enginemen who made sure their steeds went out in fine style, quietly supported by Traction Officer Bill Thorley and the then Western Region General Manager Gerry Fiennes. It was the dream of the mechanical staff at Worcester and Swindon to see these fine 'Castle' Class locomotives go out in a blaze of glory and this small band of men became dedicated to achieving it in fine style.

The 9.15am from Paddington to Worcester and the 1.15pm return became test beds for seeing what the 'Castles' were still capable of – hauling eleven coaches on a 120 mile trip, including the four mile descent of Honeybourne (Camden) Bank at 1 in 100 to test the engines' top speed. In the dining car, soup was served in larger than usual bowls and half pints of beer in pint mugs, whilst it is reputed that a timid old lady fainted away in sheer terror when her cup and saucer slid swiftly across the dining table to smash on the floor as the train careered down the curving incline. After that, there was a ban on the sale of drinks between Moreton-in-Marsh and Evesham during the trials!

Trevor Bailey of Ian Allan had been to see his good friend WR Inspector Jack Hancock one Sunday morning to discuss the prospect of running a special train as the 'Castles" swansong. Hancock specified only seven coaches so as to give the engine the best chance of achieving the high speeds and tight timings that were desired. The train would run on 9th May 1964, from London Paddington to Plymouth and back via Bristol and would be scheduled to be hauled by the three very best 'Castles' – but which were those? Hancock and his colleague, Bill Andress, would have to try several out to find out.

In 1964, there were thirty-seven 'Castles' still in service. Half were tried out, being those having no more than 40,000 miles behind them since overhaul and eight of which would be required for the special day to run the train and also act as standbys. The short list of those eight engines considered to be capable of achieving 100mph were No. 4079 *Pendennis Castle*, No. 5054 *Earl of Ducie*, No. 7008 *Swansea Castle*, No. 7022 *Hereford Castle*, No. 7023 *Penrice Castle*, No. 7025 *Sudeley Castle*, No. 7029 *Clun Castle* and No. 7032 *Denbigh Castle*. Each of these engines was sent to either Worcester or Swindon sheds, where valves, pistons and valve gear were removed and examined and any defects rectified.

Hancock rode them all and chose the Worcester route because steam was still being used on it, the Didcot and Worcester men remained conversant with steam and he could set up all the conditions required for assessing the worth of the engine in just one run: "*What I was really aiming for was to see if the loco under test would maintain steam pressure and boiler level with the use of the exhaust injector, whilst being worked constantly in the 25 per cent cut off, with full regulator opening, and whether it was capable of sustained high speed, and lastly, the general condition of the loco. The first requirement could be achieved between Paddington and Reading, the second could always be achieved down Honeybourne bank and the third, at any time.*" In all, Hancock made fourteen test trips, riding with some engines more than once after repairs. After consultation with the team and men like Norman Tovey of the Swindon CME inspectorate, he chose *Pendennis Castle*, *Clun Castle* and *Earl of Ducie* to haul the special train, with standby engines *Penrice Castle* at Old Oak Common, *Sudeley Castle* at Taunton, *Swansea Castle* at Plymouth, *Denbigh Castle* at Bristol and *Hereford Castle* at Swindon. Two firemen were to be with each engine. Andress would ride to Plymouth and back and Hancock on to London, when it was planned to do the ton.

The men clearly knew what they were doing but, with hindsight, it might be a little surprising that *Pendennis Castle* was chosen to run from London to Plymouth, being an older single chimney and lower superheat engine which, in the early stages of planning, had not even been considered. She would not

"The Great Western"

HIGH SPEED SPECIAL TRAIN

SATURDAY, 9th MAY, 1964

* * *

IAN ALLAN

The front cover of the Ian Allan brochure for 'The Great Western', the 'Castle' swansong tour from London to Plymouth and return on Saturday 9th May 1964.

A fine study of a gleaming No. 4079 *Pendennis Castle* at Swindon on 1st October 1959. As the smokebox door shedplate shows, the engine was allocated to 82A Bristol Bath Road but, as her condition indicates, had just come out of Swindon Works after a Heavy General Overhaul, which included the fitting of a new boiler. No. 4079 was here preparing to work the 11.55am local stopping service to Didcot as a running in turn. [Photo: Russell Leitch/Reverend Canon Brian Arman collection]

GWR 'Castle' No. 4079 *Pendennis Castle*, which starred in the 1925 Locomotive Exchanges, had a second attempt at fame on 9th May 1964 when booked to haul the first leg of 'The Great Western' special, sponsored by Ian Allan, from Paddington to Plymouth. She is seen here standing ready for departure at London Paddington station but at Westbury, the locomotive failed having shed her firebars due to the extremely hot fire having found porous holes within them. *Pendennis Castle*, nevertheless, went on to be bought for preservation, initially by Mike Higson and ran a few more tours before being bought by John Gretton and Bill McAlpine. In 1977, she was sold and exported to Australia but was finally repatriated by the Great Western Society in 2000.

have been if Swindon Mechanical Foreman Day had not repeatedly voiced the opinion that she could be the best of the lot, having given her a valve examination. *Clun Castle*, selected to run over the stiff Devon banks, was considered a weak engine as she did not perform at the standard 15 per cent cut off, although she alone out of the chosen three had the improvements designed by Sam Ell and Ernie Nutty at Swindon: four row superheater, double blastpipe and mechanical lubricator. *Earl of Ducie*, chosen to go for the ton on the run back to town, was also a single chimney lower superheat engine. Hancock and Andress had their reasons and, although the hoped for hundred miles an hour was not achieved, all the engines ran with great results. Actually, it was rather nice that the train ran with an example from each of the '40XX', '50XX' and '70XX' series, and with both single and double chimney types, and also both Collett and Hawksworth tenders! The mechanical department were of the view that all eight locomotives chosen were mechanically sound enough to have hauled the train.

As soon as it was known that *Earl of Ducie* was the chosen locomotive to seek to achieve the magic 100mph, the *Railway Roundabout* BBC TV team went up to Worcester and Honeybourne to film her from a flat wagon pushed by Collett 0-6-0 No. 2222, running in parallel. The illusion of speed was given by running the camera slowly when exposing film so giving fewer frames per second when screened at normal speed! Pat Whitehouse was among the film crew of course and struck up a friendship with Jack Hancock, which was to prove timely for *Clun Castle*'s future life.

The weekly notice leading to 9th May contained special instructions: ''The Great Western' high speed special train is to be signaled 4-1-4 [a special code] *and must run strictly to time.*'. Even the 8.30am 'Royal Duchy' was to be held at Newton Abbot for the special to get ahead. The load was, as specified by Hancock, seven Mark 1 coaches at 243 tons tare.

Jack Trounson, a Cornish mining engineer, passenger on the train and one of the founders of the fund to save *Clun Castle*, gives

A fine portrait study of May 1950-built BR (WR) 'Castle' Class No. 7029 *Clun Castle*, as modified in the late 1950s with a four row superheater, double chimney and blastpipe so she could compete with the 100mph diesel-hydraulics then being introduced on Western Region expresses. No. 7029 is seen at Plymouth Laira depot immediately before setting off with train No. 1Z48, the special which would attempt to take *City of Truro* 'down a peg'. Because her run was the most successful of all the 'Castle' legs on this train, No. 7029 was retained to become the last of her class in service, allocated to Gloucester Horton Road shed, and also subsequently preserved, founding the Tyseley Collection.

RIGHT: No. 4079 *Pendennis Castle* stands at the end of the Down Main platform at Westbury, having failed with melted fire bars whilst hauling the special. Concerned enthusiasts mill about but the headboards and train reporting numbers had already been removed and reattached to No. 6999 *Capel Dewi Hall*, unexpectedly on hand to take the train to Taunton. There, No. 7025 *Sudeley Castle* was waiting to take charge for the run over the Devon banks to Plymouth.

BELOW RIGHT: A day later, on 10th May, *Pendennis Castle* was photographed stored round the back of Westbury engine shed. The locomotive was not to turn a wheel again in BR revenue service, being towed back to Bristol St. Philips Marsh shed where it was officially withdrawn on 14th May. However, fortunately, that was not to be the end of its story but the forerunner to a new beginning. [PHOTOS: BOTH PAUL STRONG/NEIL PARKHOUSE COLLECTION]

a flavour of the day: '*As we moved out of Paddington, every whistle and diesel horn was sounding, with signalmen looking out of their 'boxes' and waving us on. Speed began to gain very soon and it was clear that the crew on the footplate were out for a record run to Plymouth.*'

Aptly named Driver Perfect was at the regulator of *Pendennis Castle*, driving her from Paddington and intending to get to Plymouth, but only succeeded with an engine change to unprepared *Capel Dewi Hall* at Westbury, after the Ogilvy coal melted the firebars of *Pendennis*, which were later found to be porous. But *Pendennis Castle* had put in a good effort, justifying Day's faith in her by reaching 96mph by Lavington. *Capel Dewi Hall* achieved the 47.20 miles to Taunton in 43 minutes and 11 seconds, a very creditable show. Standby *Sudeley Castle* took over at Taunton to make a spirited run to Plymouth. The passengers had now experienced three engines hauling their train so far, with two more to go. Those in the restaurant car tucked into roast chicken and chips with garden peas and new potatoes, followed by cake, pastries or cheese and biscuits whilst they checked their stop watches.

Harry Cooke, Chief Divisional Locomotive Inspector at Newton Abbot, was a master of his trade and his personal preparation of *Clun Castle*, for what became her historic and record run back over the hills to Plymouth, contributed very largely to her outstanding performance, coupled with the excellent work of the footplate crew. Harry explains: '*No. 7029* Clun Castle *was always a weak engine, but when one gets a weak loco, you work her accordingly and one thing is certain that a weak engine will not get rough riding so quickly as a strong loco. Most drivers only know one position at speed to keep the lever at, namely, 15% cut off, if she does not respond then the loco gets a bad name. Hence my reason in telling Harry Roach to work No. 7029 on the 18% cut off, but on no account to work her below that – it's the secret of No. 7029. Make sure she is getting her oil, and that all parts*

are freely oiled, then she becomes not a weak engine but a flying 'sewing' machine.'* On shed at Plymouth Laira, Cooke twice worked out No. 7029's oil pump with paraffin to get rid of all the sludge and his final act, before she left the shed, was to give the handle of the mechanical lubricator eighty or ninety turns to make sure that the oil pipes were full and the oil was reaching the valves and pistons before she turned a wheel. Cooke did this as, otherwise, *Clun Castle* would probably have reached the top of the bank out of Plymouth before the oil really began to get to her cylinders. The result of this preparation and the excellence of the crew was evident for all to see in the terrific performance she put in that day.

Sadly, the Civil Engineer had put a limit of 80mph on the line speed through Wellington, which meant that 100mph was impossible to achieve. But No. 7029's speedometer was slow, so Harry Roach, the driver, was able to take full advantage of it. He takes up the story himself: '*On leaving Plymouth my first job was to get a couple of minutes in hand by Hemerdon … the engine was in*

*Interestingly, during *Clun Castle*'s latest overhaul, completed for 2019 service, it was found that the reverser lever in the cab had been assembled incorrectly at some time earlier, which may well take account of the difference in cut off she required to perform.

GWR 'Castle' No. 5054 *Earl of Ducie* being prepared at Bristol for the last leg of 'The Great Western', with Inspector Jack Hancock watching. Hancock chose her for the run as being the most likely to achieve the sought after 100mph.

good condition … I entered Whiteball tunnel a good 8mph faster than City of Truro. *Bearing the instructions of the Div. Manager in mind it was a case of holding the train back. I have no doubt what-so-ever that if I had been permitted I would have beat the* City of Truro's *speed record. At Bristol I told the loco inspector that the engine was in perfect condition and should continue through to Paddington. I even went so far as to say,* "Give me a pilotman and I will go through myself. I have got to know this engine coming up from Plymouth and I will guarantee you 100 mph". Trounson had a similar view: '*I had never seen* Clun Castle *before, but some instinct inside me said* "You are a greyhound" – *little did I realise the thrill we were in for; No. 7029 was to prove the brilliant star of that exciting day.*' Later, it transpired that the Civil Engineer had waived the speed restriction for the special but, for some unknown reason, this had not been communicated to the various staff operating the railway on the day.

Hancock had his plan for *Earl of Ducie*. The train was sharply timed and, as Hancock was previously the Chief Running Inspector of the Bristol Division, he used to ride 'The Bristolian' regularly when hauled by 'Castles'. Based on those runs with a similar load, he had drawn up specimen running and performance logs from which he wanted Driver Fred Higby to run this special train.

Earl of Ducie's journey did not start quite to plan. As soon as the crew received the 'right away' and Higby had given a long blast on the whistle, there was a terrific explosion of steam as the heating pipe between the tender and the first coach burst. Hancock gave instructions for the heating valve to be closed. It would save steam and, as many of the train windows were open anyway, he decided

that '*the enthusiasm of the passengers would have to be sufficient to keep them warm*'.

The train failed to achieve the hoped for 100mph down the long falling gradient to Little Somerford. There was a high side wind, whilst many coach windows were open so the train was anything but streamlined, so despite instructing the driver to shorten the valve travel, the speed dropped away by almost 10mph. Hancock summarises: '*The lever was put into 30% cut off with full regulator and the speed gradually increased to 96mph and there it stuck, and no more could be got out of it.*' Hancock stuck to his plan and passed through Reading right on the dot having averaged 84mph from Didcot, even passing Old Oak Common at 82mph, only three miles from Paddington, arriving $4^1/_2$ minutes early having covered the $117^3/_4$ miles from Bristol in $95^1/_2$ minutes. An epic day but some old hands were critical of the way the engines were worked, considering that, as Harry Cooke proved with No. 7029 *Clun Castle*, more advantageous use of the valve cut off and regulator would have accomplished something better; after all No. 7029 was only thwarted from the magic ton by a speed restriction.

Maybe the last word should go to Harry Roach: '*And don't forget, if it was not for the efficiency of my fireman, Bill Rundle, the run would have been worthless.*' Men make machines go.

But that is not quite the last word is it? Both *Pendennis Castle* and *Clun Castle* are still very much with us.

And we should not forget men like Jack Hancock or Don Green. They, and others like them, became friends with the enthusiastic businessmen who bought No's 4079 and 7029 and, behind the scenes,

gave the preservationists a great deal of help, advice and confidence which enabled these and other locomotives to re-appear on the national network hauling special trains. Don Green later worked his Worcester magic to enable Tyseley to overhaul single chimney, three row superheater 'Castle' No. 5080 *Defiant* from a Barry wreck in just eighteen months to run on the main line once again. Several Swindon men worked with the Didcot team to perform similar miracles. Without them and a whole host of former BR workshop and depot men, who gave their time freely to help the preservation

cause get off the ground, we would be unlikely to have the main line steam movement today; BR would never have relented to lift the steam ban unless they trusted the men who maintained and ran the steam engines. These stalwarts were indispensible because they intrinsically knew how a steam engine worked, how to get the best out of one and worked all hours to ensure the advertised specials ran. Now, nearly sixty years later, one can pretty much count such people on the fingers of two hands and the main line preservation movement is likely to be the poorer in skill base as a result. A salutary thought.

ABOVE: *Earl of Ducie* stands at Bristol Temple Meads station ready to leave for London on the last leg of 'The Great Western', the Castle swansong tour. Expected to reach the magic 100mph, sadly the train failed to do so.

RIGHT: Surprisingly, these tours seem not to have been well photographed, particularly in colour, so this is a rare view of No. 5054 *Earl of Ducie* heading back with the return leg of the tour, passing through Little Somerford just to the west of Swindon at around 7.30pm. The booked arrival at Paddington was just over an hour later.

DRIVER **F. HIGBY**   FIREMAN **R. GITSHAM / C. RICHARDS** OF BRISTOL - BATH R^d.

Report on the performance of engine **5054** on **SATURDAY 9TH MAY 1964**
working the **6/53 p.m. SPL** from **BRISTOL T. MEADS** to **PADDINGTON**.

M.CH.	Mins.Secs.	Stations	Speed	Position of Reg.	% cut off	Water in boiler	Steam pressure.	No. of Galls. of water consumed.
00.00	00.00	Bristol T.M.	00	CLOSED	F.GEAR	FULL	225	
1.50	4.05	Stap.Rd.	40	1/2	40	FULL	220	
2.42	5.25	Ashley H.	36	3/4	40	FULL	220	
-	7.05	Horfield	36	3/4	42	FULL	225	
4.64	8.32	Filton Jcn.	44	1/4	30	7/8	210	
7.63	12.02	Winterborne	58	3/4	35	7/8	220	
10.40	14.45	Westerleigh	61	3/4	35	7/8	215	
13.05	17.10	C.Sodbury	64	3/4	35	7/8	225	500
17.50	21.02	Badminton	64	3/4	35	7/8	205	
23.31	25.25	Hullavington	86	3/4	30	7/8	210	
27.70	28.25	L.Somerford	90	FULL	30	7/8	220	
30.50	30.07	Brinkworth	84	1/2	35	7/8	210	
34.70	32.57	W.Bassett	61	1/8	35	FULL	215	
40.36	37.45	Swindon	78	3/4	25	7/8	220	
46.14	41.50	Shrivenham	82	FULL	30	7/8	220	
51.17	45.22	Uffington	86	3/4	32	7/8	215	
53.74	47.06	Challow	84	2/3	25	7/8	210	
57.26	49.30	Vantage Rd.	86	2/3	25	7/8	215	
61.18	52.00	Steventon	84	2/3	30	7/8	210	
64.50	54.30	Didcot	82	3/4	30		210	
69.23	57.43	Cholsey	80	FULL	30	FULL	220	
73.00	60.25	Goring	78	3/4	30	FULL	225	2000
76.17	62.50	Pangbourne	78	FULL	30	7/8	220	
79.07	65.00	Tilehurst	80	FULL	30	1/2	220	
81.62	66.45	Reading	76	2/3	25	1/2	220	
86.59	70.43	Twyford	72	1/3	25	2/3	220	
93.41	75.40	Maid'head	82	1/2	25	1/2	225	
99.24	79.50	Slough	80	3/4	30	2/3	210	
104.42	83.35	W.Drayton	80	FULL	30	7/8	215	
108.54	86.26	Southall	82	FULL	30	7/8	225	
112.04	88.47	E.Broadway	80	FULL	30	2/3	200	
114.38	90.32	O.O.C.West	82	FULL	30	2/3	190	
116.40	92.10	Westbne Pk.	34	1/8	45	1/3	200	
117.60	95.18	Paddington	00	CLOSED	45	1/3	200	1000

State of Weather **FINE - BUT HEAVY SIDE WIND**   Total **3500**
Class of coal   **OGILVIE - 1A**
Condition of engine   **VERY GOOD**
Load   **7/250 TONS**

Average speed Swindon to Padd **80.59 M.P.H.**

BOILER WASHED - 7/5/64
TUBES CLEANED - 7/5/64
AVERAGE SPEED - 74.1343. M.P.H.

J. F. Hancock

Jack Hancock's log of No. 5054 *Earl of Ducie*'s run from Bristol to London Paddington, showing an achievement of only 90mph. Note his comment about a heavy side wind which, together with the many open windows in the train, were put down as the likely inhibitors.

No. 7029 *Clun Castle* was much in demand for special trains following her 1964 point-to-point record run. Here she nears the top of the Lickey Bank at Blackwell on 'foreign' Midland territory with another Ian Allan special, this time from Paddington to Worcester and on to Nottingham on 29th March 1965. She was hauling nine carriages and being banked by a diesel. Pat Whitehouse is on the footplate but, as yet, with no thoughts of purchase, as No. 7029 still had a year's service left.

LEFT: *Clun Castle* was chosen to haul the 'Farewell to Steam' railtour organised by British Railways Western Region itself to mark the end of steam on its patch. The WR was the first of the six BR regions to dieselise completely, having replaced more than 3,000 steam locomotives and virtually completed a £100m diesel traction programme in a little over seven years. On Saturday, 27th November 1965, No. 7029 hauled the last official WR steam train to depart from London Paddington, running to Swindon, Bristol and then via Mangotsfield to Gloucester. The 'Castle' is seen here about to depart Bristol Temple Meads station. [PHOTO: G.R. HOUNSELL]

LEFT: On reaching Gloucester, *Clun* was replaced by a 'Western' diesel which hauled the tour to Cheltenham Spa St. James station and back. and back. The 'Castle' is seen here near the Horton Road coal stage, waiting to back down onto the returned train, which she would then haul back as far as Swindon, where she was taken off to go on shed. The tour was then hauled back to Paddington by a pair of diesels. [PHOTO: BILL POTTER]

No. 7029 *Clun Castle* arrived at Tyseley depot for preservation in 1966, having been rescued by Pat Whitehouse and John Evans after the initial public appeal failed to raise the necessary £3,000. No. 7029 was placed into a trust with representatives of the fundraisers and subsequently into a charitable company bearing her name, which has subsequently been used to own the whole of the Tyseley Collection. Although she appeared bereft of name and number plates, the originals were sold with the locomotive but, whilst she was kept in the Tyseley roundhouse, they were stored in the depot foreman's office for safe keeping. [PHOTO: P.B. WHITEHOUSE]

11. TYSELEY DEPOT
THE SHED WHERE STEAM NEVER DIED

'Tyseley is well positioned for the future of main line steam as the gateway to 'The Shakespeare Line' runs from Moor Street station, a 1909 city terminus still in original condition and deep in the heart of Birmingham, through Shakespeare's County to the international tourist destination of Stratford-upon-Avon ...'

The classic Great Western roundhouse. GWR 'Grange' 4-6-0 No. 6861 *Crynant Grange* stands under the shed's rays during its last months of service in October 1965. These mixed traffic locomotives were well capable of a fair turn of speed and were often rostered on Tyseley's best link, the 9.50pm Birmingham Snow Hill to Swindon parcels run: a 200 mile circuit from Birmingham to Birmingham with only three intermediate stops, outward via Cheltenham and Gloucester but returning via Didcot, Oxford, the Honeybourne curve and Stratford. Nowadays Vintage Trains' locomotives often put up similar feats. [PHOTO: STEVE HEWINS]

Tyseley's Great Western Railway depot in Birmingham was just an ordinary place for ordinary locomotives whose purpose was to deliver the everyday service for the people of Birmingham and the Midlands. But, at the same time, all these simple steps were far reaching in developing south-west Birmingham, enabling goods and materials to be exported and imported, commuters to travel to work and back home, and holiday makers to trip to the seaside, as well as broccoli specials that ran from Cornwall to Moor Street good yard and fast parcels trains at night. And always managed and run by dedicated and skilled people who knew their trades well.

Tyseley depot is more than what it appears to be. It has always been defined less by its geography and physical structures (even though it is the last remaining top fifty steam locomotive depot in Britain) but more by the people who were drawn to this place.

The people who served the Great Western Railway. The charismatic shedmaster who welcomed in the railway heritage era whilst his depot was still servicing steam locomotives in everyday life. The railway heritage pioneers who graduated from preserving the world's first railway to ensuring express steam locomotives had a future role to play in society. The engineers who wielded their skills and taught the next generation to execute them to perfection. All enabling the steam locomotive to remain proud and useful and to create a second innings, thus opening the eyes of an evolving society to experience and enjoy one of Britain's finest inventions.

But perhaps Tyseley depot has been defined most of all by the ideas, the energy and the determination generated and applied to make it the beacon of light that it has become in the heritage railway sector. For Tyseley is well positioned for the future of main line steam as the gateway to 'The Shakespeare Line', running from

Moor Street station, a 1909 city terminus still in original condition and deep in the heart of Birmingham, through Shakespeare's County to the international tourist destination of Stratford-upon-Avon, on the way passing through the Forest of Arden and touching the Shire of Tolkein fame. This railway was the last main line to be built in Britain before the advent of high speed railways and still retains much original infrastructure. Its future includes a designation as Britain's first heritage main line railway and its steam trains are run by Britain's first community-owned Train Operating Company having all the attributes to deliver: steam locomotives, carriages, a workshop, a running depot, skilled people, a tour promoter and a licence to operate.

* * *

From the top deck of a Birmingham Corporation tram, one could easily see the engines lined up on the Warwick Road side of the double roundhouse and factory that was Tyseley.

The Great Western Railway, in its wisdom, had purchased sufficient land to build up to four roundhouses should the need have ever arisen and in the space where the other two could have been were two single lines often crammed full of engines, their brass and copper gleaming in the summer sunshine: *Lady of Lynne*, *Saint Helena*, *Ivanhoe*, *Rob Roy*, several 'Halls' and 'Granges', and a whole host of unnamed tank engines and goods engines could be seen from this vantage point, or by peering through the spear point iron railings from the pavement.

If one was bolder and ventured into the Stygian interior of the roundhouses, there was an awesome feast of engines gathered around two turntables in the interconnected sheds, some hidden in the dark corners, others with their features picked out by the shafts of sunlight penetrating through the windows in the roof.

In the beginning, Tyseley housed seventy-two locomotives, some fostered from the nearby Bordesley shed which closed when Tyseley

opened in 1908. The new depot was to provide motive power for the expanding GWR lines into Birmingham and the new cross-country main line route through Stratford-upon Avon and Cheltenham to Bristol and Cardiff – the cut off to the south west, known to all as the 'North Warwicks.'

Tyseley also provided many shunting tank engines for the varied goods sidings and yards in Birmingham, particularly at nearby Bordesley and also Hockley, on the north side of Snow Hill station. Moor Street terminus station had a large city centre goods yard too, with under track warehouses reached by wagon lifts. Much of the paperwork for the GWR's goods service was done from a large goods office on the other side of the main line to Tyseley depot and adjacent to the four platformed junction station for the 'North Warwicks'. To complete the establishment, the depot had a large array of carriage sidings together with a vacuum plant to suck all the rubbish out from them. Hard water, better for the locomotive boilers, was even piped all the way from the other side of the City at Hockley. The depot employed over a thousand people and was the *raison d'être* of the suburb: everyone lived adjacent to the job in rows of neat terraced houses with a school in Reddings Lane. Apart from the roundhouse buildings, the goods offices and the adjacent stables for horses, all these buildings, including the original track layout for the passenger roundhouse, still survive today.

Tyseley boasted six 4-4-0 'Bulldogs' and one 'Duke', No. 3275 *Chough*, for the North Warwicks cross country services; eight 2-6-0 'Aberdares' for the heavy freight traffic to and from Bordesley yard, which classes by the outbreak of the Second World War had been replaced by the larger Churchward '28XX' and two '47XX' 2-8-0 classes, as indeed the 'Duke' and 'Bulldogs' had been by 'Halls' and 'Granges'. But most of the engines were veteran saddle and pannier tanks for the yards at Hockley and Bordesley, and for trip freight working.

ABOVE: Tyseley depot, the first of three official views taken when it first opened in 1908, with double roundhouses and a twelve road locomotive 'factory'.

OPPOSITE PAGE TOP: The pristine interior of the twin roundhouses, prior to the arrival of any locomotives.

OPPOSITE PAGE BOTTOM: The factory machine shop. [PHOTOS: ALL GREAT WESTERN RAILWAY]

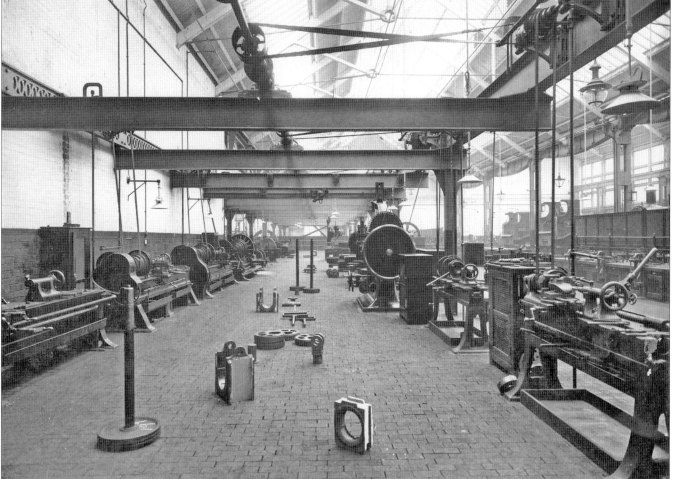

After the opening of the North Warwicks line to passengers on 1st July 1908, Tyseley for many years could boast six 'Bulldogs' and usually one 'Duke' on its roster, to operate the cross-country services. Amongst the latter were No. 3264 *Trevithick* in 1921, No. 3274 *Newquay* in 1934 and No. 3268 *Chough*, pictured here. The 4-4-0 is standing on the ash road adjacent to the coaling stage (which still survives today). Built at Swindon Works in December 1896 and originally No. 3272, *Chough* became No. 3268 during the GWR's renumbering scheme of 1912. Withdrawn in March 1939, the tender carries the GWR roundel device introduced in 1934, whilst the tender on the right is still lettered 'Great Western', which gives us a reasonable circa 1935 date for the photograph.

With the increase in suburban traffic following the opening of Moor Street city terminus in 1909, the GWR became chronically short of motive power and some surplus 'Dean Goods' 0-6-0s were rebuilt into the '39XX' Class 2-6-2Ts – a locomotive type which always looked rather odd with its straight running plate and hole in the side tanks for access to the motion. Tyseley received thirteen out of the twenty rebuilds and these lasted until ousted by the ubiquitous '51XX' Class 'Large Prairie' 2-6-2Ts, which stayed until the end of steam working.

The balance of locomotive power at Tyseley largely remained unchanged through its steam years, although gradually more modern types replaced first the Dean, then the Churchward and finally the Collett designs.

The year 1934 brought the advent of the GWR railcar and, by 1937, Tyseley had been allocated three of them – No's 2, 3 and 4. Intended to provide a fast service to Cardiff, they were the forerunners of the diesel multiple unit fleet and even came fitted with a small drinks bar at one end. Now, of course, Tyseley depot and former carriage sidings are full of the latest designs of multiple units.

Over the years, the number of engines shedded at Tyseley steadily increased, from seventy-two in 1908, to 106 in 1937 and to 116 in 1947. In particular, Tyseley became home to more freight engines

ABOVE: The ubiquitous tank shunting locomotive and lifeblood of Tyseley. Here, open cab pannier No. 2104 stands inside the roundhouse in 1930. The '2021' Class 0-6-0 was built at Wolverhampton Stafford Road Works in February 1902 as a saddle tank and was rebuilt as a pannier tank in July 1927, in which form it lasted in service until May 1951. From 1938 to withdrawal it was based at Birkenhead.

RIGHT: With the increase in suburban traffic following the opening of Moor Street terminus in 1906, the GWR became chronically short of motive power and some surplus 'Dean' Goods 0-6-0s were rebuilt into the '39XX' Class 2-6-2Ts; a locomotive type which always looked rather odd with its straight running plate and hole in the side tanks for access to the motion – wags suggested it was where a clockwork key was inserted for winding them up! Here No. 3904, spotlessly clean, runs through Snow Hill station with a freight train. On the left is a glimpse of 'Flower' Class 4-4-0 No. 4149 Auricula.

During the Second World War, a shelter was built to cover the ash roads and help hide the fires being thrown out from locomotives from German bombers. Tyseley Locomotive Works has since been constructed on this spot. Here, GWR 'Saint' Class 4-6-0 No. 2950 *Taplow Court* stands fully coaled and ready for service in April 1950. New in May 1912, the locomotive was withdrawn in September 1952. [Photo: P.B Whitehouse]

including the 'adopted' former Great Central Railway and First World War Railway Operating Department (ROD) 2-8-0s, plus more 'Granges' and some 'Manors', together with Collett '22XX' 0-6-0s and '56XX' 0-6-2Ts. Some of the 'Granges' in particular put up splendid fast performances on parcels traffic.

The first of British Railways' Riddles 'Standard' designs were released into traffic from 1951 and Tyseley gained its fair share. By 1952, the shed was allocated ten Class '3' 2-6-2Ts for suburban work but the 'masters' of the job, the GWR 'Large Prairies', were still the firm favourites of the Tyseley men and so the interlopers were transferred away to South Wales after only a few months. Despite this, sadly the dominance of GWR motive power did not last and ubiquitous Stanier 'Black Five' 4-6-0s and Class '8F' 2-8-0s, ousted from regular duties by diesels on other parts of the nationalised system, were drafted to Tyseley, along with a number of the '9F' 2-10-0s.

At the start of the *Summer 1957 Time Table*, Tyseley began to feel the first effects of the Modernisation Plan, with diesel multiple units taking over from steam on most of the suburban services from both Birmingham Snow Hill and Moor Street stations.

By 1959, the depot's allocation had shrunk to seventy-five steam locomotives, the 'Large Prairie' 2-6-2Ts becoming one of the principal casualties. Further, the 1908 steam shed was ravaged to make way for a new diesel depot. When the new diesel 'factory' opened in 1964, only the passenger roundhouse and coaling stage remained from the original buildings; the freight roundhouse having been swept away and, with it, the twelve road lifting shop, overhead 35-ton capacity electric crane, electric traverser, coppersmith, carpenters' shop and gas engine.

Near the end of the old factory's life, the Western Region decided to stage an open week at the depot and at Wolverhampton Stafford Road, to explain the railways to the public and encourage their use. Whether the object of the 'Western Week,' held from 9th-14th April 1962, was achieved is, perhaps, a moot point but, for half a crown, youngsters could take a train to Tyseley and not only visit the whole shed without interruption from the foreman and his staff but also actually enter the forbidden factory and watch the front end of a 'Castle' being hoisted into the air by the lifting gantry.

The year 1962 also saw diesels arrive in large numbers, with the Beyer, Peacock 'Hymeks' being particularly prevalent initially, until superceded by the more powerful 'Western' diesel-hydraulics which became the staying power on the 'two hour' London expresses. By 1964, many of the smaller tank engines had also been displaced by diesel 0-6-0 shunters. Still, fourteen 'Halls' and seven 'Granges' and a handful of 'Manors' remained, surviving largely on account of the Washwood Heath to Gloucester freight traffic. The run down of steam progressed, however, until by 1967 only three pannier tanks remained at Tyseley, largely for the Halesowen Basin shunt.

Towards the end of BR steam, Tyseley began to see several 'Castles', although none stayed for very long; for a brief period around 1964, five were allocated and could all be seen on Sundays. Little did the depot staff then know that Tyseley was yet to become famous for its 'Castles' …

Tyseley was never a 'top link' depot, although during its lifetime it has housed very many famous and several unusual engines. Even at the very beginning its allocation included an ex-West Midland Railway 'single wheeler' 2-2-2 tender engine, built by Beyer, Peacock as long ago as 1861. A whole line of elite locomotives were to pay

GWR 'Mogul' 2-6-0 No. 9303 is turned inside the roundhouse in June 1953. The '93XX' Series were a heavier *de luxe* version of Churchward's '43XX' Class, with twenty built in 1932. Distinguishable by their side window cabs, in the late 1950s, as the older members of the class were withdrawn, the newer '93XX's were rebuilt to lighten them and make them available for working over Blue routes. This locomotive was rebuilt in 1957 and, in common with the others was renumbered into the '73XX' Series, becoming No. 7325. Purchased from Barry scrapyard in August 1975 for preservation at the Severn Valley Railway, it is proposed to rebuild her back to No. 9303. She has run on the main line in preservation, so Tyseley depot beckons once again. [PHOTO: PAT WHITEHOUSE]

fleeting visits in the 1950s for railtour work, inspired by enthusiast societies such as the Stephenson Locomotive Society and, as we have seen, organised by the indefatigable Arthur Camwell.

One tradition quickly established from 1951 was the annual SLS Special to Swindon Works, hauled by either a last survivor of its class or by some unusual or famous locomotive. *Skylark*, *Saint David*, *Princess Margaret*, *King Henry VI* and *County of Chester* all took their turn on these trains, having been specially groomed at Tyseley the week before. The BR smokebox numberplate would be removed and, instead, the engine's numbers painted on the buffer beam in the old GWR style, the paintwork cleaned, and brass and copper work burnished as new; no one sought overtime rates on these occasions. Even the record breaker *City of Truro* and the very last working 'single wheeler', Caledonian 2-2-2 No. 123, graced the

RIGHT: Bulleid 'Battle of Britain' Class 4-6-2 No. 34051 *Winston Churchill*, now in the National Collection, steams out of the passenger roundhouse at Tyseley, preparatory to hauling an SLS Special from Birmingham Snow Hill to Salisbury, where Bulleid 'Merchant Navy' No. 35017 *Belgian Marine* took over for the run to Westbury. Then, No. 7029 *Clun Castle* brought the train back to Birmingham. I was privileged to travel on that train and wondered at the sight of *Winston Churchill* at Tyseley, whilst the trip was my first behind No. 7029. The nondescript brick foreman's office on the right of the picture is now the Tyseley Locomotive Works office.

BELOW: Tank engines at Tyseley, which was always a home to freight and shunting locomotives for the busy Birmingham goods yards at Bordesley and Hockley; there was also a goods department at Tyseley. Around 1964, a brace of '66XX' 0-6-2Ts, No's 5658 and 5684, stand under shafts of light beaming through the roof skylights together with '57XX' pannier No. 3770. Originally designated as TYS in GWR ownership, the depot was redesignated 84E in BR(WR) days and subsequently 2A when transferred to the London Midland Region. [PHOTO: PAT WHITEHOUSE]

depot with their presence, whilst being prepared for exhibition at Moor Street station.

On 26th April 1963, Southampton played Manchester United at Villa Park in the semi-finals of the FA Cup – an event which brought no fewer than eleven Bulleid 'Light Pacifics' to Birmingham with trains from Southampton and several of these engines came onto Tyseley shed for servicing. Two days later, No. 6018 *King Henry VI*, the very last 'King' in service, hauled one of 'Cam's Swindon Specials, having been specially retained some six months after withdrawal from traffic to work the train. During the week leading up to the trip, some local trains were grossly overpowered as the 'King' limbered up for the great and final day. Even after withdrawal, No. 6018 remained on Tyseley depot for a while, an awesome sight on a Sunday afternoon for a young lad to see. In September of the same year, the depot was briefly host to one of the most powerful of British express steam locomotives, 'Coronation' Class 'Pacific' No. 46245 *City of London*, on the occasion of a special working to Crewe.

Elated with 'special train fever,' Tyseley depot then proved to be a magnet for preserved steam locomotives and, strange as it will seem, these have now been resident for longer that either the GWR or BR had steam engines there. We have already read about the tank engines bought by PJG, PBW and John Wilkins, initially just for fun but then for the nascent Dart Valley Railway. Between 1964 and 1965, No's 4555 and 6435 could be seen, freshly painted in authentic GWR livery, inside the roundhouse. But even then, there was no long term thought to try to preserve the depot itself, to become the only steam shed in the whole of the United Kingdom to remain alive from the 'top fifty' such depots calculated by the number of resident engines.

Shedmaster Tommy Field was a man prepared to make decisions and stand by them. He saw no reason why No. 4555 should not be used even though it was no longer the property of his lords and masters. So, to the delight of the commuters, daily routine would sometimes be shattered by a sparkling green 'Small Prairie' on the 5.25pm all stations from Snow Hill to Knowle & Dorridge so that PJG could drive his engine, No. 4555, home from the office! On occasion, it would even be borrowed to work local pick-up freights, on one occasion even piloting a 'Hall' from Leamington on 'The Pines Express'!

Tommy was also one of the reasons why the last 'Castle', No. 7029 *Clun Castle*, came to Tyseley. Diesels had made big inroads into the steam motive power by 1966 and there was room to spare in the passenger roundhouse. In spite of withdrawal from BR service, *Clun Castle* was still in fair shape and also in great demand for enthusiast special trains. It seemed a pity to take her to Buckfastleigh on the Dart Valley, as was the original intention,

Even in 1966, the depot's last year of steam, three '57XX' Class pannier tanks, No's 4646, 4696 and 9774, were retained to work the Halesowen basin shunt. Together with the panniers at Wrexham's Croes Newydd, they were the very last Western steam locomotives of all still at work on British Railways. Here, No. 4646 stands in the former passenger roundhouse waiting for her next day's rostered work. [PHOTO: C.M. WHITEHOUSE]

By 1967, Pat Whitehouse was a main board director at construction company Cubitts, which had its monthly board meeting in London. PBW travelled down from Birmingham on the 'Blue Pullman' in the morning and, after the meeting, returned by train to Banbury. There, he left the train and walked down to the depot to where No. 7029 *Clun Castle* had been sent from her new base at Tyseley. PBW then footplated No. 7029 back to Birmingham hauling the empty car flat train to Washwood Heath – that is until the regional authorities came to know that a privately owned steam locomotive was operating their freight trains! [PHOTO: P.B. WHITEHOUSE]

The only sign of life in the shed on the last day of 1967 were the burning embers from a brazier casting flickering shadows on a silent pannier tank standing forlornly outside the shed doorway. Inside stood a Brush Type '4' diesel waiting for the new year.

ABOVE: On Saturday 4th March 1967, two Ian Allan organised special trains were run on the GWR's northern main line from London to Birkenhead to mark the end of steam and the end of the line as a through route. The first train was 'The Birkenhead Flyer', hauled by preserved 4-6-0 No. 4079 *Pendennis Castle* from Didcot to Chester, with the 'Castle' seen here shunting the train at Chester. [PHOTO: JOHN WHITELEY]

LEFT: The second special on Saturday 4th March was 'The Zulu', hauled by No. 7029 *Clun Castle*. This train also originated at London Paddington but ran by the direct route via Princes Risborough and Banbury, where No. 7029 took over the train for the journey north. Here, *Clun Castle* is seen at Saltney Junction, Chester on the outward journey. [PHOTO: JOHN WHITELEY]

Later that day, No. 7029 *Clun Castle* was photographed leaving Chester with 'The Zulu', returning to the Midlands. At Birmingham Snow Hill, a 'Hymek' diesel-hydraulic took over for the run back to London, a replacement for the originally booked 'Western'. [PHOTO: JOHN WHITELEY]

and incarcerate her in the goods shed for exhibition and only occasional forays up the sidings in the yard. So, with Tommy's agreement, No. 7029 came to live at Tyseley and she has never left! She ran several specials and also limbered up on the Banbury to Washwood Heath car flat empties for good measure, this time allowing PBW to footplate her home from Banbury. It was the only 'Castle' earning its keep in 1966.

But 'Indian summers' don't last for ever. Sadly, Tommy Field met a tragic death in a road accident and the church was packed for his funeral. In 1967, steam at Tyseley officially ended. Three GWR pannier tanks were there to the end, together with 'Large Prairie' No. 4110, retained just as a static boiler for locomotive washouts. BR then determined to demolish the passenger roundhouse and issued instructions for *Clun Castle* to leave. The only sign of life in the shed on the last day of 1967 was the burning embers from a brazier casting flickering shadows on a silent pannier tank standing forlornly outside the shed doorway. Inside, stood a Brush Type '4' diesel waiting for the new year.

But Tyseley depot never did die as expected. PBW 'pulled some strings' and took a six month licence of the coaling stage, the only building left. The interior space was extended a little so that *Clun Castle* could take up residence and plans could gradually be made for a new life. In the meantime, there were still special trains to be run. Over the winter of 1966-67, No. 7029 was housed in the diesel depot so she could be repainted properly by the family firm of B. Whitehouse & Sons and lined out by a craftsman from Swindon. She was repainted in authentic BR(WR) lined green but with 'Great Western' on her tender. There was, of course, some criticism of this in the enthusiast circles but they had overlooked that No. 7029 was the only BR-built locomotive in private ownership still running

on the nationalised system; the few others were all ex-L&NER locomotives except for sister *Pendennis Castle*, which could properly be painted in GWR livery. And BR had made it plain that they would not be amused if *Clun Castle* bore the 'cycling lion' emblem on her tender …

In March 1967, the former GWR main line to the North West from London through Birmingham to Chester and Birkenhead, was to be truncated as a through route and the express trains transferred to the newly electrified former L&NWR West Coast Main Line through New Street. So, over the weekend of 4th-5th March, no less than four special trains were run to mark this, together with the closure of Snow Hill to express trains. *Clun Castle* was used both days and the other trains were hauled by sister *Pendennis Castle* on the Saturday, both starting from London with steam from Didcot and Banbury, and with Tyseley depot's ex-LM&SR 'Black Five' No. 44680 on the Sunday, when both trains began from Snow Hill. The specials were a fitting farewell to the main line service and the evening of Sunday 5th March was an emotive occasion as *Clun Castle* bowled back to Birmingham in the darkness at more than 70mph. The sound of detonators exploding and frantic whistling deafened the centre of Birmingham as Snow Hill bade farewell to steam.

The last run had one interesting sequel. The booked fireman on No. 7029 fell ill and a replacement had to be found in a hurry. Among the passengers on the train was Bernard Rainbow, a Tyseley man and a qualified BR fireman. He willingly volunteered to 'have a go' and can be remembered running up the platform towards the engine saying "*we will be alright*". It was really just the beginning for Bernard, as he volunteered to help the embryo team formed at Tyseley to look after the preserved collection as it grew and became Depot Superintendent for many years, collecting plaudits for *Clun*'s exploits

The Tyseley preservation era begins. No. 7029 *Clun Castle* stands proudly on the passenger roundhouse turntable on Monday 6th March, bravely sporting her new preservation livery whilst all around is decay. The engine had been repainted in authentic BR passenger locomotive green but 'Great Western' lettering had been applied to the tender sides rather than the BR 'cycling lion' emblem. It must be remembered that the locomotive was by then privately owned and so could not wear the insignia of its former owners whilst still working on their track. [Photo: P.B. Whitehouse]

'Castles 'at Tyseley. No. 4079 *Pendennis Castle* (with incorrect red painted frames) sits on the turntable with No. 7029 *Clun Castle* facing on one of the turntable roads. The ladders are from B. Whitehouse & Sons, provided to assist locomotive cleaning for the weekend. The pair of 4-6-0s had completed two trips on the GWR's northern main line to Chester and Birkenhead over the weekend just past and now, on Monday 6th March 1967, they were being prepared inside the Tyseley roundhouse for Terence Cuneo to paint them on canvas. [Photo: J.H.L. Adams]

in the GW150 year in 1985 and during two Royal visits to Tyseley, working under the direction of the first Chief Engineer, Jim Kent.

Unbeknownst to many, all was not well with *Clun Castle* on her second return trip to Birmingham. Those of us on the footplate, however, were only too well aware of the position; No. 7029 was riding exceptionally roughly. It transpired that the threads on the spindle bolts on the left-hand side cylinder had stripped and the invalid limped back to Tyseley on only two of her four cylinders. If she was to run again, she would require considerable attention.

Engineering assistance was required and, fortuitously, arrived in the form of Jim Kent, lecturer in engineering at Warley Technical College and sometime volunteer with Tom and Bill Hunt, assisting with the steam engines at the Birmingham Museum of Science &

Industry in Newhall Street (since relocated as Thinktank).

During the early summer of 1967, the inside motion on No. 7029 was stripped down, repaired and re-erected, no mean task in the adverse conditions of a dilapidated roundhouse where by then there existed precious little by way of facilities. The preservationists were just beginning to learn that the purchase price of a steam locomotive was really only the entrance fee to a club which then required increasing amounts of time and cash.

But the job was completed and, in celebration, No. 7029 went to Banbury to collect the empty car flat wagons for the last time, to be followed by her famed East Coast Main Line trips with sorties over the Settle & Carlisle. Read on! The Tyseley story was only then just beginning.

12. FIRING *CLUN CASTLE* OVER STOKE, SHAP & AIS GILL
Dick Potts

'At Arlesey we touched 90 mph and kept up a high speed …'

In more than eighteen years as a fireman and driver at Tyseley, I have had many exciting trips including the last 'Star', No. 4056 *Princess Margaret*, and 'King' No. 6018 *King Henry VI* from Snow Hill to Swindon. But these were nothing to the very different experiences enjoyed whilst being one of Mr P.B. Whitehouse's 'volunteers' and assisting enginemen, who worked *Clun Castle* from King's Cross to York and Preston to Carlisle in the autumn of 1967.

During this time we had many informal discussions on how she was to be cleaned and fired, and how we could be available if needed while on 'foreign' lines. Arrangements were made with British Railways to allow us to be with the engine and, if required, to assist either the driver or fireman. This was mainly because in some areas now they had either no firemen or very few who would have had any experience of ex-GWR locomotives.

At the end of August 1967, *Clun Castle* ran light engine to Newcastle via Derby for 'clearance' trials before being sent to Peterborough, New England shed where she was to stay for a series of excursions. Six trips had been arranged with No. 7029, two of them being in balance with other preserved locomotives: No. 4472 *Flying Scotsman* and No. 4498 *Sir Nigel Gresley*.

The first trip I could attend was that from King's Cross to York on Sunday 8th October,1967. Ian Allan Ltd had arranged for 'The Silver Jubilee' special to run from King's Cross to York and back, using *Clun Castle* in both directions. As I stood, after taking a couple of photographs, admiring her, I thought of a time when I could never have imagined that I would be looking at a 'Western' engine at the head of a train at King's Cross.

But we must return to the brass and corks of No. 7029. At 10.05am, she moved her ten coach train (342 tons tare, 360 tons gross) from the platform with comparative ease and accelerated up the bank to pass Hornsey in just over eight minutes. Then we encountered numerous signal checks due to engineering work, in some instances being diverted to the slow line. But from Hatfield (we were five late but it was estimated the checks had cost a total of fourteen minutes) the pressure was applied and we enjoyed a clear road. We reached 69mph at Welwyn, 65 at Woolmer Green, 73 at Stevenage and continued to accelerate down the hill.

I was looking forward to a dash through Hitchin and I was not disappointed, as we had continued to accelerate and flashed through at 84mph. At Arlesey we touched 90mph and kept up a high speed until braking for a permanent way check at Huntingdon. We accelerated from this to 80mph after Abbots Ripon before shutting off for another check at Holme, followed by a very slow entry into Peterborough.

Arrangements had been made by our organizer, Richard Garland, for me to assist on the footplate from Peterborough up Stoke Bank to Retford and I was looking forward to a shovelling session up this famous stretch of line.

Just before starting away, I looked into the firebox and nearly had heart failure. The fire was so low! An almost even layer three to four inches thick all over the firebox was all that could be seen. I was apprehensive about the chances of great efforts with such a mere hat full of fire but I need not have worried; the Eastern men knew their stuff and I think, too, had confidence in No. 7029.

I had not bargained either for the superb quality of the hard cobbles in the tender; there were no pieces larger than five inches and almost no dust. What a contrast to the wall of boulders hidden by a muddy dust laughingly called soft coal that most Western fireman faced at the start of a journey. A much thinner fire can be allowed with hard coal and the fire built up with the regulator open while on the run.

On getting all the train onto the main line, Driver Garbutt, being of shortish stature, put his shoulder under the regulator arm and heaved it towards the roof. A flicker

British Railways Eastern Region

Regional Headquarters
Liverpool Street Station
London EC2
BIShopsgate 7600 Ext   Telex 264146   G. F. Fiennes General Manager

R. L. E. Lawrence, Esq.,
Asst. General Manager,
London Midland Region,
EUSTON.

y/r
o/r   5th December 1966.

Dear Bobbie,

          Clun Castle.   We hope to have
a small jape with her this Spring.
Patrick Whitehouse hopes that C[..] Rice
will have her in good nick.   Can you
Manage this?   (Capital M).

                    Yours sincerely,

Copy to:-
      √P. Whitehouse, Esq.,

The letter dated 5th December 1966 from Gerry Fiennes, General Manager BR (ER), to 'Bobbie' Lawrence, Assistant General Manager, London Midland Region, requesting assistance in organising the series of steam specials on the Eastern Region in 1967.

Portrait of a 'Castle'. No. 7029 *Clun Castle* stands on Peterborough shed, home for her stay on the Eastern Region in 1967, where she was well looked after by shedmaster Geoff Bird. [Photo: John Whiteley]

A Western locomotive at King's Cross – 1; Under the watchful eye of one of the 'Deltic' diesels which became synonymous with the East Coast Main Line in the post-steam era – and a type now regarded as a classic in its own right – No. 7029 *Clun Castle* backs into London King's Cross station on 8th October 1967, in order to work a special to York. Note that even the West Indian railwayman by the carriage cleaning shed in the right foreground has paused to watch this historic sight. [PHOTO: TIM STEPHENS]

A Western locomotive at London King's Cross – 2; No. 7029 *Clun Castle* stands ready to conquer the East Coast Main Line in 1967, during the 'jape' organised by Gerry Fiennes, General Manager BR (ER). [PHOTO: ERIC TREACY]

of apprehension crossed the fireman's face as he bent into the tender for the shovel. Considerable noise came out of the chimney as the reverser was wound quickly up to about 45 per cent cut off and then more gradually as we accelerated past New England shed to about 25 per cent.

We blasted towards Stoke with the feel of *Clun*'s efforts being transmitted through to us via the many vibrations common to locomotives when under pressure. These, together with the rhythm of the exhaust, gave a wonderful combined feeling of effort being exerted. We reached 60mph within three miles with the steam pressure remaining constant at about 250lbs psi with about three quarters of a glass of water in the boiler. The live steam injector was used most of the time as it put the water into the boiler quicker and kept the water level constant.

In the early stages, Fireman Hardstone and I took it in turns to shovel but gradually he allowed me to do most of the work to the summit. Some fireman would take it as a slur on their capabilities if someone wanted to assist them but I think he understood my urge to have a go. Although using a small Eastern shovel, maintaining the fire level and pressure and water was relatively easy. This excellent coal was easy to shovel too. No lumps to crack, so time was spent entirely on shovelling.

No. 7029 was now really into her stride, full regulator, 25 per cent cut off and 210lbs of steam, and the chimney rattling clean and even. A marvellous sound when in unison with the vibration, making

a co-ordinated din. With all this around me I was a happy man.

The climb from Peterborough to Stoke is about twenty miles of slowly steepening gradient, about 1 in 250 with a final three miles at 1 in 178. Driver Garbutt had got her up to 68mph at Tallington but speed dropped only gradually as the gradient got steeper and we were still doing 64mph at Corby.

Pressure was not as high as it should have been – about 190-180psi, so I thought it was time for a spell of 'Western' firing. As I pulled the shovel back from the firehole with the right hand, my left flicked the flap up to keep out the cold air. The coal on the shovel ready, the left hand pulled down the flap at the same time as the right hand moved the shovel back from the tender freshly loaded, the two hands swung the shovel towards the fire, the right hand alone pulled the shovel back out as the left hand flicked the flap up again. This was done with every shovelful of coal. It is a lot more effort but results were worth it as the pressure came back to a more comfortable 210lbs after a short time.

Meanwhile, Driver Garbutt was still sitting calmly with his hand resting on the reverser, staring at the road ahead and looking as though he had driven Western engines all his life. We passed over the summit with steam pressure at 20lbs and half a glass of water in the boiler. The 15.3 miles from Tallington to Stoke had taken us only 13.19 minutes at an average speed of 65.9mph, which I believe was quite a good performance.

Not far over the summit we suffered a severe signal check and

No. 7029 *Clun Castle* powers out of London with a 10.00am special for Leeds City on 17th September 1967, through the Gasworks Tunnels and Copenhagen Junction from King's Cross, a location usually the preserve of Gresley 'Pacifics'. [PHOTO: TIM STEPHENS]

No. 7029 *Clun Castle* leaves York for Newcastle on 9th September 1967. [Photo: John Whiteley]

came almost to a stand but the signal cleared and Driver Garbutt heaved the regulator to the full open position. The blast up the chimney was so fierce that it dislodged a large amount of rust from beneath an overbridge.

We blasted through Grantham station two minutes early. From here on the fireman and I shared the work over the easier grades, with full regulator only used for short spells. We accelerated steadily to 78mph passing Claypole, then steam was shut off for the permanent restriction of speed through Newark. Again speed rose to 69mph at Carlton and only dropped slightly to 65mph up the 1 in 100 to Tuxford. We ran quietly on to Retford covering the 62.2 miles in 59.4 minutes, or 2.5 minutes under schedule. Here I reluctantly left the footplate and rejoined my friends in the train.

After leaving Retford we suffered a permanent way slack at Sutton but soon accelerated up to 72mph at Ranskill. Easy running due to permanent speed restrictions took us to Doncaster at about 55mph. Then, running was a little better over the almost level ground to York – 63mph at Arksey and a top speed of 69mph at Temple Hirst. The 18.4 miles to Selby was covered in 16.5 minutes making an average of 66mph. A signal check, steady progress and we made a quiet entry into York, again two minutes under the booked time.

I travelled as a passenger on the return journey, the highlight of which was a maximum of 90mph near Little Bytham. Arrival was very early at Peterborough, where again No. 7029 returned to New England shed for water and fresh engine crew. The remainder of the journey was marred by numerous signal and permanent way checks but one part of it will remain in my memory.

Approaching Hitchen, I was leaning out of the window, risking the shower of ashes dropping noisily on the carriage roofs, and caught the superb sight of the train leaning into a curve of the northern approach. The intense white glare from the firebox caught the swirling steam and a spectacular stream of fire from the chimney

rocketing high into the black sky dropping slowly. The exhaust roared up the chimney as we stormed through the middle roads of the station. Many astonished passengers on the platform must have wondered what it was all about. Their view of the train must have been a wonderful sight. They would have seen the approach of two flickering headlights beneath a cascade of sparks which shot up above the steam swirling in the station lights. These lights caught the flashing brass and copper, and the thrashing of the polished steel side rods as she stormed past and roared into the distance.

She continued to the top of the hill in fine style and made a quiet entry into King's Cross two minutes late. We went home feeling very proud of our Western engine.

After the Eastern trip, the one to Carlisle was rather an anticlimax, possibly because we expected too much and several circumstances prevented any records being broken.

The trip was additional to the six already mentioned and was organised by the Locomotive Club of Great Britain. It took place on Saturday 14th October 1967. The tour started at Liverpool, a Class '9F' 2-10-0 being used to Preston. No. 7029 worked the train from Preston to Carlisle and back to Hellifield from where the Class '9F' returned the tour to Liverpool.

The crew rostered for the round trip were Lostock Hall men, Passed Fireman P.R. Norris, who became a fully fledged driver the following Monday, and Fireman J. Roach. Neither had any experience of Western engines, so we had to explain the small differences, such as the vacuum brake, injectors and firing technique, though the latter is impossible to impart to anyone in such a short time.

Before leaving the shed, we had a fresh supply of coal from the hopper but unfortunately this consisted almost entirely of enormous lumps of hard slate like coal. While watching this stuff dropping like land mines into the tender, I prophesied trouble and it came. We made the short journey from the shed to Preston station and

No. 7029 *Clun Castle* heads out of Wortley Junction, Leeds on 30th September 1967 with a train from London to Carlisle.

ABOVE: **Track to be done again in the 21st century. No. 7029 *Clun Castle* climbs to Blea Moor on the Settle & Carlisle line on 30th September 1967.** [PHOTO: JOHN WHITELEY]

LEFT: **No. 7029 *Clun Castle* stands in Newcastle station on 10th September 1967. The Tyseley team had spent virtually all night really cleaning her up for the trip back to Peterborough and she looked an absolute treat.** [PHOTO: JOHN WHITELEY]

arrived just a few minutes before the oily black '9F' brought in the special train which was made up of only seven coaches – about 230 tons. A large crowd on the platform watched us back onto the train and we left two minutes late due to the slow reloading of passengers.

At Garstang, where a stop was scheduled for photographing, I was recalled to the footplate to assist Fireman Roach. One of us cracked the lumps and then stood aside while the other shovelled. One fireman would have had a very exhausting day on his own. On leaving Garstang, we almost immediately suffered a permanent way check of 10mph. Once clear of this, the first of many, Driver Norris used full regulator and between 10 per cent and 15 per cent cut off.

Over the near level line towards Carnforth, speed rose to 52mph at Bay Horse and 67mph before shutting off for the permanent speed restriction through Lancaster.

Time was now being regained with this light load and soon we were going well, reaching 77.5mph at Bolton-le-Sands. We passed through Burton at the start of the climb at 67mph and cleared Grayrigg at 42mph. Then Driver Norton eased her down for us to get a good boiler full of water before passing Tebay. We passed Low Gill doing 36mph. and picked up a bit to run through Tebay at 56mph.

I saw none of the scenery from Tebay to Shap as it was shovel and bank all the way but our efforts got us up in six minutes and

Portrait of an 'A4', at Newcastle Tyne Dock shed on 10th September 1967. No. 4498 *Sir Nigel Gresley* was bought from BR by the A4 Society led by Julian Riddick, overhauled at Crewe Works and returned to the classic L&NER livery of garter blue with stainless steel letters and numerals. The 'Pacific' was also invited for the ECML 'jape' by Gerry Fiennes. [PHOTO: JOHN WHITELEY]

RIGHT: No. 4498 *Sir Nigel Gresley* stands at Newcastle station on 10th September 1967.
[PHOTO: JOHN WHITELEY]

ABOVE: The third locomotive involved in the East Coast Main Line extravaganza organised by Fiennes was none other than the 'World's most famous steam locomotive', L&NER 'A3 Pacific' No. 4472 *Flying Scotsman*, which had been bought by Alan Pegler. Here she is seen leaving Leeds Central for King's Cross on 'The Mercian' railtour on 16th April 1967, having taken over from *The Great Marquess* which had hauled the train from Stockport.
[PHOTO: JOHN WHITELEY]

LEFT: Earlier in the day, Viscount Garnock's L&NER 'K4' Class 2-6-0 No. 3442 *The Great Marquess* brings the same train from Stockport to Leeds, passing Foulridge. [PHOTO: JOHN WHITELEY]

we even had a bit to spare for Driver Norris to drop the reverser down a little near the summit to about 34-40 per cent cut off, and we actually accelerated to 42mph as we roared over the top through the rain sodden cutting.

Almost immediately, adverse signals brought us to a stand at Shap station, where we were blowing off, both injectors in use but with water low in the glass. Here we received instructions to proceed with extreme caution due to the flooding of the line.

Running was very erratic after this due to many checks making the controlling of the fire and steam a little difficult. We suffered a signal stop of 1.5 minutes at Eden Valley Junction because of a freight train being turned into the loop at Penrith. The rest of the journey was very quiet and eventually we were diverted to the goods lines at Carlisle No. 13 and continued to No. 11, where we arrived nine minutes early, having made a total gain of twenty-seven minutes.

Here we uncoupled and went light engine to Kingmoor shed for servicing, while the train was taken on a tour of the goods lines around Carlisle by a 'Flying Pig' (an ex-LM&SR '4F' 0-6-0).

After the Kingmoor men serviced No. 7029, we gave her a quick wipe over just before she was due off shed. What a fine sight she looked waiting to leave for Citadel station against a background of rusting locomotives awaiting cutting up.

The return trip was over the old Midland route via Settle to Hellifield. From Carlisle to Appleby, Pete Phillips assisted Fireman Roach. Most of the way the driver worked the second valve of the regulator with about 15 per cent cut off, the pressure averaging around 160-180lbs with half a glass of water. Speed reached 68mph just after Armathwaite but then steadied to about 45mph before we arrived at Appleby, two minutes up on the running time.

After leaving Appleby, No. 7029 made up a further six minutes climbing the 1 in 100 to Ais Gill. She certainly sounded as though she was being pressed hard as the crisp chatter from the chimney came surging back to us in the train. Speeds from 61mph at Ormside varied up the long climb between 53, 60, 55, 48, 50 and 48mph, and finally over the top of the bank at 50mph past Ais Gill box.

Down the long drop to Settle we never exceeded 72mph, usually running between 65-70mph. I never found the reason for this but it didn't matter too much as we arrived at Hellifield ten minutes early.

Quickly, No. 7029 was uncoupled and moved off towards Leeds to await the departure of the special behind the '9F' towards Blackburn. She then followed the special to Lostock Hall shed. Apparently the reason for this was that the clearances in the platform at Blackburn were too close for comfort. A set of Crewe men took her from Lostock Hall to Crewe and said quite a few complimentary things about her. For the rest of the journey to Tyseley a couple of Tyseley men were in charge.

The success of the Eastern Region specials in 1967, with the three privately preserved express steam locomotives *Flying Scotsman*, *Sir Nigel Gresley* and *Clun Castle*, led Gerry Fiennes to suggest to PBW that he might buy an LM&SR 'Jubilee' 4-6-0, as the last few were due to be withdrawn in the autumn of that year. Until then, there was no prospect of an ex-LM&SR locomotive being preserved for main line use. No. 45593 *Kolhapur* was chosen from the remaining few 'Jubilees' working the Settle & Carlisle trains from Leeds and here, the engine is seen in the roundhouse at Holbeck. [PHOTO: ERIC TREACY]

The originals. The first Tyseley support crew stand in front of No. 7029 *Clun Castle* immediately prior to the recommissioning of No. 5593 *Kolhapur* in 1968: (L to R): Bernard Rainbow (Depot Superintendent), Phil Gloster, 'Nobby' Styles and others. [PHOTO: P.B. WHITEHOUSE]

13. THE STANDARD GAUGE STEAM TRUST
A VIEW FROM THE 1970S
Martin Hedges – *Birmingham Post* reporter

'When you buy one of these beasts, it is really only an admission ticket to the club.'

How do you set about buying a slice of English history – which is what the Standard Gauge Steam Trust at Tyseley, Birmingham has committed itself to doing?

Well, first, you forget about the romance of steam and put from your head all thoughts of enjoying yourself, of feeling the footplate thundering beneath your feet and hearing the roar of steam whenever you feel like it. That is strictly for day dreamers. These people have developed a brand of professionalism about preservation which is to be envied.

Next you fill every available moment of your life with cajolery, scheming, negotiating, arguing, planning, pleading. You exhaust yourself with sheer physical effort – lifting, turning, scraping, polishing, bolting, painting, machining – until, just briefly, you loathe the sight of a locomotive, though you know that apart from looking good, she is mechanically sound because of your own labours.

Then what? Well then you go back for more, because what you are up to is keeping steam alive, and that is a continuing process. Those locomotives at Tyseley are not just museum pieces, shining brightly in their new paint and standing mute, only to be gazed upon. They are working engines as capable now of pulling a train as they ever were. But to keep steam alive in the way they want it, they need engineers, mechanics, fitters and general odd-jobbers; and they need workshop facilities, the wheeldrop, the spare parts and the machines to turn them.

And to provide all that, as they have done and are doing, needs money. Not simply the odd bob or two – though even they help, but a regular income of many thousands of pounds.

Progress has been tremendous but even so there are moments when hearts sink as low as the bank balance and they wonder where on earth the next few pounds are coming from. Then they get up a new head of steam and a new idea and so, once more, the balance begins to look healthier again.

Which is all well and good but shoestrings cannot support steam locomotives, as many a would be preservationist has discovered to his cost. It is not just a question of getting an old and rusty engine out of the rain which sweeps Barry Dock, painting and polishing and rust proofing her, and standing back to admire your handiwork.

Hence the birth of the Standard Gauge Steam Trust, fathered by 7029 Clun Castle Limited.

Our first home. The GWR coaling stage at Tyseley depot, taken on a six month licence at the end of steam in 1967, once the roundhouse had been demolished, and the filthiest place in any steam depot. We extended the coaling stage to take both *Clun Castle* and *Kolhapur*, and added a tool room but were obliged to leave the GWR and LM&SR Engineers' Saloons outside. We worked up to creating a workshop from there. [Photo: C.M. Whitehouse]

Bernard Rainbow and Phil Gloster stand in front of Brush Type '4' No. 1543 at Tyseley depot in the pouring rain, before hauling the only train ever to run from Birmingham's Snow Hill to New Street station, marking the closure of Snow Hill. It was a 'just had to be done thing' really, so we simply hooked up our GWR Inspection Saloon and the three Pullman Cars we then had and ran the trip for our friends. 'Mr Snow Hill' Derek Harrison, who wrote the definitive history of the station, almost missed the train at Snow Hill but we scooped him up rather like a mail bag just as the train was pulling out! Run in 1967, the exact date escapes me. [PHOTO: C.M. WHITEHOUSE]

It was in 1966 that the Swindon locomotive, *Clun Castle*, was finally acquired for Tyseley and in that year and the next, during a number of well publicised trains, her new owners quickly came to appreciate the need for skilled and regular maintenance.

In October 1967, the 'Castle' was joined by Tyseley's next acquisition, ex-LMS 'Jubilee' No. 5593 *Kolhapur* from Holbeck depot in Leeds, where she had been working summer relief trains at weekends. She was in reasonable condition, having been recently retubed but, like so many other engines of this period, repairs had been kept to a safe minimum. She was housed in the old steam shed with *Clun Castle*. Towards the end of the year, British Railways agreed that she could be moved into the diesel depot at Tyseley for an inspection and, after a thorough examination, it was there the paint was stripped off. It was found the entire top half of the smokebox was rotten and must be renewed and that other major repair work was necessary.

More work, more time and more money. But the Chief Engineer of the Trust, Mr Jim Kent, refused to be beaten and, in under four months, the engine was repaired and repainted. The work had involved having new plates rolled for the smokebox, then riveting plus renewing the cylinder bolts.

To commemorate the completion of the work to the 'Jubilee' and the opening of a new depot converted from the original GWR coaling stage at Tyseley, Terence Cuneo was invited to paint the two engines on canvas.

Jim Kent, a lecturer in mechanical engineering at Warley Technical College, became involved with *Clun Castle* when he rang Pat Whitehouse one day in 1967 and asked if he could see the locomotive, offering his help, after her valve spindle bolts stripped on the last run to Birkenhead in March: "*If I can do anything to help ...*" From then on, his help has been non-stop and so expert that *Clun* and *Kolhapur* have been saved from what could so easily have been a slow death.

To meet Jim at Tyseley and hear him talk is to know what steam preservation is really all about as far as the Trust is concerned.

"*When you buy one of these beasts*", he says, "*it is really only an admission ticket to the club. When we acquired them, they were badly run down, because they were due for withdrawal and not unnaturally only the minimum maintenance had been carried out. They were sold to us virtually as scrap.*

If you genuinely intend to preserve a locomotive and restore it as far as is humanly possible to its original condition, you are involving yourself in an enormous amount of time, work and money. You have got to try to put the clock back and repair the ravages of time. It is not just a question of cleaning the muck off and making the engine look pretty again; it involves very heavy engineering work which requires a lot of special tools such as boiler stay taps and dies at one end of the scale and the wheeldrop for removing complete pairs of wheels and axles, and a wheel and axle turning lathe at the other end.

In fact, if you are intending to go the whole hog, and that is what we are doing at Tyseley, you will need one of most of the pieces of machinery which the builders had in their works when they built the locomotives originally. Otherwise, if something goes wrong, the whole operation grinds to a dead stop, simply because you haven't got the means of putting it right."

One of the things which Jim will impress upon people is that a locomotive can be a lethal piece of machinery:

"*They aren't toys. If a boiler explodes or a serious fault develops when you are out on the track, the consequences could be absolutely disastrous.*

One of the most difficult parts of the whole business is in attempting to assess fatigue in heavily stressed members such as the draw gear. A failure in this could result in the locomotive uncoupling from the train which, to say the least, would not be funny.

So you have got to be on the lookout all the time; and you have got to know what you are looking for.

There is enormous scope for enthusiasts who have no particular skills but would like to help in some way: cleaning, polishing the engines, keeping the depot free of weeds and litter, repairs to the track and buildings and to the ancillary equipment, store keeping, cataloguing spares, rust prevention treatment and so on.

But when it comes to the maintenance of the locomotives themselves, obviously you have got to use skilled hands and then it is purely and simply a matter of bloody hard work.

So, you see, this is not just a question of standing and talking about it but of actually doing things. Only in this way can you preserve live steam successfully and give tremendous pleasure to thousands of people."

Since 1968, the Standard Gauge Steam Trust have held a series of highly successful open days to give the public a chance of seeing that 'live' steam in action. The events, which in the early 1970s attracted something like 40,000 people to Tyseley, Cricklewood (London) and Allerton (Liverpool), have been run with the co-operation of British Rail and in association with the regional morning newspaper, *The Birmingham Post*, which has produced a special souvenir edition on steam on each occasion.

It was during the run up to one of these open days that I managed to beard Jim Kent in the tool room at Tyseley to hear in detail about

Laying the foundations of the future. Gerry Fiennes, formerly General Manager of both Western and Eastern Regions, was instrumental in the two 'japes' with *Clun Castle*, as he described them. He authorised both the 1964 'Castle Swansong' Ian Allan Specials from Paddington to Plymouth, which highlighted *Clun Castle* for preservation following her record run, and also her visit to run on the Eastern Region in 1967. So Pat Whitehouse thought he would be the ideal person to hammer home the foundation peg for the new workshops at Tyseley, following the foundation of The Standard Gauge Steam Trust in 1970. Here, Gerry Fiennes brings down the mallet on the peg watched by a group of children from Hallfield School. Martyn Hedges, the journalist author of this essay, can be seen in the centre of the picture with a beard. Jim Kent, the first CME, is just above Gerry Fiennes with his pipe and PBW stands on the foundations for the Ipswich wheeldrop, holding a replica of *Kolhapur*'s nameplate to give Gerry as a present. This was another fitting connection, as it was also Fiennes who suggested PBW buy the 'Jubilee' in the first place. The GWR Hawksworth design Shrewsbury Engineer's Saloon stands in the background, ready to welcome the guests for refreshments after the ceremony. [PHOTO: C.M. WHITEHOUSE]

the amount of work involved. I fondly imagined that the activity going on around me was because the big event was only a fortnight away. Not a bit of it.

"*This*", he said, meaning the polishing, the filing, the hammering and the turning, goes on all the time, every available moment of every available day.

"*All the locomotives are subject, for example, to boiler insurance, and this entails an annual boiler inspection by the insurance company's engineering surveyor. It involves removing all the mudhole doors, all the washout plugs, the water gauge fittings, the safety valves and, periodically the superheater tubes and a selection of boiler tubes.*

Then the boilers have to be washed out ready for inspection and any repairs necessary have to be carried out to the inspector's satisfaction. This generally involves the removal of such things as wasted stay nuts from the firebox and rethreading the stays and fitting new nuts.

Afterwards there is a steam test in which the boiler inspector tests the pressure gauge against his master gauge and the safety valves are also checked."

Apart from this, there is regular checking and maintenance work to be carried out on the draw gear, the brake gear, wheel flanges and on dozens of the other vital parts of a giant locomotive.

Where is all this work carried out at Tyseley? The lighter machining operations and the making of special tools required are done in the tool room. Here, the main equipment includes a 7½in. centre lathe, an 8½in. heavy duty centre lathe, a 20in. universal horizontal miller with a vertical head and slotting attachment, a 30in. horizontal miller and a universal grinder.

On 31st October 1970, No. 4983 *Albert Hall* has just arrived from Barry scrapyard, towed up to Tyseley at 50mph still with her coupling rods fitted. CME Jim Kent braved the whole journey riding in her cab. He regarded No. 4983 as one of the best locomotives in the scrapyard, having researched that she had a light casual overhaul in 1962 at Caerphilly Works and then hardly did any serious work before withdrawal. He would have got her running in the 1970s if it was not for BR's extreme 'reluctance' to run Class '5' locomotives at that time. [PHOTO: C.M. WHITEHOUSE]

A new workshop at Tyseley emerges in September 1970. Initially, there was space for other exhibits and John Scholes, British Transport Commission Curator, lent us several items from the National Collection until the new railway museum was ready at York: Southern 'T9' 4-4-0 No. 120, 'King Arthur' 4-6-0 *Sir Lamiel*, 'Schools' 4-4-0 *Cheltenham*, Lancashire & Yorkshire 2-4-2T No 1008 and First and Third Class replica Liverpool & Manchester carriages. Here, *Cheltenham* is being shunted into the depot shortly after arrival. On the right-hand side can just be seen GWR Hawksworth 0-6-0PT No. 1501, which was en route from Coventry Colliery to the Severn Valley Railway but had called in for wheel turning on the BR depot ground floor lathe. [PHOTO C.M. WHITEHOUSE]

In the newly-constructed machine shop the equipment is to include a wheel turning and axle lathe, a 12in. centre x 6ft 6in. between centre heavy duty centre lathe, a 6ft 6in. stroke planing machine, an 18in. stroke slotting machine, a 30in. horizontal miller, a 6ft 6in. radial drilling machine and a special purpose combination machine tool specially designed for railway locomotive maintenance.

The depot also has a fully-equipped blacksmith's shop and a whitesmith's shop is soon to be installed.

The depot superintendent is Bernard Rainbow, who looks after the day to day cleaning of the locomotives and their general running maintenance. When they are out in steam, it is he who is responsible for crewing and for driving. Another driver is Dick Potts, who met Pat Whitehouse on the last trip of *King Henry VI*. There are many others, including Saltley fireman Phil Gloster (who veers towards *Kolhapur* every time), who put in countless hours of work behind the scenes.

Bernard, incidentally, got involved when *Clun Castle* was making her now-famous return run from Birkenhead on 5th March 1967. The fireman was taken ill and was unable to continue on the footplate. In desperation there was a search for a replacement until someone remembered Bernard was a passenger on that train. A message went down for him and he was seen running along the platform delightedly, calling: "*Don't worry, we'll be alright.*" They were. Pat Whitehouse recalls: "*Really, he saved us on that trip.*"

Who else is there? There's Graham Smith, a boilersmith from 'next door', Tyseley Traction & Maintenance Depot which continues to fly the flag for suburban trains, albeit diesel now; Bill Jones, a professional engineer who, with Jim Kent and Jack Silver, is

responsible for making and fitting new and reconditioned parts; together with many other willing helpers in all fields.

It is easy to see why the members of the *Clun Castle* clan were determined that what had been built up at Tyseley must not be lost – not just to them, but to us all.

That is why the Trust was born. John Scholes, the curator of the British Transport Museum at Clapham was invited to visit the depot. With him went Eric Merril, Controller of Public Relations to the British Railways Board, and Col. Simmons from the Science Museum at South Kensington. They and another visitor, Norman Bertenshaw, director of Birmingham's own Museum of Science & Industry, gave the work at Tyseley their enthusiastic approval and the idea of a charitable trust got under way.

Having found that it was possible to make this an educational charitable trust, the search began for suitable trustees. Because of the enthusiasm for the project, they were not difficult to find. Those involved in the management of 7029 Clun Castle Limited were a natural choice: Brian Hollingsworth, a joint owner of 'Black Five' No. 5428 *Eric Treacy*, by now also shedded at Tyseley, Bernard Davenport, representing the Railway Correspondence & Travel Society, Sir Peter Allen, Chairman of ICI and President of the Trust, T.C.B. Miller, Chief Engineer (Traction & Rolling Stock) British Rail, and Norman Bertenshaw, representing the City of Birmingham.

New leasing arrangements, to give the Trust both time and space, were made with British Rail and then came the new accommodation. The new shed has been built alongside the old water tower and coaling stage retained from the original 1908 GWR depot. This new shed is already an historic building, since it was

RIGHT: Early open days at Tyseley were pretty much then the only place to see standard gauge express steam locomotives in action on BR lines, albeit in 'top and tail' mode on a shuttle train on the local goods loop. But this was steep enough to hear the locomotives really bark. LM&SR No. 6201 *Princess Elizabeth* is seen here giving GWR 'King' No. 6000 *King George V* a good push at the October 1971 open weekend, held during the latter's successful trial trip from Hereford to Birmingham, two depots trusted by BR to perform. [PHOTO: C. M. WHITEHOUSE]

BELOW: Inside the new Tyseley workshop in the 1970s, with *Kolhapur* under repair, standing on the former Ipswich wheel drop with her rear driving wheel removed. In the background is BR (WR) built No. 7027 *Thornbury Castle* undergoing restoration from Barry scrapyard condition; her restoration was not completed and the locomotive was later sold once the decision had been made to transfer allegiance to repairing GWR thoroughbred single chimney 'Castle' No. 5080 *Defiant*, also rescued from Barry. The wheel lathe from Bescot depot can be seen on the left of the picture. [PHOTO: C.M. WHITEHOUSE]

the first built entirely for the housing and maintenance of main line steam locomotives since the end of steam on British Railways.

Its main function is to provide a fully covered and secure housing for up to six main line locomotives, at the same time incorporating the space for repair facilities and enough room to display the locomotives.

With a length of 210ft and a span at its widest point of 48ft, the depot has three roads. Inside there is also provision for storing a 'Pacific' locomotive and there is a wheeldrop occupying an engine's length. The central road runs the length of the shed and holds three locomotives and the third road has room for another two. Two of the tracks have inspection pits.

The new depot, incidentally, was deliberately sited to leave space alongside the water tower and coaling stage for the retention of the coal shute, which is typical of some Great Western coaling stages and the last existing one with an electrical lifting platform for ease of coal loading into the 4,000 gallon GWR tenders.

All this brings us full circle and back to the subject of money. To carry out these expensive developments and to maintain the high standard which has already been set, is going to be a vastly expensive business. Initially, the Trust has appealed for £25,000 for the new depot and a further £25,000 for future developments. I hope you feel it is worth it. I know it is.

'Resurrection of a King. Western Region's greatest steam locomotive will be ceremoniously pulled by railway enthusiasts from the stock shed at Swindon on Friday at 3pm. Strong cider drinkers particularly welcome.' Peter Prior, Managing Director of Bulmers Cider, had tracked the locomotive down at Swindon and decided to take his sons to see it as a birthday treat. He found that the Swindon Borough librarian held the key to the stock shed and was also the locomotive's official custodian. Bulmers signed a sub-lease for the locomotive on 21st March 1968 and Prior then had to remove the 'King' from the stock shed – but first replace the track. Undaunted, he seized the publicity opportunity and placed this advertisement in *The Times* on 7th August, for people just to turn up and pull the locomotive out of the shed with ropes. Some 2,000 people turned up two days later and did just that in the pouring rain! [Photo: Frank Dumbleton]

14. A 'KING' OPENS THE DOOR

'As many pioneers before him and since have found out, it never does to know everything about your subject before you dive in. Understanding the enormity of the task in detail might cause hesitation or, worse, abandonment.'

Of course, all the private express steam locomotive owners and every enthusiast everywhere wanted British Railways to relent, lift their ban and allow main line steam to run again. Sometimes, campaigns just need perhaps a new face, a little harder push and some luck – and that is exactly what happened.

Peter Prior, Managing Director of Bulmers Cider in Hereford, was driving to London and thinking about how he might widen his company's appeal and increase sales of cider. By chance, he gave a lift to a hitch hiker and they fell into conversation about steam engines, their preservation and what might be done with them. Prior learned that the first of the famous Great Western Railway's 'King' Class locomotives, No. 6000 *King George V*, still existed but was locked in a shed and all but forgotten. He reflected on this famous locomotive, its journey to the USA to star in the celebrations for the centenary of the Baltimore & Ohio Railroad in 1927, the commemorative bell it wore as a result and its accession into the National Collection. He foresaw a good marketing opportunity with this famous locomotive. There were millions of people with some interest in railways, nostalgia for the past and many people were justly proud of Britain's heritage. *King George V* would suit his purpose very well. He would rescue it.

As many pioneers before him and since have found out, it never does to know everything about your subject before you dive in. Understanding the enormity of the task in detail might cause hesitation or, worse, abandonment. No! Much better just to begin with the idea and then build on it, run ahead of the crowd and just do it. Prior was hooked. He was a determined man and once he had a good idea, he was determined to implement it but in the right way. He was, first and foremost, a businessman and not a railway enthusiast, and he was always charming and persuasive in his business dealings. The main line steam movement had found its man but by chance, whilst Prior then knew nothing of them.

Prior tracked No. 6000 down and decided to take his sons to see it as a birthday treat. He found that the Swindon Borough librarian was the locomotive's custodian and held the key to the stock shed. Bulmers signed a sub-lease for *King George V* on 21st March 1968 (even before the end of steam on BR) but now Prior had to remove the locomotive from the stock shed – and first replace the track at a cost of £2,750!

Undaunted, he seized the publicity opportunity and placed an advert in *The Times* newspaper on 7th August for people to turn up and pull the locomotive out of the shed using ropes: '*Resurrection*

No. 6000 *King George V* on the 'Return to Steam' trial trip, nearing Llanvihangel on the outward journey to Tyseley on 2nd October 1971. Swindon based Mechanical Inspector Norman Tovey ensured that the 'King' then completed the whole trial trip to Birmingham and back, via Kensington Olympia, without a hitch. In those early days it was usual to rely on such good natured expertise from BR's mechanical inspectorate and footplate staff. Quite frankly, the locomotive owners welcomed this as they had, as yet, no expertise themselves. If the 'King' had failed on this trip, there is little doubt there would have been no renaissance following from 1972. [PHOTO: JOHN WHITELEY]

No. 6000 *King George V* leaving Pilning Tunnel on the outward journey to Tyseley of the 'Return to Steam' trial trip, on 2nd October 1971. Bulmers had assembled an exhibition train of five Pullman cars repainted in its house colours, naming the cars after Directors' wives; this led Prior to search for a suitable steam locomotive to haul them and, once found, he thought it should really return to the main line where it belonged. He did not give up until he had achieved his objective. [PHOTO: JOHN WHITELEY]

The trial train arrives successfully at Tyseley on 1st October 1971. No. 6000 *King George V* and train have left the Oxford to Birmingham main line on the left of the picture (the 'North Warwicks' line heads off to the right) to call at the Down slow line platform before moving onto the depot. [PHOTO: C.M. WHITEHOUSE]

of King George V. Western Region's greatest steam locomotive will be ceremoniously pulled by railway enthusiasts from the stock shed at Swindon on Friday at 5pm. (Strong cider drinkers particularly welcome). Two days later, on 9th August, just two days before the famous 'Fifteen Guinea' last train special run by BR, about 2,000 people turned up and did just that, in the pouring rain!

Having got the locomotive out, Prior then cast around for someone to fix it, as No. 6000 had to work. BR were not interested and thus priced the job accordingly, so Prior found A.R. Adams of Newport, a contractor who fixed locomotives for the National Coal Board, and commissioned him to put *King George V* back into main line running order again. Job done, the locomotive was towed in light steam by a BR diesel to Bulmers. But, to ensure that no one tried any tricks in seeking to have the locomotive work for itself on the journey, BR insisted that the regulator was removed and, to ensure adequate lubrication, the 'jockey valve' had to be opened using a two shilling piece!

By now a picture of the calibre of man that Peter Prior was is building up but, actually, he was only just starting his journey. He was determined that *King George V* would be a public relations asset to Bulmers and so he arranged for the exchange sidings already in place alongside the factory for the export of their cider to be fettled up to take a 'King', an engine shed to be constructed and a set of five Pullman cars refurbished in Bulmer's green, red and white! The cars were converted into a museum, a bar, products display, a cinema and a dining car which retained its name, *Aquila*. A support team were encouraged to look after No. 6000, which went on to become the main line support crew, including none other than Bernard Staite, who was to become Secretary of the Steam Locomotive Operators' Association and lead the charge for the private sector when steam did eventually return to the main line again.

A grand opening ceremony was organised, with the meticulous planning of every move of the day. Invitations were sent out to witness '*the ceremonial arrival of the former Great Western Railway locomotive No. 6000* King George V *and the opening of the Bulmers' Exhibition Train*' at 11.00am on Wednesday 13th November 1968. The 'King' was back.

But still Prior was not satisfied. He wanted *King George V* back on the main line and set about finding out how to do this and what the issues would be. He tracked down the developing steam depot at Tyseley and introduced himself to PBW. He saw that Tyseley were in the process of establishing good maintenance facilities and had similar GWR locomotives. He took his and PBW's families out for a slap up lunch at Birmingham's then top hotel, The Plough & Harrow on the Hagley Road. Over fine French wine, the two businessmen pledged mutual co-operation in everything Great Western and main line, and to help each other out in a new common objective: the return of main line steam. They were to work together well, pooling ideas, business acumen and PBW's formidable BR contacts. The two men won the day through quiet, determined persuasion.

However, it was not quite that easy.

Prior, Whitehouse and the Association of Railway Preservation Society's 'Return to Steam Committee' were continually thwarted by the objections of two individuals in particular. The Chairman of the BR Board, Sir Henry Johnson, was firmly anti steam. His job was to run the real railway, look forward and not concern himself with hobbies. However, perhaps the real drive against the cause came from Philip Shirley, who was part of the Beeching era of cost cutting and largely accountable for the steam ban in the first place.

"*I could never understand their attitude*", said Prior, "*I said time and time again that there were several million people who were there*

Over 18,000 people came to Tyseley open day on 2nd October 1971, to see No. 6000 *King George V* (together with No. 6201 *Princess Elizabeth* and the home fleet) following the engine's successful trial run from Hereford. This open day was also key to unlocking the door to the return of main line steam trains, Pat Whitehouse wisely sharing the profits from the day with BR, as he was rightly keen to demonstrate in a practical way that 'steam paid'.
[Photo: C.M. Whitehouse]

waiting and wanting to love BR by seeing steam run and that they were simply being antagonised by the steam ban and all the arguments that went with it."

Persuasion and countering all the arguments why steam should not run on the main line again were not enough but, as with many things in life, fate, luck and being in the right place at the right time all played their part. It is necessary to be astute and aware if difficult objectives are to be realised. Two men had to leave their posts before it would be possible for main line steam to run again: Sir Henry Johnson and Philip Shirley. As luck would have it, they both did and more or less at the same time.

Prior and Whitehouse had many more conversations and dinners. Whitehouse had gained many friends in influential places with his contributions to the BBC TV children's programme *Railway Roundabout* and the start up of the commercially run Dart Valley Railway in Devon. As preserved steam locomotives began to accumulate at Tyseley, PBW made sure that he gained the best friends and supporters he could, by forming a charity and asking influential people to join in to help the cause. Colleagues from industry and the City of Birmingham joined but so did Terry Miller, by then himself at BRB, who had been instrumental in drawing up the BTC list of BR locomotives and rolling stock to be preserved for the nation. He became Chief Engineer (Traction & Rolling Stock) to BRB and was the driving force behind the introduction of the High Speed Train, and so was very influential in engineering matters at the Board. He was also a very sensible, likeable and affable man, with sound experience and common sense, and he helped pave the way. He sat quietly at our dining room table at home and discussed the logic of steam returning, how it could be done from a limited number of well set up depots, run by people BR could rely on, who had resources and teams of former BR locomotive men to support them. He paved the way.

Prior learned a lot from the Tyseley team. And the Tyseley team and the movement at large benefitted greatly from Prior's independence from the preservation movement, his commercial background and business connections, as well as his approaching the whole issue of getting steam back onto the main line from another

angle. Gradually the logic filtered through, fortunately more or less at the same time as the top people changed.

Sir Henry retired and Shirley returned to Australia (where, incidentally, he similarly decimated the Australian railway system!). The new Chairman of BRB was Richard Marsh, who was reputed to be 'more sympathetic to the cause.' The Deputy Chairman of BRB was Willie Thorpe, who (so Miller briefed out) was impressed with the professionalism of approach and the way in which the various open days and events had contributed to BR's coffers. They had been run without much trouble and had attracted thousands upon thousands of visitors and much publicity. The resistance was weakening and it would only take one more lucky break to push the door open – whilst, at the same time, trying to contain some of the more enthusiastic fringe.

The lucky break came shortly after these personnel changes, when those who were more sympathetic could react in the knowledge that their Lords and Masters were perhaps more likely to agree than disagree. Prior sealed the deal. He attended the premier of *Love Story* at London's West End, Leicester Square Odeon with Thorpe. As was common in cinemas of the day, a supporting educational film was also shown. This just happened to be a National Coal Board film about the preservation and operation of *King George V*. Following the screening there was a dinner at the Savoy Hotel where, at the BRB's table, Thorpe's wife fainted in the heat of the evening. Prior quickly rescued the situation and was then offered his chance in the effusive thanks he received: "*Do let me know if there is anything I can do for you in return.*"

It was then a fairly easy matter for Thorpe to convince Marsh to allow a trial trip, which had been well thought through beforehand with the help of Miller. That October, there were also 18,000 admissions, at a entrance fee of 7s 6d, to the joint BR and Standard Gauge Steam Trust open day at Tyseley, with half the profits going to BR nominated charities. The door to the main line had at last been unlocked. The wider team pushed it ajar and were rewarded by their steam locomotives being placed on the approved list.

And the rest is history.

Possibly the most perfect main line special in preservation? A full Great Western train ran from Newport to Shrewsbury and return on 3rd July 1977, with No. 6000 *King George V* hauling the Severn Valley Railway's GWR Collett carriages, including Dining cars for breakfast, lunch and tea, and the Buffet car then on loan from the National Railway Museum. Here we see the 'King' at Hereford prior to departure, at the head of the empty stock bound for Newport. [PHOTO: JOHN WHITELEY]

W. G. Thorpe Esq.

T. C. B. Miller,
Melbury House.

5478

P.1043
10.9.71

PERSONAL

Dear Chief

STEAM

As you can imagine, it did not take long for news of your decision to allow a steam locomotive to work to Birmingham to reach me and it has given immense satisfaction to those who have a genuine interest in promoting the occasional use of steam locomotives to the extent that they can bring revenue to British Railways.

I believe it is the case that Mr. Prior initially suggested that the Steam Locomotive Preservation Society should be an intermediary in promoting the use of any steam locomotives but he has since seen the wisdom of modifying this advice.

I am the Vice Chairman of the Standard Gauge Steam Trust which is based on Tyseley to which "King George V" will be working early in October but it is not because of this but rather from my personal knowledge of the people concerned with the Steam Locomotive Preservation Society and their facilities - or rather the lack of them - for maintaining locomotives in good order that I would strongly counsel caution in any negotiations regarding the use of steam locomotives on British Railways.

There are, so far as I know, only three places in Great Britain at which steam locomotives can be and are maintained in sound workable condition and these are at Tyseley, Didcot and Carnforth and if we are to avoid disasters such as the collapse of steam locomotives on the main line, it is very important that we should confine ourselves to the use of locomotives maintained at one of these places. If we allow ourselves to negotiate with the less responsible enthusiasts, amongst whom I would number some of those concerned with the Steam Locomotive Preservation Society, we will inevitably find ourselves in trouble.

- 2 -

So that we may be quite sure that we approach the future in a sensible way, should there be any prospect of continuing the occasional use of steam for short trips, I am quite sure we must not contemplate long trips.

I think Birmingham will be a very profitable centre from which to operate because we can obtain a very useful revenue from bringing people there by rail to join any steam-hauled train that we might work.

Pat Whitehouse would very much like to have an early opportunity of discussing the possibilities with you and if you will name the day, he would be very pleased to see that an appropriate lunch is provided. If I am permitted to join in as Vice Chairman and perhaps as mechanical engineering consultant, so much the better for me!

May I act as intermediary in arranging a date, time and a rendezvous?

Yours sincerely

Terry

'Dear Chief'. Terry Miller writes to W.G. Thorpe at the BR Board on 10th September 1971, to set out the case for main line steam returning: *'There are … only three places in Great Britain at which steam locomotives can be and are maintained in sound workable condition and these are at Tyseley, Didcot and Carnforth … it is very important that we should confine ourselves to the use of locomotives maintained at one of these places.'*

15. THE RETURN TO STEAM FROM 1972

'Essentially, there were to be five authorised routes,
which would allow a set number of steam locomotives to run from established depots.'

British Rail ran its last steam trains in August 1968, after which, to all intents and purposes main line steam had finished. Only *Flying Scotsman*, continued to run some excursions as its owner, Alan Pegler, had negotiated a longer term agreement; but even he was feeling the pressure of resistance and he took his locomotive off to play in the USA.

British Rail received continual buffeting from enthusiasts both openly and more tactfully seeking to facilitate the operation of privately preserved steam locomotives on the main line and there were several different, pretty continual, dialogues. The final straw was when the then chairman of the Bahamas Locomotive Society rang Sir Henry Johnson at home to plead the case. Unfortunately, the call was made at a badly chosen moment when Johnson was entertaining people to Sunday lunch. On the Monday morning, Johnson issued an instruction that all operation of privately owned steam locomotives was to cease.

But even whilst these discussions were going on, steam engines began to escape from their depots to stretch their legs from time to

time. Great Western Society tank engines featured at station open days, ran on the Wallingford Branch and also starred in filming in South Wales. The last steam locomotive of all, 'Britannia' Class 'Pacific' No. 70013 *Oliver Cromwell* ran light engine to Bressingham in Norfolk to be incarcerated in the garden centre-based museum for many years. 'Standard' Class '5' No. 73950 moved from store at Manchester's Patricroft shed down the East Coast Main Line to Peterborough, at the dead of night to avoid being seen. There were other examples but essentially these all proved the rule that steam was finished on the main line, as all these movements were delivery trips.

A few open days were also held at BR depots by friendly local staff who invited steam engines to join in. Some of these required them to run for long distances to get there from their home depots, ostensibly pulled in light steam by diesels. For example the Tyseley locomotives were 'towed' to London Cricklewood, Liverpool (Allerton) and Stratford-upon-Avon for display and demonstration in steam. These locomotives were lined up in a bizarre cavalcade of diesel, *Clun Castle*, GWR Engineer's Saloon, *Kolhapur*, LMS

During the steam ban, our locomotives occasionally managed to escape from Tyseley by being towed to various BR sponsored open days at London (Cricklewood), Liverpool (Allerton) and Stratford-upon-Avon. The formation was always locomotive followed by saloon in a convoy, so that at the destination they could be displayed individually with minimal shunting. On more than one occasion the diesel driver egged the steam locomotive crews to work the train, although strictly the regulators were supposed to be 'pegged' only to allow a small opening for lubrication. Here a cavalcade of *Clun Castle*, *Kolhapur* and 'Black Five' No. 5428 *Eric Treacy* are seen approaching Bearley on the Stratford-upon-Avon to Hatton Junction line. [PHOTO: C.M. WHITEHOUSE COLLECTION]

British Railways Board

222 Marylebone Road
London NW1 6JJ
01-262 3232 Extn. 5676
Telex 24678

CHIEF PASSENGER MARKETING MANAGER

P.B. Whitehouse, Esq.,
Standard Gauge Steam Trust,
5 Birch Hollow,
EDGBASTON,
Birmingham.

y/r
o/r P.59/J/153 - (6)   Date 26 April 1972

Dear Mr. Whitehouse,

The British Railways Board has decided that a limited number of steam hauled trains should be permitted on their lines in 1972, and a Press Announcement is being issued giving broad details. This letter is to give your Society more detailed information on the conditions which will apply.

1.   The following routes only to be used for steam traction:-

    1.1 Birmingham (Moor Street) - Didcot   77 miles

    1.2 York - Scarborough   42   "

    1.3 Newcastle - Carlisle   60   "

    1.4 Shrewsbury - Newport   94   "

    1.5 Carnforth - Barrow   28   "

2.   Only those locomotives on the list attached to be considered.

3.   Locomotives:

    3.1 To be chartered to B.R. from the Steam Preservation Society concerned for the particular run(s) concerned at a nominal charge of £1.

    3.2 To be handed over to B.R. by the Preservation Society in fit mechanical condition, to B.R. requirements.

    3.3 The Preservation Society concerned to be responsible for arrangements for fire-lighting, steam-raising, coaling, watering, fire-dropping etc. etc., to B.R. requirements and satisfaction.

    3.4 B.R. to provide Driver, Fireman and Motive Power Inspector: no representative of Preservation Society on footplate during journeys unless specially agreed in each individual case.

4.   Journeys involving steam haulage over the approved routes must be sponsored by a Preservation Society, who would be responsible for the promoting and marketing the journey(s) involved, including sale of tickets. B.R. would encourage charter trains from longer distances, with steam haulage over the approved sections of line only, to maximise revenue.

- 1 -

The 1972 experiment. Letter dated 26th April 1972 from D.V. Ellison at the BR Board to Pat Whitehouse, setting out terms for the initial experimental runs to take place in that year only. (*Continuation on page 2 oppsite*)

- 2 -

5.   Charges: Will be raised to cover all specific expenses incurred
for steam operation (e.g. staffing, provision of Inspectors, special
opening of signal boxes, police attention, special administrative costs,
locomotive examination etc.). The provision of B.R. coaching stock will
be charged for as a charter train.

6.   The Steam Preservation Society concerned with any run will indemnify
B.R. against any mishap which might occur during the movement over B.R.
lines, and take out insurance for a sum stipulated by B.R. (probably £0.75m.).

7.   Movement of steam locomotives to and from the approved lines will be
carried out by B.R. at charges to be quoted for each movement, normally by
haulage in "light steam". For short journeys, however, movement in steam
under own power might be permitted. Each case will be decided on its merits.

All applications for steam hauled journeys on the nominated routes
will be dealt with in my office, and should be addressed to Mr. J.B. Mander,
Passenger Services Officer, who will co-ordinate all activities connected
with steam traction.

The Board are entering into this further experiment for 1972 only,
and its continuation beyond this year will depend on the revenue which accrues
from the project. Financial results will be carefully monitored.

Yours sincerely,

D.V. Ellison

Engineer's Saloon, 'Black Five' No. 5428 *Eric Treacy* and BSK brake van! The trip from Tyseley to Allerton, in particular, was amazing, with travel not being permitted under the overhead electrified live wires. This meant that the locomotives had to run north via Walsall and the remains of the GWR northern main line until they got near Runcorn and then they were obliged to run under the wires over the bridge. By that time, the driver of the Class '40' diesel which was doing the towing had long since given up powering the entourage and *Kolhapur* was doing all the work!

Other open days were held at various depots around the country: Carnforth, Didcot, Ashford and Tyseley for example. PBW even managed to negotiate steam shuttle trains 'top and tailed' on the steep goods loop adjacent to the depot and so it was that upwards of 20,000 people came to the Tyseley 'zoo' to see *Clun Castle* and *Kolhapur* charging up and down the goods loop, the only privately-preserved steam hauled passenger carrying trains on the national network! They were aided and abetted by *Flying Scotsman* running an excursion train to the 1968 open day and also receiving *King George V* following its trial run in October 1971. Subsequent open days featured several locomotives which were to be approved for main line running over the years to come, including *Princess Elizabeth*, *Sir Nigel Gresley* and *Blue Peter*. There is no doubt that the existence of these private depots and their good relationships with

people who mattered at high levels within BR played a significant part in securing the return to steam for the movement as a whole.

Against this backdrop, as we have seen, a relatively new entrant in the market was able to tip the balance using his commercial flair and relative independence from the enthusiast core. Peter Prior, Managing Director of Bulmers, the Hereford cider manufacturer, was able to swing the difference but with several others coming in behind him to secure a main line future for their locomotives as well.

An embryo team had formed behind the curtain and was engaged in discussions on how to proceed by the time *King George V* ran its trial. There were still some senior people to convince at the BR Board of course but, fortuitously, after the trial, there was a change in Chairman. The wider team were then able to show that not only had the trial trip been a success but that several depots had been established with capability and which could be trusted not to let the side down. Terry Miller, who was by then working for the Board, was most helpful in pursuing the process in the right way and gently continued his persuasion behind the scenes for the benefit of all. His letter of 10th September 1971, just before the trial run by *King George V*, is illustrative of the approach which ultimately won through, although his cautionary remarks about some unnamed individuals in pressure groups is intriguing. As can be seen in his letter, Miller positioned the movement, and Tyseley, well.

The Return to Steam Committee, established by the Association of Railway Preservation Societies, comprised some notable individuals who applied their collective and individual efforts to return steam to the main line, with varying degrees of success. The Committee comprised Peter Manisty (ARPS Chairman), David Shepherd (famous wildlife painter and owner of two BR 'Standard' locomotives), Roger Bell (founder of the Princess Elizabeth Preservation Group), Mike Crewe (involved with the Middleton Railway founding fathers) and Brian Hollingsworth (on the BR Board and joint owner of 'Black Five' No. 5428). The committee's objective was to ascertain the stumbling blocks to a return of main line steam and find solutions.

Interestingly, in the light of the earlier *faux pas*, the autumn 1971 newsletter of the 'Bahamas Locomotive Society' reported: "*It should be mentioned that some locomotive owners have already been pressing for the operation of their locomotives, and in very strong terms in some cases. The BLS is NOT one of these. We have not, and will not, approach British Railways Board. We believe strongly in the policy adopted by the 'Return to Steam' committee of the ARPS; the successful operation of 'KGV' may well lead to a change in BR policy, but any independent approach to British Rail will probably 'rock the boat'.*'

So it was that, on 26th April 1972, certain locomotive owners received a very welcome letter from D.V. Ellison, Chief Passenger Marketing Manager to the British Railways Board. BR had decided that a limited number of steam hauled trains should be allowed on their network on a controlled basis. Essentially, there were to be five authorised routes which would allow a set number of steam locomotives to run from established depots. This made a great deal of sense when everyone was putting their toes in the water to start to build up a working operational relationship, the likes of which had never been seen before.

Some of the locomotives on the approved list were obviously going to be present. Their owners had seen to that and were, to a certain extent, mostly self selected. But there were also some interesting surprises: pannier tanks No's 7752 and 7760, GWR 0-6-2T No. 6697 and 'Mogul' 2-6-0 No. 5322. As we will see later, even more surprisingly, No. 7752 actually ran some trains in 1973,

mainly to Stratford-upon-Avon. But there was one famous absentee – *Flying Scotsman* was by then running in the USA.

It was down to *Clun Castle* and *King George V* to haul the first 'Return to Steam' tour on 10th June 1972. BR ran the train and took responsibility for operating the steam locomotives, just as they had always done, even using their own crews, although the private owner was responsible for all preparation and disposal, and also had to produce insurance against mishaps. *Clun Castle* came onto her train in the pouring rain at Bordesley, just outside Birmingham and then ran to Didcot. The train was diesel hauled to Hereford, where *King George V* took up the reigns for a run to Shrewsbury. The following day the trip was repeated in reverse. All went well.

Interestingly, *Clun Castle* was passed as fit for service with nothing more than a visual inspection and a trial trip to Hatton triangle '*just to see if the wheels still went round*'. Of course, it had not been long since she last ran on the main line to open days around the country and she had been continually maintained by mainly an ex-BR team headed by Bernard Rainbow, a driver fully familiar with the class. Fortuitously, at that time there were still men in BR service with all the requisite knowledge and skills and, perhaps more importantly, the locomotives selected had either still got time to run on their boiler inspections or had been overhauled at BR workshops.

BR were certainly keeping a close eye on what was going on. It is important to understand their views at the outset of permitting privately-owned main line steam to restart, especially as by the time it came to privatisation some twenty years later, knowledge and skills were to become scarce and their predictions and concerns were beginning to come home to roost. Terry Miller had advised Willy Thorpe in 1971 that, '*There are, so far as I am aware, only three places in Great Britain at which steam locomotives can be and are maintained in sound workable condition and these are at Tyseley, Didcot and Carnforth and if we are to avoid disasters such as the collapse of steam locomotives on the main line, it is very important that we should confine ourselves to the use of locomotives maintained at one of these places*'. Wise words, which in the 21st century could easily be repeated with real meaning, perhaps only with a very slight adjustment as to number.

'Return to Steam'. The inaugural authorised main line steam train after the 1971 trials ran on 10th June 1972. Tyseley's No. 7029 *Clun Castle* stands with her train at Bordesley, next to Tyseley depot, in the pouring rain ready to begin the historic journey to Didcot. There, a diesel would take over for the journey to Hereford and then No. 6000 *King George V* would run with it up to Shrewsbury. The trip would be repeated in the reverse direction on the following day. Note the Hawksworth GWR Engineer's Saloon No. 80972 behind the locomotive, then used as a support coach but in reality for entertaining suitable guests to help the continuing process to develop Tyseley as a steam centre. [PHOTO: C.M. WHITEHOUSE]

The next weekend, 'A4' Pacific No. 4498 *Sir Nigel Gresley*, also a main line preservation stalwart through the 1970s, ran a trip from Newcastle to Carlisle, over its 'authorised route', on which the engine is seen here near Brampton on 17th June 1972. [PHOTO: JOHN WHITELEY]

It was not long before we were visited by our friends at the Great Western Society, Didcot, who were at 'the other end' of the approved route between us. As it fell to me to organise many of the subsequent excursions, Jon Barlow (a founder member of the GWS) and I developed a good rapport to 'fly the GWR flag' at SLOA meetings. After all, between us and the 6000 Locomotive Association, we had two approved GWR routes to use. Here, Didcot's GWR 'Modified Hall' 4-6-0 No. 6998 *Burton Agnes Hall* has just passed Heyford near Oxford, hauling an excursion on 1st October 1972, which also used two of the Society's GWR carriages; in those days passengers could be carried in wooden bodied stock on the main line. [PHOTO: JOHN WHITELEY]

The Bahamas Locomotive Society were in the team from the beginning of the 'Return to Steam'. Although they had acquired their 'Jubilee' straight out of BR service from Stockport depot, just like we had acquired *Kolhapur* from Leeds Holbeck, neither of us had the opportunity to run our 'Jubilees' before the ban was imposed. Here, double-chimneyed No. 5596 *Bahamas* is seen at Millhouses, where the semaphore signals had recently been removed, having left Sheffield on an excursion which ran on 17th June 1973. The locomotive was then in a rather pink shade of red, which of course 'Jubilees' never carried in double-chimney form. There was no problem with passengers leaning their heads out of the train windows in those days! [PHOTO: JOHN WHITELEY]

BR authorised a total of 301 miles for use by steam locomotives. At that time, none of the routes were very heavily used, all had access to turntables or turning triangles, and depots or bases for preserved locomotives were either adjacent to such routes or nearby. The initial plan was for trains to be hauled by modern traction from a centre of population to the steam route, all as part of a longer journey, so maximising revenue for BR whilst containing the operation of steam to where it could be well managed and only permitting relatively short runs. All a far cry from the high daily mileages currently operated.

Just eight of the steam locomotives on the initial authorised list hauled twelve passenger trains in the inaugural year. In 1973, more routes were added amounting to a further 460 miles. BR technically hired the steam locomotive back from the owner and this arrangement overcame the legal responsibility for safety. The planning and coordination of trips was, however, another matter entirely and quickly became a headache for BR, which was obliged to arbitrate between the various owners, all of whom wanted to run their locomotives over the approved routes. Policy had already determined that scarcity value was required, both to maximise financial returns and minimise operational risk. So, from 1976, BR reviewed its policy and required all the locomotive owners to form themselves into one group and nominate representatives to agree an overall programme each year. This decision was conveyed to Sir William McAlpine and his henchman, George Hinchcliffe, at a lunch meeting with the then BR Chairman Sir Robert Reid. Hinchcliffe then took up the initiative and so the

Steam Locomotive Operators' Association (SLOA) was formed. This simple arrangement was to be the basis for main line steam operation from 1976 until railway privatisation in 1993.

The initial steam trips from 1972 to 1976 were not altogether best sellers and some trains were even cancelled, possibly due to fragmentation in the market, with every locomotive owning group vying for position. SLOA set up its own marketing arm, which was very ably led by Bernard Staite, formerly of the Hereford based *King George V* support group, aided and abetted by a range of Chairmen drawn largely from within the Association members. With initial guidance from BR in how trains were planned and organised, passenger numbers picked up, resulting in the number of trains increasing quite quickly. Cheap feed-in fares were offered on ordinary service trains, which widened the catchment areas for the steam trains and also added to BR's ancillary income from car parking and refreshment room catering. This policy proved successful and by 1980 there were a thousand route miles open to steam, whilst in 1981 some 100 steam excursions operated.

On 4th January 1982, the former BR regions were reorganised into business led sectors. One of these was InterCity, led by Cyril Bleasdale, which became responsible for the business planning of express passenger trains nationwide and regarded as a 'commercial railway', as opposed to Provincial Railways which was a grant supported 'social railway'. Operationally, the regions still had control. The special trains 'charter train unit' found itself within the InterCity sector and David Ward was appointed to run it. This new entity had a wide range of trains in its portfolio, and not all of them were diesel.

Bill Harvey convinced Clapham Museum Curator John Scholes to let him put the National Collection's 'V2' 2-6-2 back into working order at Norwich. Bill knew PBW from Talyllyn days and, anyway, the Tyseley to Didcot route was the nearest authorised line for steam, so No. 4771 *Green Arrow* came to Tyseley for her first runs. Two trips were run on the same day, 1st July 1972, the other train being hauled by *Sir Nigel Gresley*, with the locomotives swapping trains at Didcot. Here, *Green Arrow* ascends Hatton Bank on her first long distance charter since restoration, with GWR Saloon No. 80972 – 'The Gin Palace!' – behind the locomotive.
[PHOTO: JOHN WHITELEY]

Brian Holden was our PR man extraordinaire and knew all the local press very well. On 9th June 1974, he arranged for the *Sunday Mercury* newspaper to sponsor a special train to Didcot with No. 4472 *Flying Scotsman*. In this view, the train is seen pulling away from Tyseley along the ex-GWR Up Main Line, with two privately owned carriages on the front of the train: a Pullman car and a lovely teak-sided Gresley buffet car. In the background is Tyseley station, with the roadbridge crowded with photographers and onlookers. [PHOTO: JOHN WHITELEY]

In the 1970s, the word was 'excursion': football specials, 'Merrymaker' and Sunday mystery tours (as likely as not, ending up at Barry Island in South Wales) for 10s 6d (52.5p). Ward set to sorting it all out. Hitherto, he had coordinated the SLOA steam specials but now he had a larger 'mish-mash' of operations to knock some sense into. Which he did.

The unit commissioned the London Business School to undertake detailed research into BR's existing excursion business. Their report was uncompromising; it showed that even with full trains there was little or no money in the bottom end of the market, whereas with First Class dining and full dining trains there was considerable profit potential. So specials organised by InterCity were suddenly given a focus: smaller numbers of passengers paying a premium fare for VIP treatment in First Class and Pullman Cars with catering of comparable quality. I well remember our being invited by John Prideaux, successor to Bleasdale, on one such trip from Paddington, as he kindly requested *Clun Castle* to haul a leg on the return journey. We were met at Paddington by a very smartly turned-out train of BR Mark 1 First Class carriages repainted in the sector's 'raspberry ripple' red and white livery and given a brunch with champagne on departure. All excellent stuff!

As time marched on, further changes became necessary. BR gradually withdrew its ageing steam heated 90mph Mark 1 carriage fleet and SLOA quickly recognised that the future of its steam excursions was in jeopardy. Its owners, in collaboration with BR, had spent valuable and useful time devising a standard set of engineering manuals under the description of MT276 for

maintaining and operating steam locomotives, which worked well in practice. There was now a real danger of there being no train of carriages left to haul. At that time steam's incompatibility with modern, air braked and electrically heated Mark 1I and Mark 1II stock was absolute.

So, in 1977, thoughts turned to acquiring a suitable rake of carriages compatible with steam operation, which BR would countenance. The announcement in April 1981 that SLOA had bought a rake of eight Metro Cammell 1960s-built Pullman cars, which were dual braked and mounted on 100mph Commonwealth bogies, was the answer to a prayer. Michael Draper, then Managing Director of the Severn Valley Railway, was also Chairman of SLOA at the time and eloquently put the case to a surprised but grateful membership at a special meeting but in reality, the decision had already been made. It was that or nothing. The set was maintained by BR at Carlisle Upperby depot under contract. The train, repainted in classic Pullman brown umber and cream, made its SLOA debut behind Paddy Smith's 'Black Five' No. 5407 on the Carlisle-Hellifield 'Cumbrian Mountain Pullman' on 2nd May 1981. Yet even before that special had run, Bernard Staite was announcing that the Pullmans would form the basis of a new series of charter trains, operating in the summer months with diesel and electric haulage, under the title 'Pullman Scenic Land Cruises'. This up-market move began on Saturday 4th July 1981 over the Settle & Carlisle line and, within two years, had developed into a series of three day charter excursions to Scotland, with hotel accommodation overnight. Despite then being in what

Double-headed Great Western steam. The GWS brought two of their locomotives up to Tyseley on 19th October 1974, No. 7808 *Cookham Manor* and No. 6998 *Burton Agnes Hall*, and they are seen here near Danzey, on the North Warwickshire Line between Tyseley and Stratford. As with every private steam locomotive in those early years, these two had been bought straight out of BR service, with No. 7808 residing at Dowty's base in Ashchurch, near Tewkesbury and No. 6998 at Totnes, until the GWS organised themselves at the former GWR locomotive depot at Didcot and moved all their collection there. This was very handy for both Didcot and Tyseley, having an authorised route to run between the two approved depots. [PHOTO: JOHN WHITELEY]

The 'SLOA' Pullmans. David Ward of the BR InterCity charter train unit arranged for a rake of 1960s-built Metro Cammell Pullman Cars to be made available for SLOA to buy to be used on steam tours, as they were dual braked. Their journey into the main line steam business was somewhat troublesome, as asbestos was found and had to be stripped out, which led to further changes in the organisational structure and promotion of tours. [PHOTO: C.M. WHITEHOUSE]

was described as the worst financial recession for fifty years, the land cruise to Mallaig sold out in just nine days.

These rapid developments were to have a major effect on steam locomotive operation in many ways. Firstly, the availability of only the SLOA Pullmans dictated the number of trips which could be run. Next, their maintenance base in the north of England somewhat determined their usage. Then, the predilection of the leaders of the charter business at the time, for large 'Pacific' locomotives capable of hauling heavy trains up steep hills and with almost unlimited route availability over BR main lines, led to certain choices of motive power being selected. Consequently, these trips were not often over former Great Western main lines, nor did they very often use slightly wider to gauge GWR express steam locomotives.

To some extent this did not matter overmuch, as we were relatively happy to run *Clun Castle* only a few times a year and our small team always preferred to do so from our home base at Tyseley. Thus the Didcot route was very convenient and our friends there had an excellent depot for servicing. Jon Barlow (one of the founders of the Great Western Society) and I teamed up to plead the Great Western case at SLOA meetings and each of us occasionally had to dive into the scrum for locomotive bookings, which Bernard Staite used to arrange in the hallway of the hotel, usually in York, before dinner. I was pretty satisfied if I landed two trips a year. Jon and I used to exchange locomotives and combine trips occasionally. One year we borrowed *Evening Star*, the last steam locomotive to be built for British Railways, from the always obliging John Coiley, Keeper of the National Railway Museum. We ran two trips using the '9F' and *Clun Castle*. No. 7029 ran down to Didcot with a charter and No. 92220 brought it back, and we reversed the engines a week or two later, with the added bonus that each of us achieved a guest

locomotive for the open days we used to run. Occasionally, we took *Clun Castle* to Hereford to run on the 'other GWR route' between Newport and Shrewsbury.

Over the years, Tyseley hosted several 'foreign' steam locomotives on other people's charters. Some just called in for water, some stayed longer and featured at an open day. We were host to the 'great and the good' from 1973. Bill Harvey had convinced John Scholes, Curator at the London Clapham Museum, to let him put the absolutely marvellous L&NER 'V2' 2-6-2 No. 4771 *Green Arrow* back into working order over in Norfolk. PBW encouraged Bill to bring No. 4771 to us at Tyseley for her first trips and he brought her over from Norwich, under her own power. I well remember seeing her arrive, glistening in the evening sun and thought, "*What a beautiful engine!*". Her first preservation long haul runs were to Didcot and two trips were operated on the same day, the other hauled by *Sir Nigel Gresley*, with the engines swapping over at Didcot for the return run. We put our GWR Saloon, aka 'The Gin Palace', behind No. 4771 for the VIPs, including John Scholes, the curator of the British Transport Commission collection. My early volunteering task was wine waiter in the saloon (hence its nickname as 'awarded' by David Ward!) and, as we were bowling down Hatton Bank, I saw the speedometer in the saloon veering towards 80mph. Scholes thought we were going rather fast and asked "*How fast?*" Swiftly, I stood between him and the speedo and quipped "*Nearly 60mph*" but with a little smirk. Scholes knew very well what was going on but we all thoroughly enjoyed it. And this was all just a year after the return to steam following the ban, when the maximum speed for any locomotive was 60mph.

No. 4771 had an earlier impromptu trip out with us. Our GWR pannier tank No. 7752 was rostered for three trips to Stratford

Our 'Jubilee' managed a few trips in the 'Return to Steam' years but not without some trouble with hot axle boxes. However, fortunately, one great trip which was trouble free was a return visit to her former stamping grounds over the Settle & Carlisle line. Repainted in LM&SR red, No. 5593 *Kolhapur* ran a trip each way over the line, promoted by ourselves as Birmingham Railway Museum. The trains is seen here approaching Smardale on 21st March 1987, together with a newly acquired BFK support coach leading a rather multi-coloured train. [PHOTO: MALCOLM RANIERI]

On 25th April 1987, 'Jubilee' Class 4-6-0 No. 5593 *Kolhapur* deafens her passengers as she barks up the grade through the limestone hills at Peak Forest Junction with a Buxton-Derby train – a route not all that common for charter train use. [PHOTO: ANDREW BELL]

on two occasions that year but on the first runs we had trouble with a sticking brake on the train and stopped for a blow up. The authorities did not care for a repeat and, on the morning of the trip, it had been suggested to the inspector that No. 7752 might be failed if at all possible and indeed it was. Undeterred, our CME Jim Kent had No. 4771 taken out of the shed and a fire lit. No. 7752 dragged her up and down the yard to help create a draught to raise steam in time and so *Green Arrow* was substituted. Our passengers never complained that they had a Gresley 2-6-2 instead! So *Green Arrow* can justifiably claim to have been the first tender engine in preservation to have hauled a pre-launch 'Shakespeare Express' in BR days.

Now that main line steam was back, we turned to see what other locomotives we might be able to put back into traffic. John Scholes lent us several engines which were then in store, pending the opening of the National Railway Museum, and we toyed with the idea of returning L&SWR 'T9' 4-4-0 to the main line, as she had run excursions in BR days and would most probably have

worked alright. But she was not on the official list and, anyway, the rule was a loan for only six months at a time, so we might not have recouped our investment. We concentrated on our own locomotives and busied ourselves in medium term work on both *Thornbury Castle* and *Albert Hall*.

The obvious next candidate was LM&SR 'Jubilee' 4-6-0 No. 5593 *Kolhapur*. Jim Kent and his team had undertaken some painstaking work in 1967 tightening up loose cylinders and replacing a large part of the smokebox, and she was in working order, looking lovely in crimson red livery. We tried on various occasions to run her in the '70s and '80s but she succumbed to hot axle boxes rather too often. Nevertheless, we did have some fine trips, including both ways over the Settle & Carlisle route, providing me with a most memorable footplate trip one early sunny spring day with a light covering of snow still on the ground. We also ran some trips from Manchester to Southport, rather off-piste for us but they were fun too. The London Midland crews were glad to get their hands on her and she ran really well back on her home territory.

Lion on the main line! The amazing sight of the 1838-built Liverpool & Manchester Railway 0-4-0 'luggage engine' *Lion* on the main line, undergoing braking trials between Southport and Burscough Bridge on 12th May 1980, prior to taking part in the 150th anniversary celebrations of the Rainhill Trials. Adrian Jarvis, Keeper of the Liverpool Museum transport collection, is on the footplate clearly in his element. The two carriages are replicas, made for the 1930 centenary celebrations by the LM&SR, the leading one in blue being a Third Class carriage with no seats or a roof and the second yellow vehicle a First Class carriage in the style of former stage coaches. [PHOTO: JOHN WHITELEY]

16. BR'S 'INDIAN SUMMER' OF STEAM

'We began our contribution to the GW150 programme in style … Clun Castle was allowed out to play.
Linesiders reported that she sounded like a Spitfire roaring up Sapperton Bank …'

Lion and the 'Old Time Train' at Tyseley in October 1980, pretty much replicating the 1938 centenary train run in Liverpool by the LM&SR. The ten day event at Tyseley brought in 10,000 people. [Photo: C.M. Whitehouse]

Having cautiously put its toe back in the water for main line steam in the 1970s, and once the plan to market and run trains in co-operation with SLOA had settled down in the 1980s, BR became more interested and also more involved in special trains and events. Not only had the InterCity sector established a specialised unit which was clearly making some money but the nation's railway system was approaching sesquicentenary time – quite simply, there were many 150th anniversaries to be celebrated. These encouraged the National Railway Museum to put many very interesting steam locomotives back into steam.

First, in 1975, came the 150th anniversary of the Stockton & Darlington Railway, celebrated at Shildon with a fascinating cavalcade of locomotives and some local shuttle trains. Several of the museum locomotives which were put back into steam even ran special trains on the network as well. Those of us engaged in linesiding had a veritable field day. I will never ever forget standing with a group of 'gricers' by Gigglesworth Tunnel to watch and photograph a train from York to Carnforth double-headed by *Hardwicke* and the Midland 'Compound.' A sight for sore eyes; blink and you missed it as, sadly, the 'Compound' gave up the ghost on arrival but *Hardwicke* went on to run some shuttle trains from

Carnforth to Grange over Sands in 1976 and even double head the very last steam locomotive of all, *Evening Star*, on a special. My little Fiat 128 car ground up and down the M6 motorway from home many times as these sights just had to be seen. There was an absolutely remarkable, glorious afternoon at Carnforth depot, when *Hardwicke, Flying Scotsman, Green Arrow* and the 'B1' *Mayflower* were all in steam together!

All this was to be topped by the 150th anniversary celebrations of the Liverpool & Manchester Railway in 1980, with another cavalcade based on Bold Colliery, which proved a mouth watering occasion with some incredible resurrections: the L&MR 0-4-2 *Lion*, built as long ago as 1838 and, although much modified, still very recognisable from the 'Old Time Train' recreated for the 1938 centenary by the LM&SR; the Midland Railway 'Spinner' 2-2-2; 'Race to the North' hero and '1975 celebration veteran' L&NWR 'Precedent' 2-4-0 *Hardwicke*; and Midland 'Compound' 4-4-0 No. 1000 – just some examples of the locomotives put back into steam. This time the 'Compound' worked well and there were some memorable trips with her double-heading LM&SR 'Jubilee' *Leander*, which itself was quite a resurrection, having been rebuilt professionally at Derby Works from a Barry scrapyard wreck.

A unique sight! For the first and last time, *Rocket* and *Lion* are seen giving double-headed passenger rides at Tyseley for our 150th anniversary celebrations of the London & Birmingham Railway in September 1988, passing LM&SR 'Pacific' No. 6201 *Princess Elizabeth* for good measure. Tyseley's 'new style' open days in the 1980s hosted many visiting locomotives of all kinds and shapes. [Photo: C.M. Whitehouse]

Whilst Tyseley could not really compete with all this remarkable steam activity in the north of England, we did send our GWR pannier tank up to Shildon in 1975, primarily to operate passenger shuttles in conjunction with the exhibition there, but No. 7752 also had a place of honour in the locomotive cavalcade.

I also tempted one very tasty morsel down to us, namely *Lion*. Of course, this is pretty much completely outside the scope of main line railtours but no more so than the Talyllyn or the Dart Valley and all part of the story. Actually, *Lion* did run on the main line during 1980! The engine's visit to Tyseley in October 1980 for ten days helped put us back on the open day map and reminded me that in life one has to be bold and seize opportunities.

I had fallen in love with *Lion* when watching the film *The Titfield Thunderbolt* and dreamed of how lovely it would be if she was ever exhumed from Liverpool City's Museum. By design, as it was a good university for law, my chosen career, I went to Liverpool to study and met Adrian Jarvis, the Museum Keeper there, several times. We even talked about the possibility of *Lion* working again and he was the sort of guy who was completely up for that, especially as it had been in use on and off over the years for special events anyway and was known to work. The occasion came, of course, when *Lion* was indeed exhumed for the L&MR 150 celebrations. Quick as a flash, I wrote to Adrian and asked if he would bring the venerable locomotive to Tyseley. He simply said 'yes', although he might well have cast an eye towards some of the superb Black Country pubs as well but we were not averse to that! I organised for two of the replica Liverpool & Manchester Third Class open carriages to come from the NRM to join with *Lion* and, suddenly, we had the 'Old Time

Train' of the 1938 exhibition back, at least in part. It was quite a coup, as our open week would be the first time the public could ride behind *Lion* as part of the overall celebrations.

As we had not run such a train before at Tyseley (it had compressed air brakes on the carriages and we were 'just' a shed yard), I bunked off work from my law office in the city one morning to discuss the prospect with Major Peter Olver of HM Railway Inspectorate. I had the temerity to show him my handwritten operating proposal for the gala event. He took it and carefully read it through without saying a word. When he had finished, he completely surprised me by saying it was a fine document and had I also planned to give passenger rides? I had thought this a step too far, as we did not then have a passenger platform on the depot, nor did we have any system of interlocking points. He smiled and gently said that, if we padlocked one set of points, we could run from our turntable up to the top of our depot (about a quarter of a mile) and load passengers, using the steps on the carriages, from the brick hard standing by the turntable. Game on! I think he was just as keen as me to see the event work.

We had 10,000 visitors in ten days and I had a whale of a time driving *Lion* during the weekday school visits, learning how to stop her in reverse and fill her boiler with water from her axle pump. A complete dream come true and, oh yes, we did spend the evenings visiting 'Old Ma Pardoes' and the 'Crooked House' pubs in the Black Country. It was so much fun that we did it all over again in 1988 for the 150th anniversary of the London & Birmingham Railway and even double-headed the replica *Rocket* with *Lion*. We had the replica First Class coach as well. What a weekend!

We could not resist driving up to the south Lake District to see the National Railway Museum's L&NWR 'Precedent' 2-4-0 No. 790 *Hardwicke* running a trial trip from Carnforth to Sellafield on 22nd July 1975, after retubing. It was a really terrible wet day. My Fiat 128 car groaned up the M6 amongst heavy traffic and then we turned off to see *Hardwicke* running along the Cumbrian Coast Line with Bill McAlpine's GER saloon in tow – *Hardwicke's* motion went 'tink tink' just like PBW said it would. We were amazed when the short train stopped at the platform we were standing on and Peter Beet, the supremo at Carnforth, welcomed us aboard. We did not need a second invitation and soon we were sipping champagne in the saloon as *Hardwicke* pulled us along to Sellafield. Not in our wildest dreams did we ever imagine this! [PHOTO: JOHN WHITELEY]

Definitely a one off! National Railway Museum duo L&NWR No. 790 *Hardwicke* and MR 'Compound' 4-4-0 No. 1000 roar out of Giggleswick Tunnel on 24th April 1976, on their way from York to Carnforth. It was the only time these two fascinating locomotives were seen together on the main line and it was an almost unbelievable sight that we were so privileged to see. [PHOTO: C.M. WHITEHOUSE]

After these two events with really old locomotives, we celebrated Great Western 150 in 1985. This was such an important opportunity for Tyseley that we even moved our family summer holiday to the autumn so I could devote the time to planning and engaging with the considerable politics of the occasion.

Clearly *Clun Castle*, as the last Great Western-designed steam locomotive in BR service, had to take part but she needed a boiler overhaul. But by then, PBW had become an expert at 'grant speak' and, over the years, managed to liberate some three million pounds from public funds to establish a highly successful community training programme at our Tyseley depot. This aimed to retrain redundant artisans in order to help them regain their confidence and re-enter full time employment. Being a building contractor by occupation, this was a doddle for PBW really and he thoroughly enjoyed it. This did mean that we had the funds and could employ the

Hardwicke ran some shuttle trains from Carnforth to Grange over Sands over two days in May 1976 and every photographer in the country must have been there to witness this 'lifetime' experience. On 9th May, the 2-4-0 approaches Grange over Sands with four blue and grey Mark 1 carriages but we were not grumbling – it was far too exciting just to see her moving at speed. [PHOTO: JOHN WHITELEY]

The success of *Clun Castle*'s runs in GW150 year spurred us on to repair another of our four 'Castles', as we had obtained three more from Barry scrapyard to provide a source of spare parts 'for ever.' The initial intention was to put No. 7027 *Thornbury Castle* back into traffic as she was probably the best of the three engines obtained from Barry. But, she was another BR(WR) build and I preferred an authentic GWR-built 'Castle'. After a discussion, it was agreed that we would pull forward restoration work on No. 5080 *Defiant* (such a lovely name), as the Manpower Services Community Programme agreed to fund the cost of labour and materials and former Worcester Works manager, Don Green, agreed to supervise the work. So, in December 1986, No. 5080 was hauled to the works by No. 7760, after boiler asbestos and cladding had been removed. The restoration work to return *Defiant* to main line running order was completed in only eighteen months. No. 5043 *Earl of Mount Edgcumbe* had to wait a little longer for attention and No. 7027 never made the grade after all. New in May 1939 as *Ogmore Castle*, *Defiant* was renamed after a Second World War night fighter plane in January 1941. Withdrawn in April 1963, the locomotive then spent nearly eleven years in storage at Barry scrapyard, before being rescued in August 1974, in the state seen here [PHOTO: C.M. WHITEHOUSE]

skills needed to recertify, to the BR mantra of MT276 standard for boiler and mechanical repairs, both *Clun Castle* and our LM&SR 'Jubilee' *Kolhapur*, and also return to main line service our 'Gin Palace' GWR Shrewsbury Engineer's Saloon No. 80972, and introduce GWR 'Super Saloon' No. 9001, previously favoured by the Queen Mother. It was quite a year!

We had not then been running on the main line for a few years but, as owners of *Clun Castle*, we were, of course, invited to the planning sessions by our friends within BR. Initially, there was some rivalry and competition about who would be permitted to participate and some locomotive owners seemed to want a little more than their fair slice of the cake. By this time, the Severn Valley Railway had entered the main line frame 'big time' following Michael Draper's appearance in the General Manager's job there and he was, quite understandably, interested in *Hagley Hall* and *Hinton Manor* taking as many turns as he could get. But he had to accept our railway connections and also our ownership of a 'flagship' locomotive. *Clun Castle* was in the game.

We began our contribution to the GW150 programme in style. Through our City of Birmingham contacts, HRH The Duke of Gloucester paid us a visit. We sent *Kolhapur* into Birmingham Moor Street station with our saloons and used *Clun Castle* to bring

the Royal guest back to our depot, with the Duke riding on the footplate and taking a short turn on the regulator. The following weekend was our introduction to 'The Shakespeare Express' big time with eight trains, as you will read a little later.

Then *Clun Castle* was allowed out to play. Linesiders reported that she sounded like a Spitfire roaring up Sapperton Bank with the Gloucester-Swindon 'shuttles'. She ventured to Cardiff, double-headed with No. 4930 *Hagley Hall*. She raced up and down the Devon banks, not once but twice, double-heading *Dryslwyn Castle* from Didcot, something that we never thought we would ever see again. And she was the first locomotive to venture back into Cornwall since steam finished on BR.

GWR 'City' Class 4-4-0 No. 3440 *City of Truro*, reputedly the first locomotive to achieve 100mph, had been retrieved from Swindon Museum for the GW150 events and bagged by the SVR for repair and operation. She was due to return to her namesake city of Truro in September 1985 but repairs were not completed in time, so we were asked to take *Clun Castle* instead. We even changed her Tyseley smokebox shedplate to Plymouth Laira's designation for the event, and PBW and I spent some time in the area plotting further to build on our 1985 renaissance.

It was a simply beautiful September autumn day when *Clun*

It did not become *Hardwicke* to run tender first over Arnside Viaduct on 23rd
May 1976 – but we were not complaining. [Photo: John Whiteley]

Castle ran to Truro and back. I was delighted that we were able to
take Jack Trounson with us, who you will recall was one of the two
people who launched the fund to preserve No. 7029 in the first
place. He had not set eyes on her since BR days and the tears were
clearly in his eyes when he saw her again at Plymouth.

Clun Castle visited the half roundhouse at St. Blazey to turn and
then PBW and I took turns to ride the footplate on her return. We
did not do anything like the amount of footplating that some other
locomotive owners did, which made it ever more special when we
took the opportunity; Julian Riddick and John Cameron, both of
'A4' allegiance, must take the biscuit for footplating with rumoured
trips in the nineties at the very least …

I joined *Clun*'s footplate at Lostwithel and the crew were absolute
masters of the job, although the last steam trip they had crewed was
on a Southern 'Light Pacific' before the end of steam in Cornwall.
The line limit was 60mph and the journey seemed formed of a series
of curves but No. 7029 was up for the occasion and the needle on
her pressure gauge just hovered on the red line all the way. The
journey was magnificent and crossing the Royal Albert Bridge on
one's 'own' steam locomotive can hardly be bettered. But then, a
few days later, we were double-heading another 'Castle' over the
Devon banks whilst relaxing in 'The Gin Palace'.

By now, *Clun*'s exploits had reached head office and when we were
invited to run from Swansea to Carmarthen in September 1987, David
Ward, InterCity charter train supremo, joined us for the trip. This
resulted in *Clun Castle* being invited to run some of his prestigious

'Shakespeare Limited' Sunday lunch trains from London Marylebone to Stratford-upon-Avon. Before we could do this, he asked for a gauge testing run to check clearances in the tunnels running up to Marylebone, which we readily agreed to. On this test trip *Clun Castle* paused under a sloping roof tunnel on the approaches to Marylebone for the gap between the cab roof and the top of the tunnel to be measured. There was just sufficient clearance but we noticed some blue paint on the tunnel brickwork, clearly from some 'bouncy' diesels …

The 'Shakespeare Limited' steam-hauled Sunday lunch trains were an immediate success, although mainly hauled by 'Pacific' types. David Ward had built up an impressive charter unit within InterCity and began to branch out into BR sponsored steam trains. Ward put in hand a programme of Mark 1 rolling stock refurbishment,

involving reupholstering, recarpeting and curtain replacement and the fitting of individual table lamps, with the aim of returning respectability to carriages which had seen better days. During the second half of the 1980s, InterCity could boast five complete ten-car VIP train sets, all of which were based and serviced at London's Bounds Green depot; four of these were Mark 1 sets and the fifth was the former Manchester Pullman set. All were outshopped in standard InterCity 'raspberry ripple' livery but distinguished from ordinary service stock by having white painted roofs. This resulted in First Class dining trains taking 50 per cent market share of the total charter train market, as opposed to 23 per cent comprising private charters and only 5 per cent from steam charters.

And these were not the only changes. In 1983, the SLOA

A sight for sore eyes! *Hardwicke* double-heads *Flying Scotsman* over the viaduct at Plumpton near Ulverston in the South Lakes on 8th May 1976. Bill McAlpine's Great Eastern and Caledonian saloons are on the rear of the train. [PHOTO: JOHN WHITELEY]

An apple green double-header. L&NER 'B1' 4-6-0 No. 1306 *Mayflower* leads No. 4472 *Flying Scotsman* on an excursion from York that was bound for Carnforth on 21st September 1975. [PHOTO: JOHN WHITELEY]

Pullman set was withdrawn from service following the discovery of blue asbestos insulation in the body sides. Unable to meet the high cost of decontamination, SLOA was obliged to sell the train to industrialist Sir William McAlpine, then owner of the famous *Flying Scotsman*, as well as Carnforth depot near the English Lake District. McAlpine arranged for the asbestos to be removed and the Pullman train was hired back to SLOA for steam charter use, under McAlpine's 'Pullman Rail' banner and with former SLOA supremo Bernard Staite as Managing Director. Effectively, SLOA had not only lost its train but also its organiser. More asbestos was found in the Pullmans, necessitating a second withdrawal for attention. This was followed by a further shift with Pullman Rail also taking over operation of the Scenic Land Cruises, adding sleeping cars to the formation and confining the Pullmans to non-steam work and making available a rake of Mark 1s for steam charters. Pullman Rail was restyled Flying Scotsman Services in 1988. These trains, together with the Venice Simplon Orient Express, unleashed on an unsuspecting world in 1982 by James Sherwood of Sea Containers, cornered the luxury train market, together with the L&R Leisure Group's 'Royal Scotsman' train carrying just twenty-eight passengers, each paying around £2,600 a trip; its on-train cuisine was described as '*simply the best on any train anywhere in the world*'.

By now, BR was also running other regular steam services, beginning with a train from Fort William to Mallaig in Scotland. Network South East sector jumped on the bandwagon, as did Regional Railway with a successful summer series of steam trains over the scenic Cambrian Coast line in Wales.

These were the first steps of several which were to follow over

the next ten years or so, which would reduce the choice and control of operations by steam locomotive owners further, resulting in SLOA having less and less impact. Essentially, BR would choose the locomotives it wanted and the routes it preferred to use. In addition to BR's restrictions and choices, SLOA also introduced its own (with more than a little encouragement from BR).

SLOA management decreed there were too many new applicants for both membership and by existing members to bring more locomotives onto the main line. Amidst cries of a 'cartel', the management team introduced classifications for locomotives running on the main line: Class 'A' was the already approved list; Class 'B' was a duplicate list. This meant that if there was already a locomotive of a particular type on the 'A' list, another of the same type could only go on the 'B' list and not run at the same time as its counterpart on the 'A' list. By and large, this sorted itself out in practice, as locomotive overhauls and availability meant that few duplicates were actually presented for traffic and, when they were, an exception could usually be found.

So, we did manage to run both *Clun Castle* and *Defiant* in the same year but not at exactly the same time. All sorts of extraordinary locomotives managed to gain main line access by some means or exception or other reason: after being forbidden, Bulleid's 'Pacifics' were permitted; a Somerset & Dorset 2-8-0 gained admittance and managed a good performance over the Settle & Carlisle line; and the North British Railway 'C' Class 0-6-0 *Maude* ran over the Fort William to Mallaig route, although just once, as it set fire to swathes of gorse but we all got some good photographs!

By 1992, SLOA were somewhat concerned and, with the advent

The very last steam locomotive built for British Railways, of course earned herself a place in the National Collection. Built at Swindon in 1960, she also gained a Great Western name and was christened by Reggie Hanks, Chairman of the Western Region Board, who helped PBW and PJG acquire their GWR 'Small Prairie' No. 4555. No. 92220 *Evening Star* was allowed out on the main line, like several other NRM participants in the Stockton & Darlington 150 celebrations and became a welcome performer, until the BR Civil Engineer became concerned about her flangeless centre driving wheel running over point frogs and banned her. Here we see No. 92220 near Wennington in Lancashire on a Locomotive Club of Great Britain sponsored tour on 31st May 1975. [PHOTO: JOHN WHITLEY]

Pendennis Castle made even less runs after the 'Return to Steam' from 1972 than our own 'Castle', as she was based at Carnforth since being acquired by Bill McAlpine and she was really out of gauge for northern routes. Then, the Hammersley Iron Company in Australia contacted Bill to ask if he would part with *Flying Scotsman* and whilst the answer was 'no', they could have *Pendennis Castle*, so she was duly exported. Before she left these shores, she ran a last trip, 'The Great Western Envoy', from our depot at Tyseley to Didcot and back driven by 'our' Tyseley driver Dick Potts, actually on his first driving turn. He was lucky to have two fireman and one of those was Bernard Rainbow, our Depot Superintendent, so we were able to give *Pendennis Castle* a good send off. No. 4079 is seen here at Culham on her return run from Didcot on 29th May 1977, with guests waving from the Great Eastern saloon. Dick describes his emotions of the trip: '*As a fireman, I used to lean over the cabside and listen to the chimney roaring away and revel in the ecstacy of sound. Now here I was as a driver listening to the same music and to the feeling of a vibrant energy being exerted*'. [PHOTO: JOHN WHITELEY]

of railway privatisation and the introduction of the 'open access' concept we will read about in more detail later, they commissioned an internal report from three of its members, Clive Mojonnier (*Princess Elizabeth*), Michael Nagle (*King Edward I*) and myself. The report was to recommend the best strategy for running steam locomotives on the main line and maximise the returns to enable them to continue to run for as long as possible. The report pulled no punches. It suggested that the prime objective of all the locomotive operators had, somewhat understandably, been to run their own locomotive and SLOA's purpose had been to help them do so, which it had done by arranging a co-ordinated programme each year. No other considerations appeared to have been relevant initially. It was simply a matter of how many times a locomotive owner could operate his engine on British Rail; in some circumstances, even the fee received had been secondary.

The report continued: '*SLOA has not really been able to obtain the bargaining power of a substantial commercial organisation, as the tracks over which steam main line excursions have run belong to BR who is the ultimate decision maker, at least at present.*' Whilst SLOA did operate its own fleet of coaches under the auspices of SLOA Marketing Limited for a time, it was BR who suggested they acquire

such coaches and, later, practically ensured their subsequent sale to Flying Scotsman Enterprises following the imposition of restrictions on the introduction of asbestos regulations. However, during the time SLOA Marketing operated, commercial day to day operations flourished, albeit still subject to directions from BR as to the routes available and locomotives to be used.

Probably, the reason why commercial strategy planning was not considered in earnest was because the members somewhat rightly felt that to do so might well jeopardise the operation of steam trains on BR at all. Also, the members found it difficult to give SLOA full corporate commitment. Somewhat naturally, they were each concerned to see their own engine operate and several had stronger loyalties to private railways and steam depots where, perhaps, more of a corporate commitment existed.

The report concluded that SLOA should form a commercial corporation to own and run its own trains using member locomotives. If it did not do so, the report argued, SLOA would be reduced to a trade body, probably with less and less effect as new operators entered the market consequent on open access policies being put into practice.

And that is exactly what happened.

ABOVE: 'Royal Scot' Class 4-6-0 No. 6115 *Scots Guardsman* looked excellent in LMS black lined out in magenta and straw. Here she works one of very few specials whilst based at Dinting, on 11th November 1978, climbing towards Chinley near Buxworth. She was then owned by Peter Bill, who lived near us in Worcestershire and was keen to have his locomotive based closer to his home, so we agreed to have her based at Tyseley for a while, but neither he nor we could afford to repair her to main line standard at the time, so she now reposes at Carnforth, where their finance and facilities have put her back into action. [PHOTO: JOHN WHITELEY]

BELOW: 'Number Nine'. Steam returned to Scotland with John Cameron's 'A4' No. 60009 *Union of South Africa*, seen here leaving Edinburgh Haymarket on 14th April 1979 with a train of BR's blue and grey carriages. No. 60009 had been one of the last 'A4' 'Pacifics' to remain in service on the Perth to Aberdeen run until 1967 but, initially, only *Bittern* was chosen for preservation, by Geoff Drury, who bought it and 'A1' *Blue Peter*. He managed to run *Bittern* on a few trips before the 1968 steam ban. John Cameron ran his 'A4' on his private railway at Lochty but was soon persuaded to return her to the main line and could very often be seen on her footplate right up until her final withdrawal from operations on the national network in 2019. [PHOTO: JOHN WHITELEY]

Several LM&SR 'Black Fives' were preserved and ran on the main line. Carnforth depot, one of the initial approved main line bases, had several of course but the one shown in this picture is No. 5305, in lined black LMS livery, crossing Ribblehead Viaduct on the Settle & Carlisle route on 1st March 1980. This locomotive and Southern 'King Arthur' 4-6-0 No. 30777 *Sir Lamiel* have been well looked after by Tom Tighe and his team for many years, and indeed No. 5305 ran as recently as 2019 on Vintage Trains' second season of 'The Polar Express'. [Photo: John Whiteley]

A classic pairing in Midland red. The National Railway Museum's Midland 'Compound' 4-4-0 No. 1000 double-headed with LM&SR 'Jubilee' No 5690 *Leander* on several occasions and both looked 'just right' together. The pair are seen here, belching black smoke for the photographers, as they pass Millom. It was *Leander's* excellent and reliable runs on the main line that connected me with Bob Meanley, the locomotive's engineer, together with Graham Campion, its marketing manager. Of course, this led to Bob establishing Tyseley Locomotive Works as we know it today. [PHOTO: JOHN WHITELEY]

Snow covered mountains and icy conditions make for a fine photograph. The Midland red duo No. 1000 and *Leander* storm over Ais Gill on the Settle & Carlisle line on 12th December 1983. [PHOTO: JOHN WHITELEY]

The NRM in York opened in 1975, in the same year as the Stockton & Darlington 150 celebrations. Almost immediately, these two events added exciting and unusual steam locomotives to the main line pool, as Dr John Coiley, David Jenkinson and engineer John Bellwood formed a liberal view about enabling and promoting the use of its collection on the main line and heritage railways. The NRM had been gifted LM&SR 'Coronation' Class 'Pacific' *Duchess of Hamilton* by Sir Billy Butlin and Jenkinson hit on the idea of a '55 Club' to promote and contribute financial assistance to this fine locomotive so it could haul some of BR's 'Cumbrian Mountain Pullman' trains in particular. So, 1960s Metropolitan Cammell First Class Pullman cars *Eagle* and *Emerald* were also put back on the main line, staffed by volunteers and used for fundraising. Here we see the remarkable sight of these two cars being hauled by the NRM's

Midland 'Compound' No. 1000 leaving Marsh Lane Cutting at Neville Hill, Leeds on 7th October 1981. Even more remarkably, the support coach immediately behind the locomotive is L&NWR No. 5155, built as early as 1906. Both Pullman cars were subsequently de-accessioned, with *Emerald* going to David Smith at Carnforth, and *Eagle* eventually joining the Vintage Trains fleet and re-entering main line service in 2021. [PHOTO: JOHN WHITELEY]

The SLOA Pullman set, still in BR blue and grey, are hauled over Kettlesbeck Bridge, near Eldroth, with the snowy Cumbrian mountains behind on 12th December 1981. The motive power, completely out of context in the Northern Fells, is Southern Railway 'Light Pacific' *City of Wells* all splendidly decked out in Golden Arrow regalia. BR initially refused to allow unrebuilt Bulleid 'Pacifics' back onto the main line on account of their unusual chain drive gear but persuasion helped them relent. [PHOTO: JOHN WHITELEY]

A 'Coronation' Class 'Pacific' in her element. No. 6229 Duchess of Hamilton powers over Lunds Viaduct on the Settle & Carlisle line on 10th August 1982. Purchased for preservation by Billy Butlin, she stood on a plinth for many years outside his Minehead holiday camp, until rescued for addition to the National Railway Museum's collection and fortunately returned to main line working order. [PHOTO: JOHN WHITELEY]

The fastest steam locomotive in the world back in action. The NRM permitted its record breaker, the 'A4' Class 'Pacific' No. 4468 *Mallard*, to make just twenty-six runs over a period of five years in order to minimise boiler work to return her to the main line. Here she is seen on 11th October 1986 leaving York running southbound having just passed Holgate Bridge Junction, in a fortuitous juxtaposition being overtaken by one of her successors, a High Speed Train. The HSTs were worthy successors to the 'A4' Class, offically the fastest diesel locomotives in the world but are now largely at the end of their working lives. However, in common with the 'A4s' some fifty-five years previously, in the early 2020s they are about to enjoy an 'Indian Summer' in Scotland, on the lines from Edinburgh and Glasgow to Aberdeen and Inverness. [PHOTO: JOHN WHITELEY]

ABOVE: An unlikely candidate. After enthusiasts had bought a number of steam locomotives direct from BR, the only remaining places to find more was either on plinths at Butlins' Holiday Camps or from Barry scrapyard, where there were some two hundred to choose from. An impossible dream was to rescue the last express steam locomotive ever made by BR in 1954 – the unique No. 71000 *Duke of Gloucester*. However, by the time it arrived in the scrapyard, No. 71000 was bereft of cylinders but, no matter, a dedicated group bought the remains, replaced the cylinders with new and brought her out again on the main line, despite most people saying this was 'mission impossible.' Here, *Duke of Gloucester* storms out of Banbury on the GW Northern main line on 7th April 1990, a route she may well run countless times in the future now being based at Tyseley. [PHOTO: JOHN WHITELEY]

BELOW: GWR single chimneyed 'Castle' Class 4-6-0 No. 5080 *Defiant* tops Hatton Bank on 11th June 1988, on her first main line run in preservation, during which she even reached 80mph! 'The Red Dragon' headboard recalls her days when shedded at Swansea Landore. The circular board in the middle of the two express train lamps read 'Thank you Inner City Partnership & Sandwell College' who funded and aided her restoration in just eighteen months from scrapyard condition, under a hugely successful Community training programme which saw Tyseley return over 800 redundant people to full time employment. [PHOTO: ANDREW BELL]

LEFT: The first steam train on the Great Western main line since the 1960s. No. 6000 *King George V* leads the Severn Valley Railway's BR black liveried No. 7819 *Hinton Manor* on the 'Great Western Limited', seen here approaching Taunton on 7th April 1985. However, the trip was to end in tears with hot boxes on both locomotives, incurring BR's severe displeasure. [PHOTO: JOHN WHITELEY]

BELOW: Severn Valley power on the GW main line. No. 4930 *Hagley Hall* and No. 7819 *Hinton Manor* make a fine sight double-heading past Tavistock Junction after leaving Plymouth on 8th April 1985. Both locomotives had been restored to main line condition having previously resided in the scrapyard at Barry Island for a number of years. *Hagley Hall* had been sent down overnight from the SVR to replace No. 6000 for the return trip; fortunately, No. 7819 had been repaired overnight. [PHOTO: JOHN WHITELEY]

The classic GWR location. Enthusiasts were amazed but delighted when BR.sanctioned steam main line running over the Devon banks and along the sea wall for GW150. This pairing of the Great Western Society's 'Castle' No. 5051 *Drysllwyn Castle* leading the SVR's 'Hall' No. 4930 *Hagley Hall* make a fine sight running by Shell Cove after passing Dawlish on 7th July 1985. [PHOTO: JOHN WHITELEY]

No. 7029 *Clun Castle* climbs from Lostwithiel to Treverrin Tunnel on 6th September 1975, the first steam train in Cornwall since the end of regular steam running. This for me was a perfect trip. A beautiful late summer day and a BR(WR) train in a lovely setting pretty much as authentic as can be. Furthermore, it was a real bonus for us and an unexpected treat. *City of Truro* had, somewhat understandably, been selected for this trip from Plymouth to Truro and return but her overhaul was not completed in time. As *Clun Castle* had performed well during GW150 and we had made good connections with the powers that be arranging the detail of the specials for the event, we were asked to cover the journey. And what a trip – a steady 60mph over the Cornish main line reverse curves with the finale of being the first steam locomotive back over Brunel's famous Saltash Bridge! [PHOTO: JOHN WHITELEY]

Clun Castle again. In contrast to the reports of her attacking Sapperton Bank in spectacular and noisy fashion with the Down workings, No. 7029 here coasts back down the steep grade towards Stroud with the 10.55am 'shuttle' train from Swindon to Gloucester on 27th August 1985. [PHOTO: TIM STEPHENS]

LEFT: *Clun Castle* steams carefully off Isambard Kingdom Brunel's famous Royal Albert Bridge at Saltash on 6th September, 1985 returning the first steam train to traverse the Duchy since 1965 back to Devon.
[PHOTO: A.J. LAMBERT]

BELOW: Double-headed 'Castles' on the Devon banks. No. 7029 *Clun Castle* leads No. 5051 *Drysllwyn Castle* as they storm up Hemmerdon Bank from a standing start at Plymouth on 8th September 1985. 'The Gin Palace' has its rightful place at the head of the train.
[PHOTO: JOHN WHITELEY]

ABOVE: No. 3440 resurrected. *City of Truro* was billed to return to the main line for a second innings in preservation with the Cornish trip to her namesake town in 1985 but restoration was still incomplete. Not to worry, 1986 did see her back on the main line and she is seen here with *King George V* on 24th May near Dorrington, south of Shrewsbury. [PHOTO: JOHN WHITELEY]

BELOW: In 1987, steam returned to the highly scenic Cambrian Coast, promoted by David McIntosh of 'Provincial Railways'. The trips from Machynlleth to Barmouth (and sometimes on to Pwllheli) were extremely popular. Locomotives were drawn from a Severn Valley Railway pool comprising GWR 'Manor' 4-6-0 No. 7819 *Hinton Manor*, LM&SR 'Mickey Mouse' 2-6-0 No. 46443 and BR 'Standard' Class '4' 4-6-0 No. 75069, all authentic locomotives for the route. Here, *Hinton Manor* runs along the sea coast approaching Fairbourne on 26th May 1987. [PHOTO: C.M. WHITEHOUSE]

Clun Castle was also chosen to run between Carmarthen and Swansea in September 1987. InterCity charter train boss David Ward travelled on the train, as he had by now heard of No. 7029's good GW150 performances and he then asked if she might be available for his 'Shakespeare Limited' trains from London to Stratford. She was! No. 7029 is seen here running well through the dunes at Kidwelly. [PHOTO: BOB GREEN]

17. 'THE SHAKESPEARE EXPRESS'

'HSBC Bank was very generous to us and sold us a batch of some sixteen carriages, including vacuum braked Mark 2 TSOs, for the princely sum of £1 the lot. Bob and I split the donation between us!'

Moor Street station's last day in BR service. No. 7029 *Clun Castle* was rostered for the final train out of Birmingham's Moor Street on 26th September 1987. The terminus was slated to follow the demise of the GWR's main Snow Hill station but, very fortunately, was not demolished. The Tyseley team saw to that by holding a public meeting on the closed station as a demonstration and subsequently taking a short term licence from British Rail, with a view to preserving it as a working museum if needs be. Fortunately, it did not have to come to that as the City of Birmingham insisted that the station was preserved as part of Hammerson's redevelopment of the Bullring shopping centre. Moor Street then got really lucky, as Vic Michel, Hammerson's project manager, ensured the buildings and awnings were returned to their 1906 GWR glory as part of the station's reconnection to the network and subsequent use by Chiltern Railways. Nevertheless, it remains a private station today, still owned by Hammersons. [PHOTO: BOB GREEN]

The phone rang. It was Bernard Staite, the 'Supremo' of the Steam Locomotive Operators' Association on the other end. He was responding to our request to run a weekend of 'Shakespeare Express' trains from Birmingham to Stratford-upon-Avon, as part of our proposed contribution to the 150th anniversary celebrations of the Great Western Railway. He briefly told me that our application would be approved on the following basis: we would need to provide two steam locomotives, BR would provide the set of Mark 1 carriages it was having repainted in chocolate and cream for the year's events, we could run as many trains as we liked, the cost would be £16,000 and he wanted to know the answer within the hour. Blimey!

I received this call on a weekday evening early in 1985 and, just as luck would have it, Richard Cadge and I were in the office at Tyseley plotting some diesel charters, which we had got into the

habit of running intermittently. Ordinarily in the evenings the office would be unmanned.

We did some quick sums, consulted a few trustees and then I rang Bernard back and said 'yes'. I think he was a bit taken aback and certainly surprised we had agreed. We duly ran a series of eight trains over one weekend and took £33,000. Job done.

A simple business transaction you may say and, indeed, it was but when put in context, it was little short of remarkable. BR's policy was to run day out trains and not a series of short runs and certainly not to Stratford-upon-Avon with Great Western locomotives. They had long memories. You will have read earlier about our pannier tank No. 7752's exploits on the Stratford line and BR's preference for larger 'Pacific' types to run steam charters. But we were lucky and had the chance to live the dream as it was GW150 year and many previous taboos were about to be broken. We had always thought

ABOVE: The Birmingham spirit prevails again. A public meeting at Earlswood station campaigning against closure of the line, led by F.S. 'Derek' Mayman, a regular commuter from Danzey into Birmingham on the North Warwickshire Line, which was slated by BR for closure, not once but twice. Closure was thwarted at the eleventh hour, fifty-ninth minute by a High Court Order! [PHOTO: C.C. GREEN]

LEFT: 'Milepost 65' with Derek Mayman, the key man who never gave up in what became the successful campaign to save the North Warwickshire Line. A family special train was subsequently always run down the line on his birthday with his age on the headboard! Vintage Trains was pleased to provide the motive power free of charge by way of thanks. Here, Derek is celebrating with his family and friends at Birmingham Moor Street station and with *Clun Castle*. [PHOTO: ALAN WOOD, VINTAGE TRAINS COLLECTION]

that steam trains running between Birmingham and Stratford-upon-Avon would be marketable and now we had the chance to prove our point. We succeeded.

Over the 8th-9th June 1985, we ran eight 'Shakespeare Express' trains, four on Saturday and four on Sunday, all well loaded. We served breakfast, lunch and dinner and added two GWR saloons of our own to the train: Shrewsbury Engineer's Saloon No. 80972 and semi Royal 6-wheeled bogie Saloon No. 9001, which had a fair-sized kitchen. We provided BR(WR) No. 7029 *Clun Castle* and LM&SR 'Jubilee' No. 5593 *Kolhapur*. Sadly, the latter only made the first outward trip on the Saturday, retiring hurt with a hot box, so No. 7029 ran the rest of the weekend's trains all by

herself, which included tender first running to Stratford at up to 60mph. Apart from the 'Jubilee' misfortune, everything else ran like clockwork, together with a large and well attended depot open weekend to boot. The weekend's events gave us a true sense of purpose for the future, as our dreams and ideas had just been proven to work. Moreover, *Clun Castle* went on to run many more charter trains successfully for the GW150 celebrations, including Gloucester-Swindon 'shuttles' up Sapperton Bank, double-headed 'Castle' trips along the GW main line from Bristol to Plymouth and the first steam train over Brunel's Royal Albert Bridge to Truro in Cornwall since the demise of regular steam.

Having run the 'Shakespeare Express' weekend once, we clearly wanted to do so again and so we did on several weekends over the coming years but only as 'one off' charters. BR were still not willing to entertain a regular series of trains but, gradually, the ice was thawing in other parts of the country, particularly in Scotland where BR promoted 'The Jacobite' itself from Fort William to Mallaig.

We had one final fling in April 1990 before the advent of privatisation, which took advantage of *King Edward I* returning to the main line following its rebuild from scrapyard condition. The 'King' and No. 5080 *Defiant* ran the eight weekend trains without a hitch. They were heavy trains too, with the SLOA Pullman set being used together with our two GWR saloons again, sadly for the last time as they are wooden bodies carriages and increasing regulations were to prohibit such vehicles from being used for passengers. One bonus resulted in that each train was banked out of Stratford station for half a mile or so by the locomotive used for the incoming journey. So, by the time privatisation of the railways arrived with the Railways Act 1993, we had run four weekends of 'Shakespeare Express' trains and were itching for more.

In the early days of BR's privatisation, it was not entirely clear if or how steam train charter running would be continued, as many innovations were introduced and discussed generally within the embryo privatisation programme. Somewhat fortunately, as a commercial finance lawyer, I was heavily involved in several transactions as they came out of BR's HQ and so got to know many senior players in the newly-created industry. We began to learn the rules and contracts which would become relevant.

A simple letter to the Office of the Rail Regulator produced a response seeking a meeting to discuss the concept. A team from the ORR came up to Birmingham, intrigued at the prospect of private owners of historic machinery wanting to run them on the national network. '*No problem*', they opined. The ORR would welcome new operators of any traction, provided it complied with Network Rail's Group Standards (or any derogation). Furthermore, Network Rail were quite prepared to discuss track access agreements directly, even if steam trains were operated by a third party. Centro, the local authority transport body in the West Midlands, were also prepared to put 'Shakespeare Express' times in their regional time table. We learned that we could run (or have run for us) open access trains, provided we promoted thirteen in any one six month time table period.

In the event, we probably over engineered our thinking, as it proved relatively simple to contract with the former Rail Express Systems (RES) which had, at the outset of privatisation, been included within the sales of the freight businesses to the new American-owned English, Welsh & Scottish Railways, led by

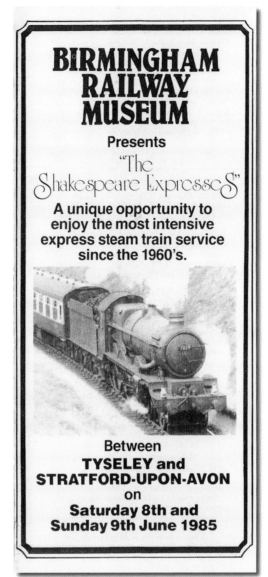

The promotional leaflet for the first weekend of 'The Shakespeare Express' trains, run as part of the GW150 celebrations.

Ed Burkhardt. It also proved pretty easy to 'bump into' Ed himself at a conference and invite him to see our steam locomotives and workshop for himself, which he duly accepted.

Meanwhile, Bob Meanley had been busying himself and his new Tyseley Locomotive Workshop team getting our train ready. He led a team of young engineers, including his son Alastair, in completing the rebuild from Barry condition of our GWR 'Hall' Class 4-6-0 No. 4983 A*lbert Hall* to main line condition and acquiring a train to run behind her. We had begun No. 4983's restoration some while ago but put her on one side for, at that time, BR were not in favour of operating Class '5' power classification locomotives and certainly not ones with wide and low hanging cylinders which restricted route availability somewhat. However, the new privatisation regime allowed us to run any traction type we wished so long as it was compliant. A two-cylinder 'Hall' Class locomotive would be ideal for 'The Shakespeare Express', as the line between Birmingham and Stratford-upon-Avon had been designed to suit GWR types of course and No. 4983 was the cheapest locomotive to put through the works in readiness. *Clun Castle* was then still being used on public driving experience courses at Tyseley depot and, in any case, unfortunately had one driving wheel tyre below regulation size, so was limited to depot and private railway use for a while.

Remarkably, during her rebuild, we found out that No. 4983 was not *Albert Hall* at all, or at least not completely so. It transpired that she had been in Swindon Works for overhaul alongside No. 4965 *Rood Ashton Hall* and that both locomotives were combined under the number No. 4983, but the main frames, cylinders, wheels and motion belonged to No. 4965 and so that is what our 'Hall' became.

We also needed a train of carriages of course. HSBC Bank was very generous to us and sold us a batch of some sixteen carriages, including vacuum braked Mark 2 TSOs, for the princely sum of £1 the lot. Bob and I split the donation between us! Vacuum brakes were no use to a 'ROSCO' Bank and parting with them to us saved storage charges. Now we had our own train of carriages as well. We were in business.

A little later on we were also able to acquire the SLOA Pullman car set too. A rather brazen call was made to the then CEO of the new company established to own and operate the famous *Flying Scotsman*. This company was clearly heading for insolvency (which is sadly where it ended up) but it owned the SLOA Pullman car set and we could do with some Pullmans to embellish the 'Standard' Class ex-HSBC carriages in providing a dining car service. The CEO sold the whole set to us and we arranged for its collection and transfer to Tyseley for assessment.

ABOVE: LM&SR 'Jubilee' 4-6-0 No. 5593 *Kolhapur* makes a return to the main line sharing the June 1986 summer weekend of 'Shakespeare Express' trains with *Clun Castle*. Here she is seen approaching the Stratford Canal aqueduct shortly before Bearley Junction, on her way to Stratford-upon-Avon. [PHOTO: VINTAGE TRAINS' COLLECTION]

BELOW: No. 5080 *Defiant* threads its way past Henley-in-Arden as it heads to Stratford-upon-Avon with 'The Shakespeare Express' during Easter 1990.

Over the Easter weekend in 1990, No. 5080 *Defiant* made one of its relatively few main line runs to date on 'The Shakespeare Express' trains operated on 15th and 16th April. Unnoticed by many, she used No. 7029's tender that weekend, which can be seen in BR livery behind the locomotive. When No. 5080 had been taken over to BR's Traction Maintenance Depot at Tyseley for her fitness to run exam a couple of days before the trip, her own tender was derailed and damaged an axlebox. There was no time for repairs so little alternative but to utilise No. 7029's tender which all worked out fine. In the days following the trip, SLOA Chairman Dick Hardy rang me to scold me for using an unapproved vehicle on BR (as No. 7029 was not then registered for main line use). I accepted the ticking off but Dick then complimented me for being a railwayman and ensuring the show went on! The train is seen here heading away from Stratford past the site of what is now Stratford Parkway station. [PHOTO: JOHN WHITELEY]

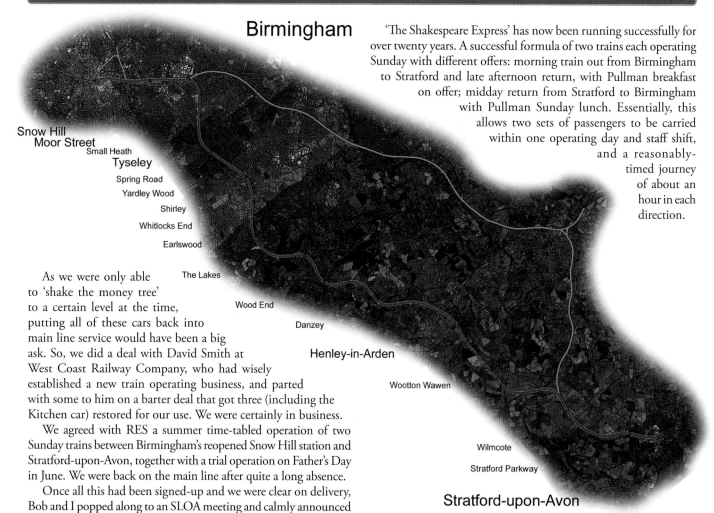

Birmingham

Snow Hill
Moor Street
Small Heath
Tyseley
Spring Road
Yardley Wood
Shirley
Whitlocks End
Earlswood
The Lakes
Wood End
Danzey
Henley-in-Arden
Wootton Wawen
Wilmcote
Stratford Parkway

Stratford-upon-Avon

'The Shakespeare Express' has now been running successfully for over twenty years. A successful formula of two trains each operating Sunday with different offers: morning train out from Birmingham to Stratford and late afternoon return, with Pullman breakfast on offer; midday return from Stratford to Birmingham with Pullman Sunday lunch. Essentially, this allows two sets of passengers to be carried within one operating day and staff shift, and a reasonably-timed journey of about an hour in each direction.

The route map of the Shakespeare Line. [ROBIN COOMBES]

As we were only able to 'shake the money tree' to a certain level at the time, putting all of these cars back into main line service would have been a big ask. So, we did a deal with David Smith at West Coast Railway Company, who had wisely established a new train operating business, and parted with some to him on a barter deal that got three (including the Kitchen car) restored for our use. We were certainly in business.

We agreed with RES a summer time-tabled operation of two Sunday trains between Birmingham's reopened Snow Hill station and Stratford-upon-Avon, together with a trial operation on Father's Day in June. We were back on the main line after quite a long absence.

Once all this had been signed-up and we were clear on delivery, Bob and I popped along to an SLOA meeting and calmly announced our 'Shakespeare Express' operation. The room full of locomotive owners went quiet. Would Tyseley really bounce back and especially with such an audacious plan to run a series of open access working time-tabled steam trains at our own revenue risk? We would and, what's more, we did!

For the Easter 1990 April weekend of 'Shakespeare Express' trains, we were privileged to be able to use No. 6024 *King Edward I*, then based at the Buckinghamshire Railway Centre. No. 6024 had been moved to Tyseley so it could undergo main line trials with us and, in return, it was the star attraction over the weekend, performing very well.
[PHOTO: JOHN WHITELEY]

No. 6024 *King Edward I* bursts out of Wood End Tunnel whilst working one of the April Easter 1990 series of 'The Shakespeare Express' trains. [PHOTO: JOHN WHITELEY]

No. 4965 *Rood Ashton Hall* heads 'The Shakespeare Express' towards Hatton Junction in 1999, the first year of the regular summer Sunday running of the service. EWS' Traction Inspector Gareth Jones was 'riding shotgun' on the footplate – a far cry from his induction to steam on the pioneer preserved railway, the Talyllyn!

It has always been thought that this type of short haul, regular operation would most probably become 'the last man standing' for main line steam trains for several reasons.

The passenger market for those who remember express steam trains and seek to ride for nostalgia is dwindling and newer generations will not necessarily travel for its own sake. Millennials, in particular, are renowned for seeking experiences and even my own children tell me that they will seek such on websites, for which they allow about seven seconds to be convinced of an offering!

Also, the national railway network has been catering for more and more trains, running at faster speeds with shorter headways, none of which have been calculated with the steam locomotive in mind. It is all very well saying that steam can run fast, and indeed it can, but the faster it runs the more wear and tear occurs. Additionally, the provision of water, fuel and servicing facilities have to be considered.

'The Shakespeare Express' is well suited to meet these points. It operates within an area where over ten million people can reach it within an hour. It runs between two key centres: Birmingham, the nation's second city and a growing tourist centre in its own right, particularly for business leisure and international tourists; and Shakespeare's Stratford-upon-Avon, which is on everyone's bucket list. Furthermore, HS2 is planned to arrive in Birmingham at Curzon Street station, alongside Moor Street station where 'The Shakespeare Express' stops. And, if that were not enough, every station along the recently rebranded Shakespeare Line has its own story to tell: Birmingham City football at Small Heath; manufacturing and 'The Workshop of the World' at Tyseley;

Tolkein's Shire at Spring Road and Hall Green; the Bus Museum at Wythall; lakes and walking at Earlswood; Wood End Tunnel; the picturesque black and white half-timbered village at Henley in Arden; and Shakespeare's Stratford. So there is much yet to be developed by 'station destinations' in their own right. Already, in association with West Midlands Trains and the Shakespeare Line Promotion Group, all the stations along the route have been adopted by community groups. So now we can begin to tell all these stories and involve local areas in the railway line in general.

To provide some future focus for these imaginative ideas, Vintage Trains has formed an alliance with the local authority body responsible for transport, West Midlands Rail Executive, to develop the Shakespeare Line as Britain's premier heritage main line railway in conjunction with the commuter traffic. Pre-coronavirus pandemic, over three million passengers travelled over the Shakespeare Line annually and the footfall at Moor Street station was seven million people. Even if not all these people return to commuter rail travel post-pandemic, the opportunity remains to encourage them to travel on 'The Shakespeare Express'.

Network Rail are also supportive of the concept of developing The Shakespeare Express service and are actively assisting with developing working timetable paths for the future so that the opportunity exists for the future to grasp. With the potential to develop the passenger market and also provide entertainment trains coupled with the prowess of Tyseley Locomotive Works and its close proximity to the Shakespeare Line, there is every reason to expect a good future for main line steam in Birmingham.

No. 5043 *Earl of Mount Edgcumbe* storms past the now demolished Henley-in-Arden Signal Box (it was to close on 23rd October, six weeks after this picture was taken) with a return 'Shakespeare Express' working on 11th September 2010. It has become a tradition for the last train of the summer season to be 'Castle' hauled but it was then unusual to see the return working also on the Shakespeare Line. This was due to engineering works on the main line through Solihull, which is the usual Sunday return route. Saturday paths have now been developed for 'The Shakespeare Express' and when introduced, scheduled to be in 2022, these trains are expected to run both ways over the Shakespeare Line. [PHOTO: MARTIN CREESE]

No. 5043 *Earl of Mount Edgcumbe* runs into Platform 4 on the fast line at Tyseley station with the afternoon 'The Shakespeare Express' on 10th July 2010. The station remains more or less complete, with all its GWR station buildings and platform awnings, and is shortly to undergo a refurbishment by Network Rail, with the assistance of the Railway Heritage Trust and a Department of Transport community grant. It will be branded as 'The Gateway to the Shakespeare Line' and, in common with all the stations along the route, it has been adopted by volunteers, in this case the Friends of Vintage Trains. In the future, the community will be able to help run their own stations. [PHOTO: MARTIN CREESE]

ABOVE: From time to time guest locomotives are invited to haul 'The Shakespeare Express'. Here, No. 4953 *Pitchford Hall* joins the GW main line at Hatton North Junction on its way back to Birmingham on 3rd September 2006. No. 4953 was rebuilt at Tyseley Locomotive Works and ran several excursions double-headed with Tyseley Collection's own 'Hall', *Rood Ashton Hall*. [PHOTO: MARTIN CREESE]

BELOW: On 12th June 2019, Andy Street, the Mayor for the West Midlands, launches the alliance between West Midlands Rail Executive and Vintage Trains to develop the Shakespeare Line as Britain's premier heritage main line railway. No. 7029 *Clun Castle* steamed to Birmingham's city centre Moor Street terminus station specially for the occasion. [PHOTO: ROBIN COOMBES]

Tyseley Trio 1: At the very end of steam at Tyseley on 7th November 1966, three pannier tanks still remained, retained to work the Halesowen Basin shunt: No's 4646, 4696 and 9774. No. 4646 was sent to Wrexham's Croes Newydd shed in 1966 in exchange for their No's 9610 and 9630, brought down to run the SLS 'Last Panniers' special train that year. No. 4646 was the last but one GWR locomotive ever to see service for British Railways. Which of the five panniers are in this picture is open to conjecture but a reasoned supposition is (L to R) No's 9610, 4696 and 9630 – the two outer panniers are cleaner and so could be the two which hauled the special; also, the right-hand engine has the inspection cover to her cylinders lifted – No. 9630 blew her cylinder cover on the special, an ignominious end. [Photo: C.M. Whitehouse]

18. A TALE OF MORE TANK ENGINES

'The first steam-hauled mixed train in eons!'

Portrait of a pannier. Immaculate No. 7752 stands on the coaling stage embankment at Tyseley in 1973, shortly after being repainted in authentic GWR livery for the first time in preservation. [PHOTO: C.M. WHITEHOUSE]

Tyseley depot has always been the home of Great Western Railway pannier tanks. Shunting, trip freights, goods work and even passenger trains on the Great Western were the preserve of these plucky, useful and efficient 0-6-0PTs, right up to the very end of steam at Tyseley.

Arthur Camwell organised a 'Farewell to GWR Panniers Tanks' railtour on Sunday 11th September 1966, featuring double-headed 0-6-0PTs. But the powers that be clearly did not think the TYS panniers were quite up to the job of a passenger train and so organised for No's 9610 and 9630 to be brought down from Wrexham for the trip. These two plucky engines gallivanted around the region, reaching 63mph near Henley in Arden and charged up the local banks, including Old Hill and Hatton. The last mentioned was to be their demise for, almost as soon as they had breasted the summit, No. 9630 blew a cylinder cover and had to be removed from the train at Lapworth, leaving her twin No. 9610 to soldier on to Snow Hill, including hauling eight carriages up the 1 in 47 bank in the tunnel!

On 7th November 1966, Tyseley depot closed to steam, with the only working locomotive remaining resident being *Clun Castle*, thus providing continuity for steam since 1908. However, once

the BR steam ban had come and gone, and the newly installed preservationists had taken a lease of the remaining area of the steam depot and built a new workshop, a new opportunity presented itself in 1973.

London Transport had continued to use GWR pannier tanks beyond the end of steam on British Rail, so that the type actually became the last main line steam locomotives to be used. On 6th June 1971, Class '57XX' No. 7752, renumbered as LT No. L94, hauled the last London Transport engineer's train from Moorgate to Neasden and starred on the BBC 10 o'clock news and in the national newspapers. Sister No. L90 (ex-No. 7760) coupled onto the train at Neasden and drew it back into the yard and that was that, apart from the now-famous 'Farewell to Steam' depot open day on 6th June 1971. LT put its last three pannier tanks up for sale by tender: No. 7752 was reputed to be in good order; No. 5764 (LT No. L95) also so but with a loose driving wheel tyre; No. 7760 had a slight bulge in her firebox.

PBW decided he would like to buy No. 7752 and bid slightly over the odds to secure her (always worth it in the long run). No. 5764 was bought by the Severn Valley Railway and No. 7760 was sold to a scrap merchant. When PBW heard of this outcome, he

Top: GWR pannier tanks No's 9630 and 9610, from Wrexham Croes Newydd shed, take the junction for the North Warwickshire Line at Tyseley with the SLS run 'Pannier Farewell' trip on Sunday 11th September 1967. [Photo: C.C. Green]

Centre: A pannier at Stratford-upon-Avon. No. 7752 hauled a four car special for the Institute of Mechanical Engineers from Birmingham to Stratford on 9th May 1973. The leading two carriages are First Class Pullman *Ione* and Third Class Pullman car No. 54. [Photo: C.M. Whitehouse]

Bottom: Main line mixed train! No. 7752 stands with empty coaching stock and a 'Fruit D' van in Tyseley carriage sidings, preparatory to her first general public main line runs on 13th May 1973. The van was added to the train to take coal and tools to Moor Sreet for the day. All done without main line certificates of approvals and the van's axleboxes were simply checked over before being attached to the train, just as it would have been in BR days! [Photo: C.M. Whitehouse]

promptly drew £1,500 in cash from his bank (about half what No. 7752 had sold for) and went to visit the scrapman. This visit resulted in us having twin pannier tanks. Both were also successfully added to the 1972 list of approved main line steam engines!

No. 7752 was delivered in working order, whilst No. 7760 would take a little longer to fix. No. 7752 went straight into depot service and led the charge for a week of school visits, then was promptly repainted into GWR green. In 1973, the tank engine even ventured out onto the main line, not once but three times. Once for an Institute of Mechanical Engineers' trip to Stratford, once for three passenger runs in a day from Moor Street and once for a TV film. It was the Moor Street trips which were to confine her to base for several years …

The IMEchE were intrigued with the propaganda emitting from the new occupiers at Tyseley: a new 20th century steam workshop was under construction to safeguard the future of main line steam. This had to be seen and what better way to experience the outcome than take a steam trip. So we organised a trip to Stratford using two of the three 1930s Pullman cars acquired from the Dart Valley Railway (and subsequently sold to the Venice Simplon Orient Express). No. 7752 acquitted herself well on the trip down the then-threatened North Warwickshire Line to Stratford, even achieving 60mph!

Once proven, we set out to run her

Tyseley Trio: 2. On 26th August 1999, all three of Tyseley's panniers, No's 7752, 7760 and 9600 were in steam together. [Photo: C.M. Whitehouse]

on passenger excursions: indeed the first-ever one was down what was to become the Shakespeare Line in modern parlance and the precursor to the subsequently-developed 'Shakespeare Express'. Three return trips were planned from Moor Street to Stratford on 13th May 1973 and seven Mark 1 carriages were used, such was the popularity of an unusual excursion opportunity.

Even after the return to steam following the three year ban, the methodology of the operation of privately owned steam locomotives on BR was pretty well just as it had always been. The charter was ordered and BR ran the train and staffed the engine. PBW was used to all this of course; shades of 1964 with No's 4555, 1420 and 6435. No. 7752 was allowed to run to the Tyseley carriage sidings to fetch the stock for the train and, moreover, we even took a GWR 'Fruit D' long wheelbase 4-wheeled wagon with us full of coal for reloading at Moor Street. The first steam-hauled mixed train in eons and no one asked to see main line certificates in those days!

On the first return trip up Wilmcote Bank from Stratford, No. 7752 struggled to a stand. There was a faulty brake on one of the carriages which leaked on (although BR subsequently blamed the engine). This caused us to lose time, so I suggested a unilateral change of plan. Why not divert the second train to Knowle & Dorridge? It would be a shorter run and surely the passengers would not mind too much, and that way we could make up time and run the third trip to the original schedule. PBW agreed, BR were 'informed' and Control made the switch. We can still recall the faces of the photographers standing on Spring Road Bridge, just after Tyseley Junction, as No. 7752 sped by on the main line rather than take a right turn towards Spring Road station! The third trip ran to Stratford as planned. It all proved jolly good fun.

BR HQ was not amused at these antics. We had arranged a

second hurrah a few weeks later to repeat the jolly and these trains were now even more heavily booked. Enthusiasts loved the idea of a main line pannier – but BR had other ideas. No. 7752 was not to be permitted to 'go'. And so it proved on the day. Undaunted, Chief Engineer, Jim Kent had L&NER 'V2' 2-6-2 No. 4771 *Green Arrow* steamed (she had just arrived from Norwich for her first run in preservation to Didcot a month later) and substituted, running tender first in the outward direction. All went very well – but BR HQ was not amused at these antics either. Apart from a couple of runs to Didcot, via Stratford, made by *Clun Castle*, in the ensuing years, it was not to be until 1985 that we were permitted to go to Stratford-upon-Avon again.

BR refused to allow any more tank locomotives to run on the main line, so we did not progress the overhaul of No. 7760 for some time. However, PBW 'fell' for No. 9600, ex-NCB Merthyr Vale Colliery, to make up a trio of pannier tanks, all of which would come in useful but later. For the next twenty years, No. 7752 was confined to Tyseley and private lines, although BR did relent and allowed it to venture to Shildon for Stockton & Darlington 150 in 1975, as they wanted some reliable small engines to run the passenger shuttle there. Plucky No. 7752 ran all the way to York and back using *Flying Scotsman*'s second tender as a water carrier.

By this time I had begun my legal career in London and was lodging with Donald Wilson of Kent & East Sussex fame. He quite understandably taunted me with requests to hire No. 7752, all of which were declined as we needed her at our depot. But to keep Donald quiet, I did say that when we had two working panniers, we would consider the loan.

When I later let slip that No. 7760 would be in working order once more, quick as a flash, Donald reminded me of my earlier

ABOVE: Reincarnated No. L60 (actually No. 7760) makes a spectacular departure from Rothley station on the Great Central Railway on 30th July 1993 with an engineer's train, recreating the sort of work GWR pannier tanks undertook when on the London Transport system. [PHOTO: MALCOLM RANIERI]

RIGHT: On 4th October 1998 Councillor Brian Bird, the head of the City of Birmingham's Leisure Services and a former Saltley-based locomotive fireman, christens No. 9600 at Tyseley on her return to service. Brian Bird was very instrumental in the early days of Tyseley's preservation, in helping secure a lease on the depot and saving Moor Street station from demolition when the Bullring shopping centre redevelopment was mooted.
[PHOTO: C.M. WHITEHOUSE]

With the encroaching vegetation and the semaphore signals in the background giving the appearance of a preserved line, No. 7760 runs into Cannock on 21st May 2000, with the second of a series of three trains from Walsall. [PHOTO: C.M. WHITEHOUSE]

comment and so it was that No. 7752 entered the hire circuit on private railways but not before I had spent a day driving her under supervison on the K&ESR! No. 7752 (and indeed No. 7760) ventured all over the country: Dorset, the Cotswolds and the East and West Midlands on hire. No. 7760 even returned to London Transport, painted in their lined red livery, to double-head with the Quainton pannier on the Metropolitan; that was to prove PBW's last footplate ride, sadly.

The prospects for the Tyseley panniers all changed following privatisation of the railways. Provided one had a traction unit which complied with Network Rail Group Standards (or appropriate derogations), it could be used on the national network. So, once *Rood Ashton Hall* was in service, Tyseley Locomotive Works turned its attention to No. 9600, to finish off its overhaul started many years before. On 26th August 1999, No. 9600 was turned out for an evening trial trip to Stratford, painted in Paddington carriage shunter lined black. Strictly unauthentic for No. 9600 but a livery several of her sisters wore in London and, arguably, more attractive than plain black.

Just as for all the pannier tank excursions in the past, No.

9600 on the main line proved a hit. This 'go anywhere' engine was soon clocking up the miles around the Midlands, including to Wolverhampton High Level on some evening beer trips for enthusiasts. In order to increase the revenue on this type of excursion, No. 7760 was returned to main line service too and double-headed panniers became the norm, after the tank engine also ran a proving trip to Stratford and then three trips in one day from Walsall to Cannock.

No's 7760 and 9600 (and subsequently No. 7752 in LT red as L94) double-headed up all the Birmingham hills and also out to Burton on Trent. No. 9600 ventured further afield to Devon and Princes Risborough and both acted as banking engines up Old Hill and the Lickey Incline. No. 7760 took the banker plunge first with two ascents of the Lickey, pushing 'Halls' up twice in one day and then making a curtain bow 'light engine' trip before returning to Tyseley. We found that just by running two such double-headed trips a year, the panniers paid for themselves, on the basis their certification work was largely done as a labour of love by the works staff, mainly in their 'spare' time. Long may they continue to provide something a little different on the main line.

A timeless quintessential English scene, as No. 9600 passes a cricket match underway at Bledlow, on a charter from Princes Risborough on 3rd July 2010. [PHOTO: ROBIN COOMBES]

Departing Leamington Spa for Nuneaton, pannier tanks No's 7760 and 9600 are silhouetted crossing the River Leam on 30th December 2001. For a few years, Vintage Trains ran a Christmas holiday steam train which was always popular. [Photo: Andrew Bell]

LEFT: The improbable continues. Access to Birmingham by any route requires hill climbing and the Lickey Incline is the steepest sustained main line climb in Great Britain, having a gradient of 1 in 37. Steam trains have routinely been banked from Bromsgrove to Blackwell since the line first opened in 1840, often by locomotives especially built just for this task, such as the 0-10-0 known as 'Big Bertha' built by the Midland Railway in 1919. In BR days, ex-MR 'Jinty' 0-6-0Ts took over and then, when the line was transferred to the Western Region, by GWR designed '94XX' Class 0-6-0 pannier tanks and even regularly by Class '9F' 2-10-0s. Here an earlier design of pannier tank, gutsy No. 9600 from the Tyseley stable, banks LM&SR 'Pacific' No. 6201 *Princess Elizabeth* up the incline on a Vintage Trains' charter on 29th May 2010. The last ever steam engine to perform banking duties under BR was No. 6947 *Helmingham Hall*. [PHOTO: ROBIN COOMBES]

BELOW: Panniers at night. No. 7752 in London Transport red livery as No. L94, together with No. 9600, stand at Worcester during a hill climbing excursion around the Midlands on 3rd November 2012. [PHOTO: MATT SPENCER]

One of the early 'foreign' residents to be based at Tyseley in the privatisation regime was Andrew Naish's 'Merchant Navy' Bulleid 'Pacific' No. 35005 *Canadian Pacific*, seen here on Gisburn Viaduct on 29th May 1999. Rebuilt 'Merchant Navy' locomotives were never painted in BR's experimental blue livery of course but Andrew liked it that way and it was his locomotive. When he later sold it, he declared he had made a slight profit of a few pounds from his ownership of No. 35005, very possibly one of the few preservationists who can say that. [PHOTO: JOHN WHITELEY]

19. OPEN ACCESS

'Now, any steam locomotive was permitted to run on the main line,
provided it was repaired and maintained to the requisite standard, and was gauge friendly.'

No. 6024 *King Edward 1* leaving Appleby on the Settle & Carlisle line on 14th March 1998. This picture rather underlines the point about the regulatory open access regime allowing change and really opening up the steam railtour market to all comers anywhere. British Rail would not have allowed a 'King' to operate over this route in the period from 1972 to privatisation – although, of course a 'Castle' did in both 1967 and for the Locomotive Exchanges in 1925. [PHOTO: JOHN WHITELEY]

Nearly everything changed with the Railways Act, 1993. British Rail was torn asunder. A new track authority was formed and initially sold on the stock market as Railtrack plc but Government later realised the stupidity of that decision – what right-minded country would sell its essential infrastructure, especially when it required so much capital improvement which was, in reality, only fundable by Government? So, investors lost much of their money when Railtrack was tipped into insolvency and recreated initially as an 'off-balance sheet' replacement called Network Rail. With ever increasing infrastructure renewal costs, this entity eventually became 'on-balance sheet', which meant effective nationalisation by another means. Great Britain plc was stuck with paying for the upgrading costs of its ancient railway infrastructure.

Passenger services were franchised out but the basis of this changed so many times over the ensuing thirty years that it was difficult to keep track. Sometimes the franchises were simply management contracts to run a social service, sometimes they were subsidised passenger train performance specifications, sometimes they required private operators to pay a premium (none of those lasted very long, as everyone overpromised) and just one or two, like

Chiltern Railways were, more sensibly, long term contracts requiring the private company to improve and extend infrastructure and run a better service. But in railway history, thirty years is a long time and changes to design and ownerships were frequent.

Some services were simply sold to the highest bidder – train manufacture and maintenance, infrastructure and freight. With the sale of the freight companies also went the ability to operate steam locomotives on the main line: the steam operating safety case. Americans Wisconsin Central entered the fray and scooped all three heavy freight offerings (the freight business had been artificially split by British Rail prior to but in anticipation of privatisation), together with the Rail Express Systems parcels business (with the steam safety case) and amalgamated them into English, Welsh & Scottish Railways. None of the passenger franchises included a steam safety case or subsequently developed one. British Rail were effectively out of the steam business again, as well as being out of any business.

A guiding principle of rail privatisation was 'open access'. In essence, provided an organisation could obtain a licence to operate (by having fit and proper people, a safety management

Another Great Western 4-6-0 in the North of England, No. 5972 *Olton Hall* runs between Hellifield and Carlisle at Selside on 4th December 1999. No. 5972 is owned by David Smith, who is based at Carnforth and became the first owner of privately preserved steam locomotives to succeed in gaining an operating licence, subsequently running countrywide, including the most successful, 'The Jacobite', a regular operation from Fort William to Mallaig. It was that route, and in particular the Glenfinnan Viaduct, which featured in the Harry Potter movies together with No. 5972, now better known to an extremely wide audience as maroon-liveried *Hogwarts Castle*. [PHOTO: JOHN WHITELEY]

system and requisite insurance), it could operate trains anywhere with appropriate track, station and depot access agreements and qualifying traction and rolling stock. Steam was permitted providing it was maintained and managed pursuant to Network Rail Group Standards and an appropriate maintenance policy. Of course, it also had to fit within the loading gauge (the space envelope between the tracks, stations and structures). Steam was able to squeeze through the eye of the needle as long as it operated within these parameters. The world was about to become steam's oyster once again.

All this was immensely interesting and useful to me as a commercial finance lawyer with a great interest in railways. My law firm became even more interested in me, especially as we represented Asea Brown Boveri (who manufactured trains) and Via Générale de Transport (who ran railway and metro services in France). It was rather like being a pig in the brown stuff, especially as no one in the early days had any practical experience of what privatisation meant. 'Big wig' City lawyers had dreamed up a complex contractual matrix based on the utility sector, which really did not suit railways very well, as trains run best on an integrated command and control system. Inventing a contractual matrix instead often meant two people doing one person's job, as there were now so many interfaces between infrastructure, operation, systems and trains that 'each side' needed its own teams when previously one would do. But, for a lawyer, this was heaven. All contracts needed specifications on who would do what, with lots of 'boiler plate' for when things went wrong. All this was exacerbated by the introduction of private sector insurance to the risk analysis and also independent regulation of nearly everything (except rolling stock leasing). These changes were

brought home very heavily indeed at the Ladbrook Grove disaster, when a Thames Trains Turbo multiple unit ran into a Great Western High Speed Train just outside Paddington. Quite apart from the loss of life and the terrible mess of mangled steel and aluminium, the new contractual and risk regime meant that sorting out all the issues would take months when, before, British Rail would simply have accepted responsibility, cleared up the mess and carried on.

What has all this got to do with main line steam and Tyseley's locomotive collection you may well ask? Well quite a lot.

Privatisation would change the approach to railway operation in our country completely and many of the previous arrangements would simply evaporate, almost overnight. No longer would any 'friendly arrangements' or 'locomotive type preferences' avail in relation to running steam charters. This was advantageous to us. No longer would 'Pacific' or Class '8' powerful locomotives necessarily hog the charters.

I met some very interesting and useful people and found myself quite willingly swept up in the forces of change, which not only assisted my career and the prospects of my firm but also took me to far flung foreign parts (such as Africa and Asia) following my clients.

Immersion in the new system and meeting the new people was to prove very useful to Tyseley but we also allowed the time for all this new information and contacts to sink in and develop before we used them to advantage. Sometimes, it is better to be the second or third mover.

In any case, Tyseley was then in no position to run its steam locomotives on the main line. Although *Clun Castle* had had a good innings in the '80s, sadly one driving wheel tyre had

Steam on the Royal Train! It does not get much better than this. No 6233 *Duchess of Sutherland* has just passed Horton in Ribblesdale on 22nd March 2005, hauling the Royal Train with HRH The Prince of Wales on board. The crimson-liveried 'Pacific' was the first steam locomotive in private preservation to haul the Royal Train, with Queen Elizabeth II on board during her Golden Jubilee year in 2002. [PHOTO: JOHN WHITELEY]

succumbed to *anno domini* and was a millimetre or so below the minimum radii for main line work, so she was effectively confined to depot or private lines. *Kolhapur* needed boiler work. *Defiant* was now active and, indeed, in one good year in the late 1980s we ran all three locomotives in the same year. But the Government's employment community programme, which we had husbanded to help redevelop our Tyseley depot and improve our locomotive and rolling stock collection, as well as retrain over eight hundred formerly unemployed artisans, had come to an end. The resulting redundancies had severely damaged our bank balance.

Furthermore, the upgrading of the Inter City and 'Flying Scotsman Enterprises' charter businesses, in BR times, had largely ruled out Great Western 4-6-0s, not least for political reasons but also due to their restricted route availability when much of the main line steam action moved northwards.

So, for a while, we settled into hiring locomotives out to private railways and running driving experience courses for the public at Tyseley. So successful was the latter that we did deals with the Battlefield Railway and later the Great Central Railway to offer experiences on their lines as well. But whilst that was a short term win, it was curtailed long term as those lines, and others, simply climbed on that band wagon. Nevertheless, we did have *Clun Castle*, *Defiant*, *Kolhapur*, panniers No's 7752 and 7760, and two industrials – *Henry*, a Hawthorn Leslie 0-4-0ST, and *Cadbury No. 1*, an Avonside 0-4-0T – in operation, which was not bad and they all brought in hire fees.

We also got to know Graham Oliver, then Managing Director of the Great Central Railway, through the good offices of Bob Meanley, who 'turned up' at Tyseley looking for something to do after the LM&SR 'Jubilee' 4-6-0 *Leander* had been sold by its owners Messrs Clark and Ford, the GCR's guiding minds. Bob had managed the engineering and operation of *Leander* and very well too, as this

locomotive was often in operation and found consistently reliable.

I was first introduced to Bob on a *Leander*-hauled Settle & Carlisle trip by Graham Campion, the Commercial Manager for the locomotive. I found Bob and his wife, Maureen, a delightful couple, bunkered down in their support coach with their one year old son called Alastair. Bob can talk for England of course but very interestingly and, for some reason or other we soon fell into discussing manufacturing locomotives. PBW, some friends and I were members of something called the 'Grand Junction Club', a hedonistic dining society of railway minded individuals, and during one very boozy champagne lunch at Viscount Garnock's house, we had fallen to discuss making an L&NWR 'George V' 4-4-0, one of PBW's favourites and a certain missing link in the ranks of preserved locomotives. But Bob said why not make a 'Bloomer'? A what?

Co-incidentally, Dick Hardy was then the very sensible and practical Chairman of SLOA and at one dinner we were discussing this ridiculous idea when Dick declared that there were still three 'Bloomer' original tenders in existence, as water carriers: two at Nantwich and one at Machynlleth. So we began to make a 'Bloomer', or rather Bob did. This brought him into the fold at Tyseley as PBW, using his 'grant speak', found nearly enough (but sadly not quite enough) money to make one. A 'Bloomer', by the way, is the nickname for what was a trend-setting single-wheeler steam locomotive built for the L&NWR in the 1850s. The 'Bloomer' represented a landMark 1n locomotive design as, 170 years ago, this locomotive type, a 2-2-2 with 7ft diameter driving wheels, was pulling trains between London and Birmingham at speeds up to 70mph in just two hours, door to door. It was the 'Concorde' project of its day.

The Bloomer's design was at the forefront of technology, with such innovations as a high pressure 120psi boiler, superior valve design, patented firebox designed to run on coal not coke and a hopper grate for removing ash and clinker.

The scenery in this picture shows why 'The Jacobite' is probably Briatin's most successful main line steam train these days. It is operated by West Coast Railways twice daily between April and October, and runs over the stunning West Highland route from Fort William to Mallaig. Here, LM&SR 'Black Five' No. 45407 passes the end of Loch Eilt on 28th September 2007. [PHOTO: JOHN WHITELEY]

L&NER 'K1' Class 2-6-0 No. 62005 climbs from Glenfinnan towards Mallaig on 1st October 2007. Members of the 'K1' Class were frequent performers on this route in steam days. [PHOTO: JOHN WHITELEY]

Designed by James McConnell, the London & North Western Railway's Chief Engineer, in collaboration with Charles Beyer, the great German engineer who went on to found the famous railway builder Beyer, Peacock & Co. in Manchester, the locomotive was nicknamed after campaigning American feminist Amelia Bloomer. At that time, anything novel or striking was likely to be labelled as a 'Bloomer'. Her reforms in dress revealed ladies' legs – the locomotive revealed its 'naked' driving wheels and the lower part of its 'anatomy'!

Bob set to and designed a replica, then began to build it. He could see that Tyseley was struggling for cash to put its locomotives back on the main line and we could both see that 'now' was probably not the right time to do so. So, after some discussions with Graham Campion of the GCR, the concept of that line's 'big engine' policy was born and *Clun Castle* and *Kolhapur*, along with No. 7760 and our two GWR Saloons, moved to Loughborough and were put into service. These moves enabled the locomotives to see use on the GCR and at their expense but we could still enjoy them, even if they were not on the main line. The move could also have formed the basis of a complete transfer of operations if it became impractical to continue at Tyseley. After all, in the early 1990s, we had little money or engineering expertise, although we did have a very well equipped workshop and lots of lovely steam locomotives.

Bob's day job was developed at Babcock Power and his steam locomotive expertise derived in a practical way, 'on the job', from BR enginemen, whilst mending and operating steam locomotives on the main line and private railways, and not just *Leander* either. Bob will proudly tell you that he is the only person now living who has driven the GNR 'Stirling Single.' He determined to take a 'sabbatical' from designing power stations and rolled up at Tyseley to see what could be made of it.

We had sort of begun a commercial enterprise at Tyseley Locomotive Works already. Harry Hill was then our CME, with excellent credentials in engineering management from Bellis & Morcom in the Midlands, aided and abetted by Don Green from Worcester Works. Working together, they were instrumental in enabling *Clun Castle* to be fit for GW150, plus *Defiant* to be rebuilt from scrap in just eighteen months and then go on to race from Banbury to Tyseley, reaching 80mph on her first long haul main line tour. And previously, Jim Kent and his team had worked wonders in collecting and renovating to exacting standards much running shed type machinery; a good example of such being Jim's demonstration of operating the former Bescot multi-purpose lathe whilst balancing on it a 50p piece on its edge without it falling over.

So we had the machines and tools and much else besides. Bob added the expertise and contacts and 'TLW' began its commercial offering to heritage railways and main line locomotives. Step by step Bob built up the business, reinvesting surplus into our development and the collection, first into finishing the restoration of *Rood Ashton Hall*, then panniers No's 7760 and 9600, and then moving on to the 'impossible' project of *Earl of Mount Edgcumbe*. That was really my fault. It would have been so much simpler to repair either *Clun Castle*, *Defiant* or *Kolhapur* really but, at that time, all were still working and earning us money on driving courses or hire to private railways and it seemed wise to leave them be for now. Also, restoring

The Railway Touring Company, established by Nigel Dobbing, promote many main line steam excursions and also overseas tours. One of the former is the 'Cotton Mills Express', which runs from Lancaster to Blackburn. Here, LM&SR 'Jubilee' 4-6-0 *Leander* is in her element amidst appropriate scenery climbing to Copy Pit at Cornholme, between Burnley and Todmorden. This line was to be one of the last bastions of time-tabled steam haulage on British Railways in 1968. [PHOTO: JOHN WHITELEY]

The Pioneer High Speed Train. The Community Programme job creation scheme we ran in the 1980s, returning over 800 redundant people to full time employment, had some useful spin offs for us. One of these was the ability to make most, but not quite all, of a replica of one of McConnell's 1860s L&NWR 'Large Bloomer' single wheelers, which hauled express trains from Curzon Street to London Euston in two hours. After the job creation scheme ended, we have been able to progress construction step by step pursuant to kind donations and legacies. In December 2019, the large 7ft driving wheel was fitted before the locomotive was exhibited at the Warley Model Railway Show at the NEC. [Photo: Robin Coombes]

the Earl was an emotive thing. She had a superb reputation as a 'good' Castle in GWR and BR days and, if we were able to recreate that, then she would be a very much needed morale booster. After really quite tricky times over the previous ten years or so, when our funding nearly ran out, we needed that.

Precision engineering is not delivered in a day and requires lots and lots of time, expertise, patience and money. But a realistic blend of each, coupled with a manageable main line steam programme, building each stage incrementally, began to work and then flourished. From being one of the first in the field of owning preserved steam locomotives and promoting their operation on the main line, moving to swimming in a pond with bigger and more political locomotive 'fish', we morphed back into the First Division and created the regular operation of the summer Sundays 'Shakespeare Express', which even ran in the working time table, operated initially by EWS from 1999.

Bob's arrival at Tyseley created a safe pair of management hands on the spot. As my sister always reminds me, everything has its time and place. All our locomotives were safe within a complex but unbreakable charitable legal structure and, moreover, we had steadily increasing financial surpluses derived from the Tyseley Locomotive Works business, together with a growing team of experts. And, for the second time at Tyseley, son was following father: Alastair Meanley showed from a very early age an uncanny aptitude in knowing how a steam locomotive worked. The collection was in good hands. All this allowed me time and space to bring up a family, develop an international railway projects law practice

and have a 'sabattical' myself, helping the nascent Welsh Highland Railway to be rebuilt and chairing the oldest railway company in the world, the Ffestiniog Railway.

Of course, whilst all this was going on, main line steam still ran but not in the same way as before. Oh dear me no! Everything was completely different.

New tour promoters entered the fray. One in particular called 'Days Out', formed by Melvyn Chamberlain, made dramatic changes. Out went the cautious and realistic approach of running trips from sensible base depots over reasonable routes for a steam locomotive to handle in terms of distance and capacity. In came 'thrashes' of hundres of miles from city centres, including London, and up and down the arterial main lines of Great Britain: the East Coast Main Line, the West Coast Main line and the Great Western Main Line, as well as various Southern routes. Frankly, anything went. It was all little short of astonishing, following the quite understandable constraints required by BR and the original advice to BRB by Terry Miller. All the previous rules restricting numbers and types of locomotives and where they could run simply went out of the window. Open access prevailed and steam went everywhere.

In 1994, music producer and rail enthusiast Pete Waterman bought the former BR Inter City charter train business, promising sixty-five trips in the following year and a hundred in the year after that.

Rail Express Systems were busy guys as, initially, it was the only company qualified to operate steam trains on the main line and both Pete Waterman and Melvyn Chamberlain had to contract with

Not to be outdone in the ability to run nearly everywhere under the open access regime, West Coast Railways operated Vintage Trains' 'The Cornishman' tour on 15th May 2010, which was double-headed by No. 4965 *Rood Ashton Hall* and No. 5043 *Earl of Mount Edgcumbe*. The pair are seen here climbing Whiteball Bank on their way from Bristol to Plymouth. [PHOTO: ROBIN COOMBES]

Steam in Birmingham New Street's station was not initially permitted as it is classed as an underground station. However, as parts of it are nevertheless in the open air, Bob Meanley gently encouraged Network Rail to permit steam operations there. Initially, locomotives were carefully positioned in the open air, always with little smoke and ensuring that they did not blow off. Appropriately, to begin the trials, LM&SR 'Pacific' No. 6201 *Princess Elizabeth* stands at New Street on 11th July 2010. Even more interestingly the train was bound for London Euston down the West Coast Main Line.
[PHOTO: MARTIN CREESE]

RES to have their steam trains run. Of course, once this was appreciated, all claims of exclusivity evaporated, as anyone could charter RES to run their own trains. All great fun of course and enthusiasts understandably had a whale of a time but market expectations were set very high now.

Regulations and standards were key but, by this time, steam locomotives were well past their sell-by date. Until now, owners could 'get by', as their locomotives largely had unused life left in them when they were withdrawn, as their end of life had been brought about by political and accounting reasons rather than fatigue. Of course, this is a generalisation but provided one had engineering knowledge, the right locomotives could give the best chance to hold the fort.

Tyseley's locomotives, bought directly from BR and London Transport, were far from 'basket cases,' although they were certainly tired. Some of the locomotives we had bought from Barry scrapyard were very well chosen by Jim Kent. We had scoured the scrapyard in the early 1970s and Jim had selected the best. *Albert Hall* had a Light Casual overhaul at Caerphilly almost immediately before being put into the scrapyard as a complete locomotive; as she was not in there long, she was towed up to Tyseley still with her coupling rods on at 50mph! Bob Meanley led a team of young engineers, including his son Alastair, in completing her reincarnation, but as No. 4965 *Rood Ashton Hall* as, during her rebuild, it was found that *Albert Hall* and *Rood Ashton Hall* had been combined to make one good locomotive on the latter's frames. Pannier tanks No's 7752 and 7760 had been well looked after by London Transport and even repaired at Eastleigh Works; they came with a whole load of spares too. So it was quite understandable that Bob chose these three first to put back into service, the order of priority wholly depending on the amount of work needed to get them back in conditon. And now, any steam locomotive was permitted to run on the main line, provided it was repaired and maintained to the requisite standard, and was gauge friendly.

English, Welsh & Scottish Railway was formed in 1996, having acquired RES and all the long haul freight businesses from BR apart from Freightliner. So, as we read in the 'Shakespeare Express' chapter, it was EWS who operated our trains from the outset of our return to service. But after a while, their prices increased and our surplus decreased. Something had to be done. By now, David Smith, a coal merchant and locomotive owner, had formed his own train operating company, following his initial experiences chartering trains mainly in Scotland. Like us, David had watched the slow but steady disintegration of SLOA and its effectiveness, and seen new boys on the block coming in to promote trains on the

privatised railway with little or no knowledge of steam engineering or operating processes.

BR offered a good pension scheme and many people who were aged in their 50s at the time of privatisation somewhat understandably did not care for the wholesale changes being introduced. In my legal career I could see the detail of this: employment contracts were changing, free travel passes were being cut away, staff reductions were possible on account of amalgamations and the closures of workshops and depots. Good skilled and knowledgeable people, nay real railwaymen, were available. David seized his moment, formed West Coast Railway Company and set up to run his own trains from Carnforth depot, which he had acquired from Sir William McAlpine, as even the Flying Scotsman entrepreneurship had waned and the famous locomotive changed hands with disastrous results. The old order was over but the expertise at the level it mattered – those who really knew how to run trains – was still available; just.

WCRC steadily built up its operations, not just with steam but also in diesel, infrastructure services and charters. David took over BR's successful Scottish steam operations and developed 'The Jacobite' into Britain's most successful main line steam operation. EWS was subsequently acquired by the German Government and so its steam safety case became owned by Deutsche Bahn. Now there were two players in the market place and, for the first time ever, promoters had a choice of operators.

David Smith and James Shuttleworth kindly came down to my law office in Birmingham for a chat with Bob and me. David has always been a man of his word and a straight talker. It was easy to

In late summer, David Smith's LM&SR 'Royal Scot' 4-6-0, No. 46115 *Scots Guardsman*, now in authentic BR express passenger locomotive green livery, powers past Langcliffe on the Settle & Carlisle line with 'The Waverley' on 5th August 2012. [PHOTO: JOHN WHITELEY]

At the same location seven months later, with a change in season to very early spring, Jeremy Hosking's BR 'Pacific' No. 70000 *Britannia* passes at the head of another Vintage Trains' excursion on 2nd March 2013. Jeremy Hosking has since formed his own train operating company, Locomotive Services Limited, based at Crewe. New into service from Crewe Works on 5th January 1951 and the first of the fifty-five strong class, they were named the 'Britannia' Class as a result. One other, No. 70013 *Oliver Cromwell*, has also survived to be preserved. [PHOTO: JOHN WHITELEY]

Vintage Train's immaculate No. 5043 *Earl of Mount Edgcumbe* crosses the River Aire at Bretherton, alongside Ferrybridge power station, on her run from Tyseley to York for the Christmas Market on 14th December 2013. Since this picture was taken, the power station has closed and five of the eight giant cooling towers have been demolished by controlled explosions. [PHOTO: JOHN WHITELEY]

On 12th April 2017, main line steam hit a new high in preservation when newly built 'A1' 'Pacific' No. 60163 *Tornado* ran at 100mph on the East Coast Main Line at night on an organised trial. The promoters always sought to run their locomotive at 90mph on occasion and who could resist seeking the 'magic ton.' Ambitions have perhaps been scaled back a little since, as the practical limit for steam on the main line nowadays is 75mph for large wheeled express locomotives. Although it is rumoured that *Tornado* was not actually the first steam locomotive to reach 100mph in the preservation era ...
[PHOTO: ROBIN COOMBES]

reach terms for operation and even better to know that they would be delivered and continue to be delivered. I could rest easy in the main line steam world and concentrate on my family, legal career and certain world famous Welsh 2ft narrow gauge railways. Bob ably ran 'TLW', which by then comprised locomotives, a train, a workshop, an operating depot and a tour promoter, having left the operation itself to EWS in the formative years of privatisation and Tyseley's rehabilitation from the financial doldrums. By now, we had all attributes except one to run main line steam trains. The only aspect we did not have was a licence – but we did not need one. The relationship with WCRC saw to that and, very largely, their drivers Ray Churchill and Ray Poole were assigned to us to enable us to run our trains with the home team firing and guarding.

All was well with our world, for the time being.

To a large extent we were then able to follow in the slip stream where others had paved the way, opening new routes and opportunities. This enabled us to run away from our immediate home patches of the Tyseley to Didcot and Hereford to Shrewsbury routes, and gallivant in wider fields. We took double-headed Great Western locomotives pretty much everywhere: up Shap to Carlisle and back over the famous Settle & Carlisle route; and down the GWR main line to Plymouth. *Earl of Mount Edgcumbe* even managed to reach Edinburgh, the Forth Bridge and Stirling in Scotland, the first time a 'Castle' had ever been to that part of the United Kingdom! We promoted several celebratory 'non-stop' runs with the kind cooperation of First Great Western and Network Rail: *Earl of Mount Edgcumbe* re-ran 'The Bristolian' from London to Bristol and back, nearly at the original crack timings. She also re-ran 'The Cheltenham Flyer', narrowly achieving a non-stop run by careful enginemanship running up to a red signal at Reading, managing to reach it just after it had turned from a red aspect. No. 5043 even beat her sister *Clun Castle*'s record run from Plymouth to Bristol without trying, this achievement largely being due to sustained high speed running at a constant 75mph, something largely unheard of in 1964. Perhaps the hardest won non-stop was

'The Inter City' from Birmingham to London, where it was brought home to us just how tough that route is. You can read about some of these runs from the 'driver's eye view' in the next chapter.

As if that was not enough, we kept two out of our three GWR pannier tanks running, albeit limited to 45mph. When double-headed, they could shift ten carriages and everyone thought such trips delightful. Pannier tanks are economical yet powerful locomotives and we found that around two main line trips for them each year sold well and paid all their operating costs. What is not to like?!

We also used guest locomotives from time to time to provide variety and different routes. 'Merchant Navy' No. 35005 *Canadian Pacific*, rather fetchingly but inaccurately in BR experimental blue, was one of the first; then Bob's previous charge LM&SR 'Jubilee' *Leander* and also some of Jeremy Hoskins' collection – *Nunney Castle*, *Bittern* and *Britannia*. Some of the TLW outshopped contract engineering locomotives also took turns, particularly two GWR 'Hall' Class 4-6-0s, *Kinlet Hall* and *Pichford Hall*, often double-heading with our own *Rood Ashton Hall*; they made a fine sight.

I suppose one should always expect the unexpected but we did not and so we learned another lesson. Our locomotives and carriages were all vacuum-braked (although the Pullmans are dual-braked and we do have some air-braked Mark 2 First Class cars in stock). Effectively, this meant we could only run with WCRC, as DB Cargo did not operate vacuum-braked stock, However, with the arrangements we had in place, this did not matter; well, until it did matter.

As we have already discussed, steam locomotives were, by now, largely past their sell-by date. By this I mean two things. In times past, each locomotive would routinely be put through works at intervals and renewed as necessary; after some time, it would become obsolete as a new design took over. This somewhat natural engineering process had been arrested after BR finished with steam: there were no workshops running steam locomotive production line engineering and so everything had to be dealt with individually, as required, by a nascent cottage industry. Furthermore, few footplate

A steam-hauled time-tabled train or, as it is known in Germany, *Plandamph*. No. 60163 *Tornado* heads the 10.44am Skipton-Appleby public service train at Langcliffe on the Settle & Carlisle line on 14th December 2017, replacing the normal diesel multiple unit. These trains ran on three consecutive days and were the first time-tabled ordinary main line passenger steam trains to run in England for over fifty years. They were run by a collaboration of Northern (the franchise holder), Network Rail, DB Cargo (the steam locomotive operator), the A1 Steam Locomotive Trust and the Friends of the Settle & Carlisle, together with Bauer Media (who came up with the idea) to help revive the economic fortunes of the S&C line and publicise its highly scenic route, under the banner: 'I ♥ S&C'. [PHOTO: JOHN WHITELEY]

crew were being trained and most of those who were so qualified did not drive steam all the time. Was there an accident waiting to happen?

Unfortunately, there were several.

Perhaps it all started with a few engines hitting buffer beams a bit hard at terminal stations. That just made a paragraph in the journals but the engineering effect could be more serious: leaking stays in the firebox perhaps. Then, on 1st October 1994, L&NER 'A2' Class 'Pacific' No. 60532 *Blue Peter* was booked to work from Edinburgh to York on the East Coast Main Line. When starting away from Durham, the locomotive was opened up for the climb up the rising gradient to Relly Mill. At this point, *Blue Peter* 'lost her feet' and went into a wheelslip that was uncontrolled for many seconds before the crew regained control. These locomotives have steam chests and, even when closing the regulator, there is still steam unleashed. Such a rush of steam caused water carry-over and mangled some of the locomotive's running gear. She was an unmoveable cripple on the main line. Quite apart from the damage to the locomotive (repairable with loads of cash) and reputation, there were now performance penalties to be paid. In the new privatisation regime, only three minutes' leeway is permitted; over that and the operator gets fined.

Unfortunately, that was not the only accident. *Princess Elizabeth* 'lost some motion parts' on the move, 'Battle of Britain' Class 'Light

Pacific' *Tangmere* threw a connecting rod onto the ballast whilst at speed and, somewhat later, new build 'A1' 4-6-2 *Tornado* also shed some of its motion on the East Coast Main Line. Whilst in the past these sorts of things perhaps happened all the while, the volume of steam locomotive running compared with the incidents in times past was then almost immaterial. Indeed, people still recount the good but true yarn of a driving wheel falling off GWR 'Saint' No. 2933 *Bilbury Court* when hauling a cross country train through Olton, near Tyseley depot in 1930. The driver still managed to nurse the locomotive onto the depot whilst only fitted with five driving wheels! The trouble is that, nowadays, steam locomotives are very much in the limelight and incidents of various kinds like these get into the headlines quickly and make people worry about maintenance regimes and skill sets.

By far the worst event was not an accident at all, very fortunately, but it was to have severe ramifications for a while. In August 2006, the Rail Accident Investigation Branch issued the following statement:

'*At around 17:25 hrs on Saturday 7 March 2015, train reporting number 1Z67, the 16.35 hrs steam hauled charter service from Bristol Temple Meads to Southend, passed signal SN45 at danger. Signal SN45, which is situated on the approach to Wootton Bassett Junction, was being maintained at danger to protect the movement of a scheduled passenger train. At the time that the incident occurred, this scheduled*

'The Scarborough Spa Express' is another of Britain's regular main line steam train services promoted and operated by West Coast Railways, running between York and Scarborough in the summer months, Here LM&SR 'Jubilee' Class 4-6-0 No. 45690 *Leander* (this time in BR lined black passenger livery) leaves York under the wires on 6th September 2018. [Photo: John Whiteley]

passenger train had already passed through the junction. No injuries, damage or derailment occurred as a result of the incident.

Train 1Z67 was operated by West Coast Railways and consisted of the steam locomotive Tangmere and thirteen coaches. Although Tangmere is a heritage locomotive, it is fitted with modern safety systems including the Automatic Warning System (AWS) and the Train Protection and Warning System (TPWS).

RAIB's investigation has found that signal SN45 was passed at danger because the driver did not reduce the train's speed on approach to the signal. This meant that he was unable to stop the train in time, once he realised it was at danger. The driver had not reduced the train's speed because he had not seen the preceding signal, which was at caution and should have alerted him that SN45 was at danger. He missed this preceding signal because he had become distracted by activity within the cab and possibly also because he was experiencing a higher workload than normal.

Train 1Z67 also passed signal SN45 at danger because the TPWS system was unable to reduce the speed of the train by automatically applying the brakes. This was because TPWS had been rendered ineffective by Tangmere's crew when they had isolated the AWS system in order to by-pass an automatic brake application which had occurred at a speed restriction. Isolating AWS in this way was in contravention of the relevant rules but RAIB has found that it had almost certainly become an accepted practice among some train crews on this locomotive. This was probably because warnings from AWS were not always apparent to drivers, who were also anxious to avoid delays resulting from brake demands. Measures intended to prevent the misuse of AWS isolations had either not been adopted by West Coast Railways or had not been effectively implemented.

The RAIB found three underlying factors. These were that the AWS system on Tangmere was installed in a way which meant that warnings from the system were not always apparent to drivers. In addition, the investigation found that a speed restriction which was in place on approach to the junction was based on incorrect information and had been implemented in a way which did not conform to the relevant rules and standards. The investigation also found that West Coast Railways had a weak safety culture and that this had affected the way its staff observed rules and instructions.'

As these points unfolded, they were reported widely and, of course, came to the notice of the board of trustees of Vintage Trains Charitable Trust. We were immediately affected as WCRC had its operating licence suspended, which meant that it was unable to operate any of our charter trains. We lost a considerable amount of money as a result; fortunately, Tyseley Locomotive Works remained profitable, so we kept our head above water.

The non executive trustees, in particular, were adamant that our charity could not be put in this position again. We debated whether we should simply stop promoting main line steam specials altogether, wait for things to calm down (assuming they did) or seek to carry on with a third party. Having got this far over many years, we were not the type of people to give up now. We did wait a while but the prognosis was not encouraging for some time. We discussed operations with other possible parties and nearly concluded terms but the volume of our business was not then sufficient to convince a third party to take on the operational aspects of both steam and vacuum brake.

So, we decided to see if it was possible to run our own trains!

Reputedly the World's most famous steam locomotive, L&NER 'A3' Class 'Pacific' No. 60103 *Flying Scotsman*, now part of the National Collection and based at the National Railway Museum in York, passes through the staggered platforms of Ribblehead station on a Manchester (Victoria) to Carlisle train on 4th December 2019. More commonly known to enthusiasts as L&NER No. 4472, *Flying Scotsman* here wears BR livery and sports the BR number she carried from 30th December 1948 until withdrawal on 15th January 1963, when she was sold to the businessman Alan Pegler. [PHOTO: JOHN WHITELEY]

In the late 1960s, LM&SR 'Jubilee' Class' 4-6-0s were synonymous with the Settle & Carlisle line and ran many excursions from Leeds (where the last of the class were based) to Carlisle in particular. No. 45562 *Alberta* was one of the final few of the class to survive until the end of steam on this route in 1967 but only one of the Leeds 'Jubilees', No. 45593 *Kolhapur*, made it into preservation, now based at Vintage Trains' Tyseley depot, albeit paired with *Alberta*'s tender. In recent years, David Smith's 'Jubilee' *Galatea* has been renamed *Alberta* and repainted into authentic BR express passenger locomotive lined green so as to remember the 1967 excursion days. Here she passes Salt Lake cottages on the approach to Ribblehead on the Settle & Carlisle line on 12th February 2020. [PHOTO: JOHN WHITELEY]

On 9th February 2019, LM&SR 'Jubilee' No. 45596 *Bahamas*, fitted with a double chimney and blastpipe, roars through Ribblehead on the Settle & Carlisle line on her first main line excursion for twenty-five years since being repaired at Tyseley Locomotive Works, pursuant to a Heritage Lottery grant and after a restoration cost of nearly one million pounds. Note stations on this line have also received the heritage treatment. [Photo: John Whiteley]

On 5th August 2020, No. 70000 *Britannia* hauls one of Locomotive Services Limited's steam specials just south of Leominster, an excursion from Exeter to Shrewsbury. Steam haulage was from Bristol and the tour ran via the Severn Tunnel and round the Maindee East Junction to North Junction curve at Newport to head directly to Shrewsbury along the Welsh borders. The return was the same way along this popular and scenic route for main line steam trains. Now there are four companies operating express steam trains on Britain's main lines, together with the North Yorkshire Moors' own time-tabled trains to Whitby. However, in 2020 there were not so many main line steam runs due to the coronavirus pandemic lockdowns and social distancing requirements but LSL operated a mixed formation complying with the reduced seating requirements. [Photo: Robin Coombes]

20. *EARL OF MOUNT EDGCUMBE'S* NON-STOP RUNS

'On arrival at Gloucester, I spoke to Mathew Golton about the timings.
"Oh don't worry about those", he said, "We've got other plans".'

'THE BRISTOLIAN' – Bob Meanley

Much of *Earl of Mount Edgcumbe*'s considerable reputation as a 'flyer' had been gained from her regular working of 'The Bristolian' express between London Paddington and Bristol Temple Meads. The celebration of GWR175 in 2010 provided the opportunity to turn back the clock for more than fifty years. However, running a steam train non-stop from Paddington to Bristol and then back again poses all kinds of difficulties, fitting in with the frequent high speed services running today, to say nothing of the removal of water troughs, which made such non-stop runs possible in the past. The water problem was overcome by including a converted GUV 'water carrier' in the formation, linked to and marshalled next to No. 5043's tender; and much detailed planning went into the pathing and operation of the train. But everyone – First Great Western, Network Rail, West Coast Railway Company and Vintage Trains – wanted this to happen and, as they say, 'where there is a will there is a way' and the problems were overcome.

The months of scheming and planning came to an end shortly after 11.30am on a beautifully sunny 17th April morning, as driver Ray Poole opened the regulator on No. 5043 and moved the eight coach train out of Platform 3 at Paddington. Pathed along the main line to Maidenhead, speed reached into the mid 70s and we were on the relief line, as scheduled, and out of the way of the following HST bang on time. And this precise running continued through Reading and Didcot. Another 'pinch point' came as we ran slowly along the relief line on the approach to Challow, as we waited for another HST to overtake. It did, and shortly after 1 o'clock and with speed in the 60s, we cruised through No. 5043's birthplace, Swindon. And now the 'plan' went out of the window and the on board planners took over. Running over a section where the train was booked to average little more than 50mph, speed began to increase and we were soon into the 70s. The travelling controllers had seen an opportunity to get to Bristol earlier and had told the crew to go for it. Seven minutes early at Chippenham became ten minutes by Bath and, a rousing 76mph near Keynsham saw us arrive at Bristol Temple Meads almost eleven minutes early.

Non-stop express steam! On 18th June 2011, No. 5043 *Earl of Mount Edgcumbe* approaches Bath's Sydney Gardens with 'The Bristolian', running non-stop to London Paddington, arriving forty-four minutes early and only five minutes over the 1950s BR timings. [PHOTO: ROBIN COOMBES]

Perhaps the ultimate Great Western Railway image for the 21st Century? No. 5043 *Earl of Mount Edgcumbe* roars out of the western portal of Brunel's famous Box Tunnel at 75mph, on the Down run of 'The Bristolian' on 17th April 2010. During the 'Indian Summer' of Western Region steam, 'The Bristolian' was Britain's fastest scheduled steam hauled express trains and only locomotives in the best condition were normally rostered. *Earl of Mount Edgcumbe* was one of those locomotives and so we simply had to repeat the experience, with many thanks to First Great Western, Network Rail and West Coast Railway Company for rising to the occasion with us and easing the path. [Photo: Bob Green]

We had taken 133 minutes 9 seconds for the 118 miles and 26 chains, an average speed of 53.3mph. We had our 'Castle' haulage, we had our non-stop run but, as we enjoyed the sunshine, moves were afoot to add the third 'Bristolian' element – sustained speed.

By the time No. 5043 and its train had left Platform 3 at Bristol Temple Meads shortly after 5 o'clock, some intense *ad hoc* planning had arrangements in place to allow a much faster return to London than the schedule required. And what a run we had! With a careful start, just avoiding a threatened signal stop on the approach to Bristol Parkway, driver Andy Taylor took the 'Castle' quickly into the 60s. Soon, after the minor summit at Badminton, No. 5043 was galloping along at around her permitted speed of 75mph and there, with just a couple of minor fluctuations, we remained for the next ninety miles! This was as close to the experience of the high speed 'Bristolian' as we are likely to get nowadays and the miles just flew by. Swindon station saw us running twelve minutes early and doing 72mph. By Didcot, our advantage had increased to almost twenty-one minutes and, by Reading, to a massive twenty-five and a half minutes.

The miles continued to fly by as we ran under green signals almost all the way to Paddington. And, just before 6.52pm and more than forty-four minutes early, the 2010 version of 'The Bristolian' came to a stand in Platform 1. We had taken just two seconds under 110 minutes, only five minutes longer than the schedule allowed in 'the good old days.' Our end-to-end average had been 64.2mph and, for the hundred miles between mileposts 108 and 8, we had averaged

72.8mph, an unprecedented achievement by preserved steam, despite minor checks approaching Didcot and Reading. Indeed, from Swindon in, we had beaten the sixty-six minutes allowed for the 1958 train by nineteen seconds.

It had been a remarkable performance and No. 5043 and her crew deservedly took the spotlight. But such achievements depend on many people and organisations, and none of this could have been achieved without the crucial and enthusiastic contributions of Network Rail, First Great Western, West Coast Railway Company and their staff. For a day, thanks to their professionalism, we had been able to turn the clock back more than fifty years and enjoy again the glamour, the atmosphere and the sheer excitement of the steam hauled 'The Bristolian'.

'THE MARYLEBONE FLYER' – Ray Churchill

I had been asked to work a job from Tyseley on 6th April 2013, along with Fireman Alastair Meanley and Guard Phil Allison. The train was titled 'The Marylebone Flyer' and it would start from Birmingham Moor Street station bound, obviously, for London Marylebone station. It was billed as non-stop. Now running a steam operated train over a distance of over a hundred miles without stopping is a very tall order indeed these days. "*Wait a minute*", I hear you say, "*back in steam days most regions had their non-stoppers, some travelling 400 miles or so, how come a mere 112 miles is so difficult?*". In steam days, those non-stoppers were given priority and woe betide anyone who stopped them! If the signalman let a freight

Around five miles and five minutes later, No. 5043 *Earl of Mount Edgcumbe* hurries 'The Bristolian' past a group of well wishers in Sydney Gardens, Bath. For those wondering about the photographer's supersonic mode of transport – this picture was taken by his wife, dropped in position first! [PHOTO: JOAN GREEN]

train through when he had only just got time to clear the section before being put inside but the driver dawdled along stopping the non-stop, both the signalman and the freight train driver would 'get the papers' as we say. In other words 'Please explain'. Our 'non-stop' this day would get no such priority, steam charters are at the bottom of the pile; a steam charter might get stopped if a flock of geese wanted to fly over. The trouble is, although our locomotive has a maximum legal speed of 75mph, modern traction runs up to anything from 90 to 125mph and more, and where we might take 'x' amount of time to reach our maximum speed, they can reach theirs in a quarter of the time.

One of the biggest headaches in running steam on the main line today is water or the lack of it; where to get it and how to get it. As far as Tyseley is concerned, it's Bob and Alastair Meanley's job to sort this out but it will not bother them for this trip as we have now got a GUV (General Utility Vehicle) that has been converted to carry water to within its weight limit constraints and that will be enough to get us to London without stopping. Coal will not be a problem either, so all we have got to do now is the running.

'Heh heh heh', that's the hard bit, if there was only us on the line it would not be a problem. I could just set the controls and read the *News of the World* for a bit, but it is not that simple. "*Do they not give you a path to run to?*", I hear you ask. Well, yes. The Network Rail backroom boys burn the midnight oil and come up with a plan that will steer us through the myriad of other trains that will occupy the line during our journey, but it is still a minefield. In order to give us that path they may have to time us through a section or two that is too tight; in other words we cannot keep that time and we will lose a minute or two, but we will get it back on easier sections.

We are in Moor Street now ready to depart bang on 09.57, but the signal remains resolutely red. I look back and there is our guard, Phil Allison, standing with his green flag at the ready. Just as I am wondering if anybody has told the signaller we are ready, I see the cause of our problem. A Chiltern service has just run into the Up Main line platform bound for Marylebone. Oh dear, we have now got to follow it all the way. Very often when waiting to leave a station of any size you will be booked to follow a fast train and it is not hard to see why. I have already mentioned the different

RIGHT: No. 5053 *Earl of Mount Edgcumbe* powers along the GW main line near Yatton with the 21st century 1-Zulu-48 on Saturday 10th May 2014. This run was always planned to be a non-stop trip, if possible, to recreate and pay homage to sister *Clun Castle*'s record point to point run from Plymouth to Bristol in 1964, recounted earlier. What we did not expect was for the *Earl* to beat her sister's timings by some three minutes. The benefits of sustained 75mph running and some careful on board communication between Network Rail and its control made this remarkable event possible. So we have some unfinished business with *Clun Castle* one day …! [PHOTO: ROBIN COOMBES]

BELOW: Seconds later, 1-Zulu-48 flashes by. 'The Bristolian' often recorded 100mph in BR (WR) days and who knows now if *Earl of Mount Edgcumbe* achieved such a milestone on these trains in ordinary service but it is nice to think she might well have done. Her double chimney and four row superheater 'front end' modifications, well designed by Sam Ell and Ivor Huddy at Swindon, put all the modified 'Castles' in a good position to run this train in the upgraded diesel timings during the changeover years. This image also well illustrates the modern railway and its now 'day to day' speeds often well over 100 mph within which steam now has to find a path running at its maximum permitted speed of 75mph. The 100mph sign is actually a speed restriction board. [PHOTO: ROBIN COOMBES]

speeds and acceleration; the Chiltern will get away from us in due course and it gives the next train behind – us! – maximum headway. Aha, we get a signal, Phil toots his whistle and waves his green flag and I ease No. 5043 *Earl of Mount Edgcumbe* out of the platform, through the crossovers and onto the Up Main. Now my immediate headache is that the Chiltern stops at Solihull (more than likely), Dorridge (probably), Warwick Parkway (possibly), Warwick (not sure), Leamington (definitely), Banbury (undoubtedly). The trick is to keep far enough behind so that it does not stop us, and me not to stop someone else; "*Simples eh? Yur Wight!*".

I let No. 5043 make slow acceleration and by Dorridge we are up in the 70s. So far so good. On the approach to Hatton I shut-off and let her lose a bit of speed as she will gradually get it back on the descent. The trouble is, if the Chiltern does stop at Warwick Parkway, it is not many minutes before it also stops at Leamington. Thought it was too good to be true; adverse signals at Warwick. I bring the speed down far quicker than normal to increase the time to reach the red. Come on get it going. Dropping down under the canal bridge now and I can see the red signal. Ah it has turned yellow, but I do not apply steam as the next red signal is at the end of Leamington platform; rolling towards that now and it turns yellow. That chap in front will be going hell for leather now I hope and so I risk a smidgen of steam. The next signal is green, my favourite colour!

With any luck we should not see the Chiltern again, even though it stops at Banbury. I can get stuck in now on the climb up through Fosse Road and Harbury Tunnel. Through Fenny Compton now and still going well, all greens through Banbury but on the approach to Aynho Junction we get yellows; surely I have not caught it up here? We slow down to nearly 10mph before we can proceed, so the climb up to Ardley was taken quietly, therefore imagine my surprise when I learned later that we had started a fire there. This bloke will surely stop at Bicester which is about five miles down the road but we keep on getting green signals so keep on going. Alastair is doing his usual sterling job of keeping me well supplied with that elasticated water vapour known as steam.

Haddenham & Tame Parkway, Princes Risborough, High Wycombe, Whitehouse Tunnel (now where have I heard that name before?) and we are still going. Oh-oh spoke too soon, yellows ahead; I steadied up to about 30mph and we keep going. At Gerrards Cross, we get the road and pass a multiple unit in the platform. I learned later that we were booked to pass it there. It is not the one we have been following from Birmingham but a stopper from Aylesbury that joined our route at Princes Risborough. It is fortunate that we are able to pass it here or else it would have surely caused us to stop. We soon gather speed on the downgrade but adverse signals again cause me to brake heavily yet again; what now? Despite my best efforts it looks like a stop is inevitable with us now down to walking pace with just over two hundred yards to go before the red signal. Andy Taylor, our Operations Manager, is riding with us as Traction Inspector. So he picks up the GSMR Radio Telephone and contacts the Signalman at Marylebone to find out what is wrong. It seems that the signaller wanted to discuss the fire we had started at Ardley. This was the first we had heard about it. For goodness sake what was the point of discussing it here? Andy managed to persuade the Signaller to let us go into Marylebone and we will talk about it there and with about ten yards to spare, before having to stop, we get a green signal; Phew! I yank open the regulator; they told me later a great cheer went up in the train. That was too close for comfort.

We arrive in Marylebone about nine minutes late, which was a shame as it was unnecessary; but we had achieved our goal – a non-stop run. But only just.

So the next time you are out on a steam charter, spare a thought to all the effort that goes into making it work, all the planning and pathing. The day before, when the fitness to run examination of the locomotive takes place to make sure everything is up to scratch and the paperwork is submitted to officialdom; it cannot run without it. And last, but by no means least, the train support crew who keep the locomotive serviced whilst out on the road, often having to perform some lousy tasks, and the passengers informed. It is all great team work and something we can all be proud of some fifty years after express steam trains finished on British Railways.

'THE CHELTENHAM FLYER' – Ray Churchill

I knew it was possible that I might work 'The Cheltenham Flyer' some weeks before but I never count my chickens so to speak, so when Andy Taylor, our Operations Manager, gave me the outward job I was delighted, until that is I saw the timings. We were allowed 63 mins from Reading to Paddington, a distance of only 36 miles. I wondered if we might be prosecuted under the Trades Descriptions Act. 'Cheltenham Flyer'? More like 'Cheltenham Crawler' or 'Cheltenham Snail Pace'. The glitter had suddenly gone out of the job. The train was to be hauled to Gloucester by diesel with us on No. 5043 *Earl of Mount Edgcumbe* attached to the rear travelling at a maximum speed of 60mph tender first. Not a pleasant experience. On arrival at Gloucester, I spoke to Mathew Golton about the timings. "*Oh don't worry about those*", he said, "*We've got other plans*". Mathew, a member of the First Great Western team, plus a man from Swindon Control are hopefully going to steer us through to Paddington non-stop. The man who is going to boil the water for me to do the job is fireman Alastair Meanley.

We leave Gloucester on easy steam as the Welsh coal we are burning needs time to get hot, but after negotiating the Up Curve onto the Bristol line I get more serious with No. 5043. Bob Meanley, Alastair's dad and Tyseley's Chief Engineer, is also on the footplate and is in radio contact with the team on the train. He is just receiving the first set of instructions which he relays to me. We have to be at St. Mary's Crossing for such and such a time and at Kemble at so and so time. We have just got into our stride, when two yellows loom up heralding the approach to Standish Junction, where we are going to turn left at a speed of 40mph, if the signals will let us, for the long climb to Sapperton. I don't press No. 5043; on the lower slopes it is not serious and I stick to a speed were I can ease the regulator to come to 50mph for the reverse curves at Stroud without touching the brake. St. Mary's Crossing is reached in good time and I apply more steam and lengthen the cut-off to the steepening gradient. I have to be careful here, I don't want to cause any fires or that will blow the job altogether but, at the same time, I want to make a decent climb of it. I do not think fires will occur as there has been recent rain and there is a lot more greenery about. Every so often I add another notch to the cut-off. At about 35 per cent I decide that is enough and we plunge into Sapperton Tunnel, where I keep both hands on the regulator ready to slam it shut should she lose her feet on the wet patch, but she does not slip. The 30mph summit speed could have been bettered but I did not want to take any risks.

Kemble is reached with time to spare and Bob's next instruction is to go at train speed to Swindon. We arrive there on a yellow signal and Bob spies an HST just leaving the main line platform. Whoa steady boy, we are slowly heading up Platform 1 towards a red signal; it goes to yellow, phew! I ease No. 5043 forward, the next signal eventually going green. We have now to go hard to Challow, where we will be put onto the 4-mile long relief line, then go steady while

The world's fastest train. The classic and distinctive 'Cheltenham Flyer' headboard was recreated specially for this train, again hauled by No. 5043 *Earl of Mount Edgcumbe*, on 11th May 2013. As driver Ray Churchill recounts, the trip was so nearly not a non-stop run but the tantalising easing up to the red signal at Swindon, which then turned orange in front of the engine, made the trip even more exhilarating. The *Earl* is seen here on the climb out of Stroud, with around two miles of the bank up to Sapperton Tunnel still ahead of it. Notice the polished embellishments to the buffers! [Photo: Robin Coombes]

Another classic Great Western setting. No. 5043 *Earl of Mount Edgcumbe*, running on the slow relief lines at the head of the 'Cheltenham Flyer', is overtaken in Sonning Cutting by another iconic train, a diesel-powered InterCity 125 HST, arguably the best train ever made. [Photo: Bob Green]

Steam trains in the dark are always evocative and none more so than this sight of No. 5043 *Earl of Mount Edgcumbe* roaring out of Snow Hill Tunnel and through the Down Main platform at Moor Street station hauling the InterCity special Christmas shopping train to London on 13th December 2008, shortly after 8 o'clock. On the adjacent line, a West Midlands Class '150' diesel unit pauses on its routine suburban service. The contrast in styles and purpose could hardly be greater. The photographer describes his experience: *"I wanted to capture steam in a city centre urban environment, bursting out from a subterranean world into a brightly lit station. This was in the fairly early days of digital and this was really pushing the boundaries with a Nikon D300, so is far from technically perfect. However, what it lacks in technical sharpness is made up in power, impact and drama. The image captures exactly my emotions of first anticipation, a light glimpsed in the darkness of the tunnel, the burst of steam, the extreme sense of motion, of heraldic headboard, copper capped chimney and red buffer beam. A blur of gleaming green and polished brass, of being enveloped in warm rushing air, lights from the carriages, turning around and seeing a red tail lamp disappearing into the distance. And finally a feeling of privilege to be a witness to a moment of such drama and spectacle."* [PHOTO: ROBIN COOMBES]

one comes by, then be turned out behind it, all without stopping. At Uffington I expect to see two flashing yellows to tell me that the route is set for the relief but it's green. We must be doing better than they thought because we're staying main line. Steventon then they say but, no, we go all the way to Foxhall Junction before we are turned onto the relief to go through Didcot.

Alastair has had a couple of occasions today when the needle on the pressure gauge was not where he likes it, nudging the red line. I can tell because if there's a need to be running on say 25 to 30% cut-off the crispness goes out of the exhaust and a glance across at the pressure gauge will tell me it's dropped to 200lbs or just under. As I said earlier we are burning Welsh coal and one of its nasty little habits is to form a thin layer of clinker over the fire bars, which stops the fire from breathing properly, so you do not get enough heat to create a full head of steam. Toffee on the bars I call it. When this has happened, Alastair has reached out a fire iron called a chisel bar or slice and rifled it down the firebars, breaking up the clinker and letting the fire breathe again. When it is nice and bright, he fires it again and the needle is back on the mark. When your fireman can read a fire, see what is wrong and put it right that is when you know you've got a good'un. But I must stress that even when you know what is wrong, its not always possible to put it right on the main line and you might need to be in a siding to put it right. Alastair Meanley is a very good fireman and I know of no one who could better him and if he was my son, I would be very proud of him, not only for that but for his engineering skills also, but I digress.

We are some way down the relief before that HST overtakes us. We are nearing Reading now and I need to keep my wits about me. Reading is being rebuilt and re-signalled and it is going to take a little while to get used to it. All the signals are green and that is a great help. We are through there now and Bob tells me we are going out fast line at Ruscombe, but we may go back onto the relief at Dolphin Junction. Not if I can help it and nor do we, and we blaze along the main line towards Paddington. I shut off at Ealing Broadway, even though we are some five miles out we easily have enough speed to take us right in. I will have to apply the brake in a mo' to bring us to 50mph at Kensal Green, then further on it drops to … oh lore I have spotted two yellows up ahead, so I apply the brake to bring us down to creep mode, Bob has a word with the brains who tell us we need the 10.21 to vacate Platform 3 so we can run in there. I consult my watch, 10.20 and he has not even got the road they say, 10.21 … 10.22 … 10.23 … come on we are approaching a red signal, do not let it all fall down now. At last! I see the nose of an FGW HST slowly making its way over the layout, its back end disappears. We get a yellow, hooray … the next one goes to green, that will take us right in and we pull up in Platform 3 some 40 minutes early, non-stop. I get down onto the platform to take a photo of No. 5043. That done,

I am besieged by our passengers congratulating me, photographing me and wanting to be photographed with me, but it is not me who should be taking the accolade, it is those guys in the train without whose help it could not have been done non-stop; and Alastair, of course, who just happened to put coal on at the right time in the right place. I just tagged along for the ride and operated the controls. One or two came and said I was becoming an expert at the 'creep', as I had to employ the same method on 'The Marylebone Flyer' to keep it non-stop. Yes I said I can see that in future I'm going to be known as 'That Creep Churchill'. See you next time!

Ray Churchill, 21st century express steam train driver, relaxes at Tyseley Locomotive Works on the footplate of a pannier tank. Ray began his railway career at Bescot depot in the Midlands as a cleaner and became a passed fireman there in 1966 and driver in 1972. He retired from English, Welsh & Scottish Railway in 2001 but returned to driving main line specials for West Coast Railways in 2002, which he described as *'the icing on the cake'*. He retired again in 2016 but was approached to join the nascent Vintage Trains to help it establish its footplate team and enjoyed driving both *Clun Castle* and *Bahamas*. A final highlight for Ray was driving turns on 'The Polar Express', where he recalls the huge pleasure and emotional experience he felt from seeing the faces of hundreds of delighted children and parents. With the onset of the covid pandemic and approaching 80 years of age, Ray decided then to hang up his main line boots but will, no doubt still be seen driving a pannier or two at Tyseley from time to time. [PHOTO: ROBIN COOMBES]

The original Tyseley 'factory' repair shop on 29th September 1948, nine months into the British Railways era and interestingly housing around a dozen locomotives, which is similar to the current capacity of Tyseley Locomotive Works. In the left foreground is '5101' Class 'Large Prairie' No. 5162, built at Swindon in November 1930, which appears to have a fair amount of chalked instructions on its bunker side. The 2-6-2T had probably been allocated to Tyseley from new, the shed boasting a total of thirteen of the class in 1934, including No. 5162. In spring 1949, it came out of Wolverhampton Stafford Road Works and went into store at Swindon Stock Shed for around three months, before being sent to Swansea Landore shed. It never returned to Tyseley and was withdrawn from Gloucester Horton Road in July 1958. Next along is 1941-built 2-8-0 No. 3833, which within a month would be in Swindon Works, and right at the back is 'Dukedog' 4-4-0 No. 9025, which was stored in April 1956 and withdrawn in August 1957. [Roger Carpenter Collection]

21. TYSELEY LOCOMOTIVE WORKS
AND THE RENAISSANCE OF *CLUN CASTLE*

'The repair of No. 7029 has undoubtedly been entirely at the level that might have been expected of a heavy general classified repair carried out at Swindon Works.'

Tyseley depot was built by the Great Western Railway in 1908. It has been in continuous use for the heavy maintenance and repair of steam locomotives ever since and has been able to turn out a steam locomotive for service every day since it was opened. In addition to its two engine roundhouses for storage and day to day maintenance, Tyseley depot also had a factory workshop, capable of heavy intermediate repairs to around a dozen steam locomotives at any one time between heavy general overhauls, which were usually carried out at either Swindon or Wolverhampton (Stafford Road).

All these facilities were destroyed when the depot was converted into a diesel traction maintenance depot from 1964, with the factory being the first to go, followed by the goods engine roundhouse and then the passenger roundhouse building. But we were left with the original track layout, trackwork and turntable from the passenger roundhouse, and the coaling stage, with its now unique electric hoist to enable soft Welsh coal to be tipped into the locomotives waiting below. More recently, the depot staff club has been donated to us to incorporate into our visitor, passenger and community activities. We have a good rapport with landowner Network Rail and fellow occupier, West Midlands Trains, which operates the diesel traction maintenance depot and still uses the original GWR carriage sidings, where even the vacuum plant house remains (once used to draw rubbish from carriages to a central location).

But we have had to rebuild from there. In 1970, a new workshop building was erected adjacent to the coaling stage and, in 2013, an erecting shop with travelling crane was added to enable more engineering to take place under a single roof, the latter being partly funded by a European Regional Development Fund Grant.

In 1997, the trustees agreed to promote the engineering activities under the brand of Tyseley Locomotive Works, run by Bob Meanley. Over the next two decades, engineering activity steadily increased and Tyseley evolved into a national centre for steam railway engineering and express steam train operation but still with

Inside the new erecting shop at Tyseley Locomotive Works, with two heavy general repairs in view at a cost of £2 million between them – Bahamas Locomotive Society LM&SR 'Jubilee' Class No. 45596 *Bahamas* and Tyseley Collection No. 7029 *Clun Castle*. Both locomotives are in course of reassembly, with *Bahamas'* boiler on the left-hand side ready to be retubed. [PHOTO: ROBIN COOMBES]

Above: The boiler is lifted off No. 5043 *Earl of Mount Edgcumbe* in readiness for her ten year internal and external boiler examination during 2020. [Photo: C.M. Whitehouse]

Below: Alastair Meanley, TLW General Manager, supervises firebox repairs. [Photo: Robin Coombes]

occasional open days and behind the scenes tours.

Over the past ten years, TLW has consolidated its reputation as one of the top heritage traction repair and restoration facilities in the UK. Its skilled staff tackle increasingly complex repairs and even undertake building new steam locomotives, despite not having a production line capacity and needing to carefully manage its supply chain for materials.

In 2018, Tyseley Locomotive Works was presented with an Engineering Heritage Award by the Institute of Mechanical Engineers, at a ceremony on Tuesday 18th September. Mr Tony Roche, the President of the Institution unveiled a commemorative plaque, together with Alastair Meanley, the Works Manager. The plaque '*recognizes both the importance of the engineering and educational aspect of the steam railway depot, which gives visitors a taste of the thrill of seeing a live steam locomotive*'. Previous winners of Engineering Heritage Awards include Alan Turing's Bombe at Bletchley Park, the E-Type Jaguar and Concorde supersonic airliner.

The quality and process of the engineering work carried out at Tyseley Locomotive Works can well be illustrated by describing the heavy general repair recently undertaken to No. 7029 *Clun Castle*.

ABOVE: We acquired much machinery and tooling from all manner of depots when steam ended on BR. This Noble & Lund wheel turning lathe came from nearby Bescot depot and has been invaluable, as it is one of the few remaining in the country capable of turning tyre profiles on driving wheels up to 7ft diameter, as well as axle journals. Dean Morris, long standing machinist and fireman, is in command. [PHOTO: ROBIN COOMBES]

LEFT: The unveiling. In 2018, Tyseley Locomotive Works was presented with an Engineering Heritage Award by the Institute of Mechanical Engineers at a ceremony on Tuesday 18th September. Mr Tony Roche, the President of the Institution, unveiled a commemorative plaque, together with Alastair Meanley, General Manager. The plaque 'recognizes both the importance of the engineering and educational aspect of the steam railway depot, which gives visitors a taste of the thrill of seeing a live steam locomotive'. Previous winners of Engineering Heritage Awards include Alan Turing's Bombe at Bletchley Park, the E-Type Jaguar and Concorde supersonic airliner. [PHOTO: ROBIN COOMBES]

RIGHT: Tyseley Locomotive Works staff group together for a celebratory photograph on the occasion of the Institute of Mechanical Engineers' award on Tuesday 18th September 2018. [PHOTO: ROBIN COOMBES]

Trial nameplate fitting. *Clun Castle* is one of the very few working express steam locomotives still to retain a complete set of her original plates. The name and numberplates were acquired with the engine but the smokebox plate was missing; fortunately, it turned up in an auction and when the owner heard we had the rest of the set of plates, he kindly donated it. [PHOTO: ROBIN COOMBES]

A HEAVY GENERAL CLASSIFIED REPAIR FOR
CLUN CASTLE – Bob Meanley

Steam locomotives can be very demanding things to maintain. In particular, regulations require boilers to be thoroughly overhauled at maximum intervals of ten years. *Clun Castle* has seen various periods in storage and under such repairs in the intervening years. In between repairs, it has seen much use on the main line and on preserved lines. Perhaps the best known workings were operating the first ever train in BR's 'Return to Steam' programme in 1972 and its outings during 1985 when, in celebration of the 150th anniversary of the Great Western Railway, it roamed far and wide across lines of the old company, even penetrating into Cornwall. But fortunes wane for engines and organisations and this was true for both *Clun Castle* and what had become the Birmingham Railway Museum. Around the time of the expiry of No. 7029's last boiler certificate, the BRM had been enduring some hard times and had just begun the process of reestablishing itself on what were then the main lines of Railtrack. Many years of use, on both main lines and preserved lines, had caused considerable attrition of the overall condition of *Clun Castle*, despite several periodic repairs, and it was certainly no longer in the condition that it was when purchased from BR. It became apparent that nothing short of the sort of general repair which Swindon Works used to regularly carry out would suffice to bring the locomotive back to the condition required for main line operation in the twenty-first century. But the timing was then not right to start such a repair; indeed the funds were not available to do so. Tyseley Locomotive Works had successfully returned No. 4965 *Rood Ashton Hall* to main line service and this was proving to be something of a gem. The consequence of the

success of that repair had brought about an intent to return the derelict hulk of No. 5043 *Earl of Mount Edgcumbe* to working order. To some extent, this usurped No. 7029 and this was particularly so when No. 5043 participated in a 50th anniversary re-run of No. 7029's famous record Plymouth to Bristol run in 1964. In the hands of driver Ray Churchill and (lone) fireman Alastair Meanley, *Earl of Mount Edgcumbe* was to shave a full three minutes from *Clun Castle*'s record, despite having a heavier train, perhaps leaving the challenge of unfinished business.

Nevertheless, the success of *Earl of Mount Edgcumbe*'s re-introduction to service brought about not only the will to properly repair *Clun Castle* but also a revenue stream to help fund such a repair. *Clun Castle* was also to reap the benefits of the expanded capabilities and new facilities of what has become Tyseley Locomotive Works; the new workshops in particular, matched by growth in skills of its workforce, have meant that the repair process has been able to be accomplished far more effectively than would have been the case even twenty years ago. Nevertheless, No. 7029's repair has still seen an input of over 30,000 man hours to return it to the condition which can be seen today.

The repairs to *Clun Castle* commenced during 2010, which was coincidentally the year of celebration for the 175th anniversary of the GWR. Whilst shed mate No. 5043 was away raising the Great Western flag on such seminal events as the first non-stop 'Bristolian' expresses for over fifty years, *Clun Castle* was gradually being dismantled at Tyseley. The necessity of many repairs to a steam locomotive can be determined before this process begins, but there are always hidden extras which only become apparent when the locomotive is taken to pieces – or stripped in railway

We like to keep our cab interiors spotless! No. 7029 *Clun Castle* is ready for the road again. The exhaust steam injector piping is on the left-hand side and the original GWR Automatic Train Control system on the right-hand side (look for the black and yellow dial above the alarm bell and battery box). The steam chest pressure gauge, referred to by Bob Meanley in the text, is next to the vacuum train pipe reservoir gauge in the top right corner of the picture. Whilst many will say this is not original, in actual fact the Western Region trial fitted two 'Castles' and two 'Kings' with this arrangement, and our installation has been made in exact accordance with the drawings which were made at the time of the WR trial. [PHOTO: ROBIN COOMBES]

parlance. This process always presents surprises – some good, most bad! The evolving repair of No. 7029 has proven to be no exception to this rule. It has undoubtedly been entirely at the level that might have been expected of a heavy general classified repair carried out at Swindon Works, in the days when steam traction was still a commodity which was highly valued and accorded the very best of attention.

Stripped down to a point where there was virtually nothing left to unbolt, the repair has attended to literally everything which was either known beforehand or which has become apparent as work progressed. On the locomotive, the boiler was removed from the frame, all wheels also removed, as was the bogie, and obviously all of the valve motion, pistons and valves. The tender too was stripped to its component parts, with the tank removed, revealing a considerable amount of work.

The boiler has required the removal and renewal of the smokebox in its entirety, a new front tubeplate, repairs to wasted sections of the barrel external to the tubeplate, renewal of all crown stays and many steel and copper side stays. At the firebox end, lower sections of the throatplate, large sections on both sides of the wrapper plate and corners and lower section of the backplate have all been renewed, with repairs also being carried out to the foundation ring. As a result of all this work, the foundation ring has been completely reriveted, in addition to the reriveting of the firehole door. All small boiler tubes, together with the superheater flue tubes and elements have been renewed and fitted, as have new inside and outside steam

pipes. The smokebox has been fitted with our own design of self cleaning smokebox and spark arrestor screens, which has proved so successful in No. 5043 over the last nine years. Substantial repairs were also required to the feed water dispersal trays inside the boiler. The normal renewal of all washout plugs, mud doors and fusible plugs has been carried out.

Repairs to the frame have mainly centred on the renewal of much of the rear dragbox, cab floor structure and lower cab sides in order to replace extensively corroded material. The axleboxes were one of the pleasant surprises, in that only the rear (or trailing) axlebox guides were sufficiently worn to require correction using our own design of horn grinding machine, all others showing little sign of wear despite the many years since they last received attention at Swindon. The axleboxes concerned had their liners reset and machined to suit the repaired guides (horns). New bearing brasses have been made and fitted to the trailing coupled axleboxes. All axle centres have been checked and reset to correct centre distances, again using gauges manufactured at Tyseley.

The wheels have come in for some extensive work, having been retyred at a cost approaching £50,000. It is a sobering thought to realise that each coupled wheel tyre alone cost £3,000 before any work whatsoever was carried out to machine it to size and fit it to the wheelset. Alongside this, the axle bearing journals have been examined and rectified as required to bring them back to correct standard and all axleboxes have been remetalled in order to bring them back to new condition.

The first moves of No. 7029 *Clun Castle* after her heavy general repair at Tyseley Locomotive Works in 2019. Alastair Meanley, TLW General Manager, who masterminded the overhaul, is justifiably at the regulator. All went well, with virtually no snags. [PHOTO: ROBIN COOMBES]

ABOVE: *Clun Castle* breathes life once more after its extensive refit by Tyseley Locomotive Works. It is running on the track leading directly from the passenger roundhouse turntable to the main line. No. 7029 has now been in charitable ownership within the Tyseley Collection for over fifty years, considerably longer than the sixteen years of BR (WR) ownership. [PHOTO: ROBIN COOMBES]

ABOVE: The locomotive is recommissioned at the TLW public open weekend on 29th October 2017 by two of the first volunteers who were pivotal in enabling charitable operations to begin here after the end of BR steam working: Bernard Rainbow and Phil Gloster. [PHOTO: ROBIN COOMBES]

Not a bad recreation of a traditional engine shed! Although only constructed in 1970, the workshop has developed a patina of its own over time and so fits quite well into the original surroundings of the depot which have been there since 1908: the GWR-built coaling stage is on the right and even the blue brick floor is original. The two locomotives epitomise the smaller end of the Tyseley Collection: Class '08' 0-6-0D No. 13029 is retained in its original livery and with its early BR number, to commemorate that it was originally delivered new to work in the adjacent Bordesley Sidings. GWR 0-6-0PT No. 9600 is one of three in the collection and was bought out of service in 1973 from the National Coal Board's Merthyr Vale Colliery, having begun her working life at Swindon depot and works in February 1945. [PHOTO: ROBIN COOMBES]

Over the years, Tyseley open days have featured a very wide range of differing locomotive types. Here, on 25th October 2013, an interesting group are juxtaposed: L&NWR 'Coal Tank' No. 1054, owned by the National Trust, is coupled to LM&SR 'Pacific' No. 6201 *Princess Elizabeth*, with the National Railway Museum's GWR flagship No. 6000 *King George V*, No. 71000 *Duke of Gloucester* and GWR '28XX' Class 2-8-0 No. 2885 behind. Of this grouping, only the '28XX' goods locomotives were indigenous to Tyseley. [Photo: MARTIN CREESE]

The locomotive line up around the former passenger roundhouse turntable is often a sight for sore eyes, as there is really nowhere else such a spectacle can be seen and enjoyed. On 25th October 2013, No. 4983 *Rood Ashton Hall*, No. 6000 *King George V*, No. 5043 *Earl of Mount Edgcumbe*, No. 71000 *Duke of Gloucester* and 2-8-0 No. 2885 line up facing the turntable. [PHOTO: MARTIN CREESE]

Three 'Castles' at Tyseley in June 2018: No. 5080 *Defiant*, No. 5043 *Earl of Mount Edgcumbe* and No. 4079 *Clun Castle*. [PHOTO: ROBIN COOMBES]

Tyseley Locomotive Works has become well known for its open weekend locomotive cavalcades, with three and, sometimes, four express steam locomotives coupled together for the sheer fun and excitement of the spectacle. Here the crowds enjoy No. 4965 *Rood Ashton Hall*, No. 5043 *Earl of Mount Edgcumbe* and No. 46233 *Duchess of Sutherland* charging past.
[PHOTO: ROBIN COOMBES]

At the front end, the cylinders have been examined, new pistons have been fitted to remachined piston rods, all four valve chests have been re-bored; valve rings, valve spindle sleeves and all gland rings and bushes have been renewed. All four sets of slide bars have been reset and fitted with new packings. This revealed one of the surprises in that at some time in the distant past the top and bottom right-hand outside slidebars had been reversed to try to rectify a prior defect in their alignment, and this took not a little effort to rectify and reset them correctly. This misalignment had led to quite extensive wear to a cylinder liner which has had to be renewed as a consequence and it is obvious that the engine had run for a number of years in BR service with this defect. The cylinder drain cocks were deemed to be beyond repair and have been renewed. On the lubrication front, the cylinder lubricator has been completely stripped down with all seals renewed, and the associated pipework has either been repaired or completely replaced to finally expunge the evidence of years of wear and abuse collected during No. 7029's BR career. One extra which has been fitted to the cylinders is a connection to a steam chest pressure gauge in the cab. Whilst many will say this is not original, in actual fact the Western Region trial fitted two 'Castles' and two 'Kings' with this arrangement, and our installation has been made in exact accordance with the drawings which were made at the time of the WR trial.

The valve motion has had many of the bronze and white metal bushes renewed or repaired, in particular all of the connecting and coupling rod bushes have been renewed. The pivot pins and bushes for the outside rocker arms, which transmit motion to the outside valves, needed a substantial amount of work to restore them to good order, again simply because of wear and tear. Several of the joint pins within the valve motion have also required replacement. The reverser in the cab has required extensive work, including renewal of the complex screw therein. Looseness of the components within the reverser in the cab can lead to heavy vibration which can drastically increase noise levels within the cab due to severe knocking, and it is to be hoped that future crews appreciate the effort which went into this item!

All steam fittings and pipework have been repaired, or in some instances renewed, in particular the driver's brake valve and injector steam pipes in the cab have been replaced. We are particularly proud of the fact that most of the boiler cleating plates are still the original BR items which were on the engine at the time of purchase. Much care has gone into repairing these items in order to bring them back to a presentable condition but, in particular, one of the boiler barrel panels carried distinct evidence in the form of heavy creasing due to having been folded back to attend to a boiler repair. This had been clearly visible in some photos of the engine taken during the BR years and, indeed, beyond into preservation. We consider that it was worth preserving the original material, after all there are not many engines still operating today with original BR cleating panels which look as good as the ones on No. 7029.

The tender required considerable work too. The removal of the tank from the frame revealed a very sorry state which almost suggested complete renewal. In the end, the TLW team salvaged the side and rear panels after a lot of hard work and they have been fitted with zinc anodes (as fitted to canal boats) as a measure which will hopefully reduce future corrosion rates. For the rest, the whole of the floor, tank top and baffles have been replaced, leaving just the original sides and rear. Whilst normally out of sight, there is actually a large amount of timber packing of various thicknesses installed between the top of the tender frames and the tank, and this too has been replaced with good quality timber, which hopefully will be far more resistant to decay than the original wood used by the GWR. The frame too required considerable attention to replace corroded metal within the front and rear dragboxes, together with the top plates between tank and frame. Wheel tyres and journals have been remachined and associated bearings have been remetalled. As with the engine, all bearing springs have been repaired or in some instances renewed at a total cost for the whole locomotive and tender of over £12,000.

Nearing the completion of the repair work, focus has of necessity moved onto repainting and lining the locomotive in paint which has been carefully matched to a 1956 Swindon paint sample. Work has also focused on fitting the modern electronic systems required before the engine may operate over Network Rail lines. This includes the TPWS system for train protection and warning, OTMR data recording equipment and GSMR radio communication equipment, all of which can add upwards of £50,000 to the repair bill.

In conclusion, all of us at Tyseley Locomotive Works hope and expect that No. 7029 will prove every bit as good as its shed companion No. 5043 and that the pair of them will continue to uphold, and indeed further enhance, the reputation of the GWR and its 'Castle' engines.

POSTSCRIPT

Of course, none of this would have been possible without the help and assistance of so many people – those who have donated money to the *Clun* appeal, the management, the staff and volunteers of Tyseley Locomotive Works, West Coast Railways and its VAB, Network Rail, and our suppliers and subcontractors, together with a host of well wishers too numerous to mention.

Finally, special word must go to our General Manager, Alastair Meanley, who has managed this project from beginning to end.

On 9th October 2018, Vintage Trains Limited ran its first steam main line trip as a licenced community owned train operating company. No. 4965 *Rood Ashton Hall* powers through Wilmcote station under the lovely ornate GWR lattice footbridge with a test train run to assess crew competencies under the new regime. We are fortunate indeed that the Birmingham to Stratford-upon-Avon route passes through a number of stations that retain original buildings and features, which have been beautifully painted in an approximation of the GWR's original light and dark stone colours. Apart from the new safety and disability compliant platform surfaces, one has to look hard to spot the other signs of the 21st century, such as CCTV cameras and dot matrix train indicators. [PHOTO: ROBIN COOMBES]

22. SO, YOU WANT TO RUN YOUR OWN TRAINS?

'The whole steam main line movement is at a tipping point and will need to engage co-operatively in many ways to survive.'

This simply was not possible on the main line until 1993, as the railways were nationalised and run by British Railways as a monopoly. However, members of our team could and indeed did run their own trains in a variety of other places: on private miniature, narrow and standard gauge railways, with a variety of regulatory oversight on some of these. We had started off on the standard gauge by simply watching, riding and photographing trains. Then, our involvement incrementally increased: we chartered trains from BR, which simply meant we paid them a fee to run a train. Then we bought our own locomotives. This required a little more effort but initially not a lot more. We had to find somewhere to keep these locomotives. We chose Tyseley depot as it was not far from home, could be reached on a Sunday afternoon between lunch and supper, and we had become somewhat used to the place following its association with Cam's SLS Specials to Swindon. Then, BR still did everything for us or nearly so; some of our volunteers who were then also BR footplate crew willingly and voluntarily undertook some of the operational and light maintenance work, signed off by BR.

Once BR had determined to rid itself of steam in 1968, our involvement and obligations stepped up. We had to enter into longer term property deals, we sourced patterns, parts and machinery, and built a workshop. Some of this was done without cost, as time and materials were, to a very large and kind extent, freely given but, even in 1970, we had to raise about £25,000 (nearly £340,000 in 2021 terms) just to put up the workshop and install the wheeldrop and lathe. Then BR, quite rightly, brought in MT276, a document setting out overhaul and maintenance standards which we were required to work to. BR came to inspect and approve the processes and the outcome, and checked locomotives and rolling stock were fit to run each operating day. So we needed skills, equipment and money to comply. We had these in varying amounts and quality as time went on during the '70s and '80s.

Then, with privatisation from 1993, the bar to engineering and operating was raised higher. MT276 was not mandated anymore. It was up to us to devise a safety management system, and operating and maintenance policy to deal with our own repairs and maintenance, and any operations the private sector wished to conduct. Train Operating Companies would have to do their own fitness to run exams but processes and examiners would still be checked and audited. All this quite naturally required more time, paperwork and considerably more money. For example, it was

No. 7029 *Clun Castle* powers through Leamington Spa on 1st December 2019 with an early Vintage Trains Limited charter to Bath Christmas Market. The first vehicle behind the locomotive is a former BR General Utility Vehicle (GUV) converted to a water carrier. Nowadays, there are no facilities for steam locomotives to take either water or coal once out on a journey and supplies either have to be delivered to the locomotive at prearranged stops or taken with the train. Note the station was part way through a repaint into GWR heritage colours. [PHOTO: ANDREW BELL]

Vintage Trains Community Benefit Society members salute the return to steam of Tyseley Collection's flagship No. 7029 *Clun Castle* at Tyseley Locomtoive Works on 28th October 2017. Seven hundred members of the public subscribed for £1,100,000 capital, enabling the first community owned main line train operating company to become licenced to run express steam trains. This was the first of yet more steps which will need to be taken over the coming years to build a sustainable base of engineering, operating and commercial skills to keep main line steam alive. Moreover, further development of both Tyseley depot and the adjacent Shakespeare Line between Birmingham's Moor Street city terminus and the international tourist destination of Stratford-upon-Avon will be a focus for many years to come. But the genesis exists. [Photo: Robin Coombes]

no longer simply sufficient to rely on equipment and materials acceptable to BR, everything had to be subject to ultrasonic testing for flaws and cracks. If new material was introduced into a locomotive, its origin and composition had to be approved and checked. Network Rail introduced Group Standards setting out all the detail of the requirements and processes. Some of this did not suit steam locomotives, of course, and so derogations had to be obtained, meaning justification for doing something in a slightly different way and proving it was still safe.

As the main line railway became busier and faster, more stringent safety standards were introduced. Our GWR locomotives already had an Automatic Warning System for signaling installed in the cab; this provided audible noises depending on the 'colour' of the signals and even put the brakes on if the driver did not acknowledge either an orange or red signal. But, as each accident brought new solutions to prevent reoccurrence, additional safety precautions were introduced step by step and, indeed, are still being introduced, either to seek to reduce operational risk or improve train control. We were obliged to fit tachograph-style data recorders, radio communication, and train protection and warning systems to our locomotives. This meant boxes and wiring hidden in tool boxes, under dragboxes and wiring in new pipes amongst the frames. The cost of all this ran into tens of thousands of pounds of course and, all the while, the cost of repairs also grew as the cost of labour and materials increased, assuming each were available in the right quality and volume at all. Fortunately, we had amassed a quantity of spare parts at the beginning of our standard gauge preservation days from depots and workshops which had closed and, if we had known then what we know now, we would have collected a great deal more. Some material is difficult to source and we are now obliged to go to France for some axle material and as far away as South Africa for locomotive driving wheel tyres for large wheeled express steam locomotives, where there is only a single supplier.

But all this is just the precursor to actually operating your own trains on the main line.

Of course, just operating a train is simple enough if you know how to do it. Cylinder drain cocks open, reverser in forward gear, brakes off and regulator open. But the railway is a stranger place now. Even the track gauge has a slightly different rail profile. And the less said about the overall loading gauge the better, especially if you have a Great Western designed locomotive, as they are slightly wider than many. Amazingly, one or two owners are even altering their locomotives, providing narrower cylinders or reduced height chimneys so they fit the loading gauge easier and so have a wider range. The all encompassing height mantra of 13ft 1in. is also a challenge but I defy you to notice the reduced cab height on our 'Castles'; its all about keeping the same profiles and angles. Nowadays, the loading gauge is measured by laser with a few millimetres added here and there. No longer are railwaymen expected to know all this amount of detail and so, occasionally, everyone can be 'taken by surprise' when a platform coping stone or two gets pushed out of alignment by weeds and causes a gauging issue.

But, before a single train can run on the main line, you need an operating licence issued by the Office of Road & Rail (ORR). Before this can be issued, you need a team of '*fit and proper people*', a safety certificate, access agreements and public liability insurance. The safety management system encompassing competence and methodology is all important for both safety critical operation and requisite skills and knowledge. Once this has been demonstrated in writing and on the ground in practice, its maintenance and continuous improvement needs to be embedded in everything one does.

As the railway is no longer an integrated system, there are many and varied organisations to deal with, ranging from Network Rail as owner and manager of the infrastructure, interfaces with other train operators and industry bodies, together with access arrangements for track, stations and depots and much more besides.

Beneficially, a Train Operating Company (TOC) can bid for time table slots and has a 'seat at the table' for things such as proposals to make alterations to the network. Currently, we bid for charter paths but we also have working time table paths for our 'Shakespeare Express' trains, which enables us to operate at much shorter notice and, providing we use these paths, to keep them year by year. This provides us with commercial certainty and an increasing ability to plan ahead in the tourist market place. But even so, charter paths are still the last to be allocated and so it can be rather like a game of musical chairs. If a franchise train operator wanted an extra path, it could request one, which might mean the charter path was no longer available. The only way to be certain about train paths is to apply for 'firm rights', but this means committing to a minimum amount of trips. 'The Jacobite' has gone down this route with good success.

All this requires detailed knowledge of how the modern railway works and funding of course, both to enable operations to begin in the first place and also to provide working capital through the start up period until ends meet. We determined that £850,000 would be necessary to begin operations with the financial model we began with, which included some 'non passenger' activities such as new train mileage accumulation and night-time water jetting operations in the winter months.

In order to raise such a sum, we determined to make a share issue which offered community participation. We thought that the public would like the opportunity to subscribe for a share in a railway operating company which ran express steam trains offering the 'Great British Breakfast' in our Pullman cars, champagne dinners and also simply tourist trips in carriages with big picture windows. We chose the relatively new Community Benefit Society model, but made it charitably controlled by the Vintage Trains Charitable Trust. The CBS model offers commercial and withdrawable shares which have a right to interest, once the business has settled down and is into profit, and an entitlement for the member shareholders to withdraw their funds in certain circumstances. The objective of a CBS is engagement by its members as well as having a commercial return. Our design and promotion worked and we raised £1,100,000; a not inconsiderable sum, which enabled us to get started and also make some improvements to our train. As with pretty much any type of heritage train operation, it is almost certain that fundraising will need to go on for ever, to cover, at the very least, major overhauls and refurbishments which can very rarely be met from operating revenue alone. But that aspect of fundraising is the preserve of Vintage Trains Charitable Trust, our managing charity. Our operating company 'simply' pays hire fees for the use of traction and rolling stock, which is supposed to be calculated to cover day-to-day running costs and maintenance.

All of this, and more, needs to be considered and established before a steam locomotive ventures out onto the network. And 'all of this' needs to be constantly maintained 'in good standing' and continuously improved all the time as well. A culture. A way of life. Every day.

But we now have what we believe is the only train operating company licenced to run express steam trains which is owned by the people of Great Britain and open to all. We are very proud of that. However, we have only just begun the operating journey and only just in time. The main line railway is a very different place

A picture that epitomises what drives us on: No. 5080 *Defiant*, No. 5043 *Earl of Mount Edgcumbe* and No. 7029 *Clun Castle* stand under the night sky at Tyseley Locomotive Works, reminding us of the enormous amount of effort and goodwill that enabled this line up in the first place and also reminding us that our work is never finished. *Defiant* will probably require £1 million to be spent on her before she once again treads the main line boards. [Photo: Robert Falconer]

Pullman restaurant car service. Most current day charters rely on bookings from passengers who want more than just a train ride behind a steam locomotive – and what better way to travel than to dine as well. Fortuitously, BR ensured a train of 1960s Metro Cammell Pullman cars were retained for steam charters and several of these can now be enjoyed on special trains run by West Coast Railway Company and Vintage Trains. As these cars were made in Birmingham by a company who exported carriages worldwide, this adds to Vintage Trains' pioneering story well. [Photo: Taliesin Coombes]

now compared with the 'steam friendly' arena of even the 1960s. And there are precious few people who still intrinsically know and understand how to repair, maintain and operate steam locomotives safely and commercially at up to 75mph. The whole steam main line movement is at a tipping point and will need to engage co-operatively in many ways to survive.

Over the last seventy years, we have learned a great deal and achieved many things but now we cannot simply react to circumstances and work out how to overcome the next obstacle put in front of us. We must now plan ahead to a much greater extent to ensure we have the cash and the skills necessary to enable express steam trains (and, of course, our tank engines too) to continue to operate at speed. We need to spend time developing our Community Benefit Society model so that this process becomes more routine and engages well with both internal and external stakeholders. We are very fortunate to be based in the City of Birmingham, which welcomes 'The Shakespeare Express'

in particular and is also prepared to help us, on occasion, with grants and assistance to employ more people and train them in useful engineering skills at our Tyseley Locomotive Works. Network Rail and the West Midlands Rail Executive are also supportive. These stakeholders can all see that the future of express steam trains on the Shakespeare Line, connecting the large industrial conurbation in the West Midlands with the international 'bucket list' tourist destination of Stratford-upon-Avon, is worth putting some collective effort into.

We have always considered that what we do at Tyseley is what the Great Western Railway might have done if they had continued to exist after 1948 and decided to keep a few of their steam locomotives running, even after they had modernised their railway – which they would have done.

If you want to find out more, volunteer to help, join us in any way or simply find out when our express steam trains are running, please look at our website: www.VintageTrains.co.uk

23. HOT CHOCOLATE

'What would the GWR have done in our place if it had continued to exist to the present day?'

'The Polar Express' arrives at Birmingham Moor Street station behind No. 4965 *Rood Ashton Hall* especially renamed *Polar Star*, in the weekday rush hour during December 2018, fully booked with over three hundred enthusiastic passengers for the theatrical performance on board. [PHOTO: ROBIN COOMBES]

"All Aboard!" cried the Conductor. A crowd of people, largely dressed in pyjamas, followed him and his guiding handlamp across the concourse at Birmingham's Moor Street city-centre station. It was a weekday rush hour evening and hundreds of busy commuters were hurrying to catch their train home. But, alongside platform 3 stood *Polar Star*, a gleaming green locomotive wreathed in steam, its brass and copper adornments sparkling in the station lights against the night sky. At each carriage door stood a happy, laughing chef dressed in white, complete with chef's kitchen cooking hat. The smell of hot chocolate and cookies pervaded the air. The show was about to begin.

Vintage Trains ran a series of sixty-five trains in the evening rush hour periods and at weekends during the month of December from Birmingham Moor Street station to the 'North Pole' at Tyseley in both 2018 and 2019. This intensive period of operation comprised four trains on each operating day, running in and around the busy Chiltern Railways service and into a city terminus station. Fortunately, Tyseley is well served with an additional track for empty coaching stock workings from Moor Street station to the carriage sidings at the depot. Effectively, this means we only have to run 'The Polar Express' trains for some 250 yards on the main suburban

lines between the station and the empty carriages line, which helps time table pathing and performance enormously.

We carried 50,000 passengers in these two December periods and entertained them in a 'moving theatre' for an hour's experience. The station and train were full of 'singing and dancing chefs' and, of course, Father Christmas visits every person to give them their very own silver bell, all requirements detailed by the Warner Brothers' franchise, very well managed by Rail Events and American Railway Heritage, who contract for very many 'Polars' in the USA.

We came across the 'Polars' quite by chance really when our family were on holiday in the USA. It has become my custom to get to know heritage railway places and their people as I travel around the world, both for business and pleasure. It is always fascinating to compare notes between new friends as to how operations begin and develop. There is always much to learn and also to offer.

One such family trip was to Durango in Colorado to see the famous Silverton Line of the Denver & Rio Grande Western Railroad, running through the amazing Animas Canyon using yellow clerestory roof cars hauled by huge 8-coupled narrow gauge steam locomotives. As usual, I had written ahead to introduce myself and to ask if we could see the locomotive depot and workshops.

Although a theatrical experience for families and the general public, our 'Polar Express' was an authentic train as well, as can be seen here with No. 4965 *Rood Ashton Hall* standing in the 1909 Great Western city terminus station at Moor Street. Pretty much the only additional adornment was the headlight on the smokebox. [PHOTO: ROBIN COOMBES]

"What a fantastic experience! We loved The Polar Express, Moor Street was magical and the old steam train was beautiful. I would love to thank Chef Gingerbread & Chef Cindy, they were amazing super friendly and made our time on The Polar Express magical, a must for all who love Christmas."

'All Aboard!' The conductor leads passengers, largely dressed in pyjamas, through the iron gates onto the platform at Moor Street at the start of 'The Polar Express' experience in 2018.
[PHOTO: ROBIN COOMBES]

The conductor clips the golden ticket on board the train. [Photo: Robin Coombes]

On arrival in our Durango hotel, there was a message from the railway to call when we were settled in, together with a kind gift of railroading hats for our children and some videos.

So, on the appointed day, my son Stuart and I presented ourselves at the Durango ticket office and asked for Al Harper (we presumed the depot manager), who was going to show us around. When Al duly arrived, he was not wearing boiler suit or overalls as expected but much more finely dressed. He turned out to own the railroad and several others besides! We had a great tour, inspected his favourite locomotive and were invited to lunch. He carefully explained how he had adapted the Durango end of the D&RGWR to accommodate family rides of an hour's duration and engaged with Warner Brothers to develop various character franchises. We had a deal.

It was immediately obvious to me that his D&RGWR 'model' of operating was something we should seriously consider when the opportunity arose. Such franchises provide ready made access to huge new markets, both to railways in general and steam trains in particular, largely sold on social media. I was absolutely amazed when watching 'sales' on Facebook in the office at Tyseley in real time, to see how quickly 'posts' and 'shares' were made. Of course, the entertainment and its price are not for everyone and there were some very 'vivid' comments about that. But the trick is to pass over those and watch those who do buy; they also link their friends to the page and so do our advertising for us. Just like the chain letters we were encouraged to write at school.

Of course, operating The Polar Express Train Ride is an enormous effort, on top of all the other things we do and are required to do at Tyseley. But, in addition to helping to pay the bills, such trains reach out to new people and in a different way. Effectively, we are offering a musical and theatrical performance on the main line railway. Whilst some enthusiasts may say this is not for them (and they do not have to book of course) or it is unauthentic, maybe we should now ask ourselves what is authentic?

What would the GWR have done in our place if it had continued to exist to the present day? We are in the tourist and entertainment business now and our steam locomotives have a real purpose in what they do. They are not museum pieces. They are works of engineering, still capable of performing to their design specification, at speed on the main line and earning revenue to enable them to keep on doing so. Moreover, they require team work to operate in the first place. Steam locomotives do not function at a few taps of a computer, they require real and deep knowledge, and skill to work. Many different skills have to meld together in a single team to deliver the output: a revenue earning train. Many people gain immense satisfaction from their participation, whether it be helping the train to operate or simply enjoying the ride.

And some of our trains are as authentic as we can get in the 21st century: we can still provide a GWR designed 'Castle' 4-6-0 express steam locomotive running hard at 75mph on Britain's main line railway well over fifty years since the state ceased using them in revenue earning service. Long may it continue.

'Right away' for 'The Polar Express'. A green light and a friendly wave from a station porter as the train leaves the station and heads into the night for the journey to the North Pole. [PHOTO: ROBIN COOMBES]

Vintage Trains Community Benefit Society:

A Train Operating Company owned by the people of Great Britain and running express steam trains

TYSELEY LOCOMOTIVE WORKS

Warwick Road, Tyseley, Birmingham B11 2HL